Asymmetric Crisis in Europe and Possible Futures

The crisis in Europe is often discussed as a crisis of European integration or a crisis of national economies within Europe. Both, the 'methodological Europeanism' and 'methodological nationalism' miss out the important links between economic and political processes at different spatial scales within Europe, and hence, asymmetries and phenomena of uneven development. In addition, a systematic discussion of possible scenarios based on a sound analysis of the causes of the crisis and the implication of anti-crisi policies lacks.

This volume seeks to close this gap by systematically integrating the analysis of economic policy or 'technical' solutions to the crisis within a broader framework of political economy. It argues that combining critical political economy approaches and post-Keynesian perspectives allows for a systematic understanding of the economic and political dimensions of the crisis. Although both approaches have the capacity to deal within asymmetries and uneven development, the heterogeneity in Europe has been an often largely neglected dimension of analysis. However, this recent crisis has shown that this is an essential dimension which has to be addressed in order to better understand the dynamics of European development and integration. Hence, this book aims to deal with asymmetries in Europe and to bridge the gap between the two perspectives.

This work will initiate an integrative debate that is crucial for a deeper understanding of the current crisis and is an important resource for all students and scholars of international political economy, European political economy and European politics.

Johannes Jäger, Professor for Economics, University of Applied Sciences BFI Vienna, Austria.

Elisabeth Springler, Programme Director, University of Applied Sciences BFI Vienna, Austria.

RIPE Series in Global Political Economy

Series Editors: Jacqueline Best (University of Ottawa, Canada), Ian Bruff (Manchester University, UK), Paul Langley (Durham University, UK) and Anna Leander (Copenhagen Business School, Denmark)

This series, published in association with the Review of International Political Economy, provides a forum for current and interdisciplinary debates in international political economy. The series aims to advance understanding of the key issues in the global political economy, and to present innovative analyses of emerging topics. The titles in the series focus on three broad themes:

- the structures, processes and actors of contemporary global transformations
- the changing forms taken by governance, at scales from the local and everyday to the global and systemic
- the inseparability of economic from political, social and cultural questions, including resistance, dissent and social movements.

The RIPE Series in Global Political Economy aims to address the needs of students and teachers. Titles include:

Transnational Classes and International Relations
Kees van der Pijl

Globalization and Governance
Edited by Aseem Prakash and Jeffrey A. Hart

Nation-States and Money
The Past, Present and Future of National Currencies
Edited by Emily Gilbert and Eric Helleiner

Gender and Global Restructuring:
Sightings, Sites and Resistances
Edited by Marianne H. Marchand and Anne Sisson Runyan

The Global Political Economy of Intellectual Property Rights
The New Enclosures?
Christopher May

Global Political Economy
Contemporary Theories
Edited by Ronen Palan

Ideologies of Globalization - Contending Visions of a New World Order
Mark Rupert

The Clash within Civilisations
Coming to Terms with Cultural Conflicts
Dieter Senghaas

Capitalist Restructuring, Globalisation and the Third Way
Lessons from the Swedish Model
J. Magnus Ryner

Transnational Capitalism and the Struggle over European Integration
Bastiaan van Apeldoorn

World Financial Orders
An Historical International Political Economy
Paul Langley

Global Unions?
Theory and Strategies of Organized Labour in the Global Political Economy
Edited by Jeffrey Harrod and Robert O'Brien

Political Economy of a Plural World
Critical Reflections on Power, Morals and Civilizations
Robert Cox with Michael Schechter

The Changing Politics of Finance in Korea and Thailand
From Deregulation to Debacle
Xiaoke Zhang

Anti-Immigrantism in Western Democracies
Statecraft, Desire and the Politics of Exclusion
Roxanne Lynn Doty

The Political Economy of European Employment
European Integration and the Transnationalization of the (Un)Employment Question
Edited by Henk Overbeek

A Critical Rewriting of Global Political Economy
Integrating Reproductive, Productive and Virtual Economies
V. Spike Peterson

International Trade and Developing Countries
Bargaining Coalitions in the GATT & WTO
Amrita Narlikar

Rethinking Global Political Economy
Emerging Issues, Unfolding Odysseys
Edited by Mary Ann Tétreault, Robert A. Denemark, Kenneth P. Thomas and Kurt Burch

Global Institutions and Development
Framing the World?
Edited by Morten Bøås and Desmond McNeill

Contesting Globalization
Space and Place in the World Economy
André C. Drainville

The Southern Cone Model
The Political Economy of Regional Capitalist Development in Latin America
Nicola Phillips

The Idea of Global Civil Society
Politics and Ethics of a Globalizing Era
Edited by Randall D. Germain and Michael Kenny

Global Institutions, Marginalization, and Development
Craig N. Murphy

Governing Financial Globalization
International Political Economy and Multi-Level Governance
Edited by Andrew Baker, David Hudson and Richard Woodward

Critical Theories, International Relations and 'the Anti-Globalisation Movement'
The Politics of Global Resistance
Edited by Catherine Eschle and Bice Maiguashca

Resisting Intellectual Property
Debora J. Halbert

Globalization, Governmentality, and Global Politics
Regulation for the Rest of Us?
Ronnie D. Lipschutz, with James K. Rowe

Neoliberal Hegemony
A Global Critique
Edited by Dieter Plehwe, Bernhard Walpen and Gisela Neunhöffer

Images of Gramsci
Connections and contentions in political theory and international relations
Edited by Andreas Bieler and Adam David Morton

Global Standards of Market Civilization
Edited by Brett Bowden and Leonard Seabrooke

Beyond Globalization
Capitalism, territoriality and the international relations of modernity
Hannes Lacher

Global Public Policy
Business and the countervailing powers of civil society
Edited by Karsten Ronit

The Transnational Politics of Corporate Governance Regulation
Edited by Henk Overbeek, Bastiaan van Apeldoorn and Andreas Nölke

Critical Perspectives on Global Governance
Rights and Regulation in Governing Regimes
Jean Grugel and Nicola Piper

National Currencies and Globalization
Endangered Specie?
Paul Bowles

Conflicts in Environmental Regulation and the Internationalization of the State
Contested terrains
Ulrich Brand, Christoph Görg, Joachim Hirsch and Markus Wissen

Beyond States and Markets
The challenges of social reproduction
Edited by Isabella Bakker and Rachel Silvey

Governing International Labour Migration
Current Issues, Challenges and Dilemmas
Edited by Christina Gabriel and Hélène Pellerin

The Industrial Vagina
The Political Economy of the Global Sex Trade
Sheila Jeffreys

The Child in International Political Economy
A Place at the Table
Alison M.S. Watson

Capital as Power
A Study of Order and Creorder
Jonathan Nitzan and Shimshon Bichler

Global Citizenship and the Legacy of Empire
Marketing Development
April Biccum

The Global Political Economy of Intellectual Property Rights,
Second Edition
The New Enclosures
Christopher May

Corporate Power and Ownership in Contemporary Capitalism
The politics of resistance and domination
Susanne Soederberg

Savage Economics
Wealth, Poverty and the Temporal Walls of Capitalism
David L. Blaney and Naeem Inayatullah

Cultural Political Economy
Edited by Jacqueline Best and Matthew Paterson

Development, Sexual Rights and Global Governance
Resisting Global Power
Amy Lind

Cosmopolitanism and Global Financial Reform
A Pragmatic Approach to the Tobin Tax
James Brassett

Gender and Global Restructuring
Second Edition
Sightings, Sites and Resistances
Edited by Marianne H. Marchand and Anne Sisson Runyan

Variegated Neoliberalism
EU Varieties of Capitalism and International Political Economy
Huw Macartney

The Politics of European Competition Regulation
A Critical Political Economy Perspective
Hubert Buch-Hansen and Angela Wigger

The Political Economy of Global Remittances
Gender and Governmentality
Rahel Kunz

A Critical History of the Economy
On the Birth of the National and International Economies
Ryan Walter

The International Political Economy of Transition
Neoliberal Hegemony and Eastern Central Europe's Transformation
Stuart Shields

The Global Political Economy of Trade Protectionism and Liberalization
Trade Reform and Economic Adjustment in Textiles and Clothing
Tony Heron

Transnational Financial Associations and the Governance of Global Finance
Assembling wealth and power
Heather McKeen-Edwards and Tony Porter

The Capitalist Mode of Power
Critical Engagements with the Power Theory of Value
Edited by Tim Di Muzio

The Making of Modern Finance
Liberal Governance and the Gold Standard
Samuel Knafo

The State of Copyright
The Complex Relationships of Cultural Creation in a Globalized World
Debora J. Halbert

Transnational Financial Regulation after the Crisis
Edited by Tony Porter

The Political Economy of Global Capitalism and Crisis
Bill Dunn

Global Capitalism
Selected Essays
Hugo Radice

Debtfare States and the Poverty Industry
Money, Discipline and the Surplus Population
Susanne Soederberg

Currency Challenge
The Euro, the Dollar and the Global Financial
Miguel Otero-Iglesias

Fringe Finance
Crossing and Contesting the Borders of Global Capital
Rob Aitken

Asymmetric Crisis in Europe and Possible Futures
Critical Political Economy and Post-Keynesian Perspectives
Edited by Johannes Jäger and Elisabeth Springler

Asymmetric Crisis in Europe and Possible Futures

Critical political economy and post-Keynesian perspectives

Edited by
Johannes Jäger and Elisabeth Springler

Routledge
Taylor & Francis Group
LONDON AND NEW YORK

First published 2015
by Routledge
2 Park Square, Milton Park, Abingdon, Oxfordshire OX14 4RN

and by Routledge
711 Third Avenue, New York, NY 10017

First issued in paperback 2016

Routledge is an imprint of the Taylor & Francis Group, an informa business

British Library Cataloguing in Publication Data
A catalogue record for this book is available from the British Library

Library of Congress Cataloging in Publication Data
Asymmetric crisis in Europe and possible futures : critical political economy and post-Keynesian perspectives / edited by Johannes J?ger and Elisabeth Springler. – 1 Edition.
pages cm. – (Ripe series in global political economy)
Includes bibliographical references and index.
1. Europe–Economic conditions–21st century. 2. Europe–Economic integration. 3. Financial crises–Europe. 4. Europe–Politics and government–21st century. I. Jäger, Johannes, editor. II. Springler, Elisabeth, editor.
HC240.A848 2015
330.94–dc23
2014038308

ISBN: 978-1-138-23946-3 (pbk)
ISBN: 978-1-138-79076-6 (hbk)

Typeset in Times New Roman
by Taylor & Francis Books

Contents

List of illustrations

Figures

Tables

Contributors

Joachim Becker, Associate Professor of Economics at Vienna University of Economics and Business, Vienna.

Hans-Jürgen Bieling, Professor for Political Science at the Eberhard Karls University in Tübingen, Germany.

Alan Cafruny, Henry Bristol Professor of International Affairs at the Department of Government at Hamilton College Clinton, New York.

Mònica Clua-Losada, Lecturer of Political Sciences at the Department for Political and Social Sciences, Universitat Pompeu Fabra, Barcelona.

Heiner Flassbeck, Professor of Economics of the Hamburg University of Economics and Politics and was Director of Globalization and Development Strategies, UNCTAD.

John Grahl, Professor of European Integration at the Middlesex University, UK.

Laura Horn, Associate Professor of International Relations and European Integration at the Department of Society and Globalization at the University of Roskilde, Denmark.

Johannes Jäger, Professor for Economics, University of Applied Sciences BFI Vienna.

Karsten Köhler, Economist at Kingston University, UK.

Costas Lapavitsas, Professor of Economics at the School of Oriental and African Studies (SOAS) at the University of London, UK.

Torsten Niechoj, Professor of Economics and Political Science at Rhine-Waal University of Applied Sciences in Kamp-Lintfort, Germany.

Lukas Oberndorfer, Adviser for European Law and European Studies at the Department for EU and International Affairs at the Austrian Chamber of Labour.

Magnus Ryner, Reader in International Political Economy at the Department of European and International Studies at King's College London.

Elisabeth Springler, Programme Director, University of Applied Sciences BFI Vienna.

Engelbert Stockhammer, Professor of Economics at Kingston University, UK.

Jan Toporowski, Professor of Economics at the School of Oriental and African Studies (SOAS) at the University of London, UK, and Visiting Professor of Economics at the University of Bergamo, Italy.

Rudy Weissenbacher, Researcher and Lecturer at the Department of International Economics and Development at the Vienna University of Economics and Business, Austria.

Angela Wigger, Lecturer for Global Political Economy and International Relations at the Department of Political Science at Radboud University Nijmegen, Netherlands.

Acknowledgement

The idea for this book can be traced back to the discussion of the financial crisis in Central and Eastern Europe in a Jean Monnet Lecture series for our Masters students funded by the European Union. The series attempted to integrate economic and political perspectives, and took place in Vienna from 2010 to 2013. During this period the crisis not only hit the New Member States but practically all European economies were affected, and European integration was in a critical situation, too. Given the severe problems which were arising and the difficulties for common approaches to deal with them, it became necessary to discuss European developments in an alternative and integrative way by focusing on economic and political aspects. Based on such a promising alternative approach, the book attempts to provide a sound analysis of the reasons for the crisis; it also investigates different European scenarios of the future and the conditions under which they may materialize. The emancipatory concern which drives this book is very much inspired by the Critical Political Economy Research Network, which organized several workshops on different aspects of the European crisis. We wish to thank all the organizers and participants; several of them also have provided a chapter for this collected volume.

We are very grateful to all the editors of the RIPE Series who shared our idea of integrating the perspectives of post-Keynesian and critical political economy approaches on the crisis within this volume. In particular we wish to thank Ian Bruff for his constructive criticism and for all his substantial support from the very early stages until the end of this project. Many thanks also to Joachim Becker and Magnus Ryner for their highly valuable feedback on different aspects of the book. We are grateful also to the anonymous referees and their helpful comments. At Routledge, we wish to thank Nicola Parkin and Peter Harris for all their straightforward support for this volume. We would also like to thank Helmut Holzinger, Managing Director of the University of Applied Sciences BFI Vienna, who strongly supported the project and provided all the necessary research funds which allowed us to realize this book.

Finally, we are sincerely indebted to all our contributors, who managed to write along the suggested lines and titles we provided them with. This volume attempts to open up a debate among the alternative approaches of post-Keynesians and critical political economy scholars on European integration and its crisis. We are confident that this will substantially enrich the ongoing discussions on possible emancipatory European futures.

Johannes Jäger and Elisabeth Springler

Abbreviations

BRICS	Brazil, Russia, Italy, China, South Africa
CDFTA	Comprehensive and Deep Free Trade Agreement
CEE	Central and Eastern Europe
CFSP	Common Foreign and Security Policy
COM	European Commission
CPE	Critical Political Economy
CSDP	Common Security and Defence Policy
DG ECFIN	General Directorate for Economic and Financial Affairs
DWSR	Dollar Wall Street Regime
EBRD	European Bank for Reconstruction and Development
ECB	European Central Bank
ECSC	Economic Coal and Steel Community
EEC	European Economic Community
EFSF	European Financial Stability Facility
EFSM	European Financial Stabilization Mechanism
EIB	European Investment Bank
EMF	European Monetary Fund
EMS	European Monetary System
EMU	Economic and Monetary Union
EP	European Parliament
ERM	Exchange Rate Mechanism
ERT	European Round Table
ESM	European Stability Mechanism
ETUC	European Trade Union Confederation
EU	European Union
FDI	Foreign Direct Investment
FPÖ	Freiheitliche Partei Österreichs
FRG	Federal Republic of Germany
FSAP	Financial Services Action Plan
GCC	Gulf Cooperation Council
GDP	Gross Domestic Product
GIIPS	Greece, Ireland, Italy, Portugal and Spain
GIPS	Greece, Italy, Portugal, Spain

GSP	Growth and Stability Pact
ILO	International Labour Organization
IMF	International Monetary Fund
IPE	International Political Economy
LOLR	Lender of the Last Resort
LTRO	Long Term Refinancing Operations
MENA	Middle East/North Africa
MoU	Memorandum of Understanding
NAFTA	North American Free Trade Agreement
NATO	North Atlantic Treaty Organization
NGCA	National General Collective Agreement
NICs	Newly Industrializing Countries
NSA	National Security Agency
OECD	Organisation for Economic Co-operation and Development
OMT	Outright Monetary Transaction
PIIGs	Portugal, Italy, Ireland, Greece
PKE	Post-Keynesian Economics
REFIT	Regulatory Fitness and Performance Programme
SEA	Single European Act
SGP	Stability and Growth Pact
TFEU	Treaty on the Functioning of the European Union
TSCG	Treaty for Stability, Coordination and Governance in the Economic and Monetary Union
TTIP	Transatlantic Trade and Investment Partnership
ULC	Unit Labour Costs

Debating the future of Europe

Critical political economy and post-Keynesian perspectives

Johannes Jäger and Elisabeth Springler

The crisis in Europe is often discussed as a crisis of European integration or a crisis of national economies within Europe. Both, the 'methodological Europeanism' and 'methodological nationalism' fail to consider the important links between economic and political processes at different spatial scales, and hence, asymmetries and phenomena of uneven development. In addition, a systematic discussion of possible scenarios based on a sound analysis of the causes of the crisis and the implications of anti-crisis policies is still missing. This volume seeks to close this gap by systematically integrating the analysis of economic policy or 'technical' solutions to the crisis within a broader framework of political economy. We argue that combining critical political economy approaches and post-Keynesian perspectives allows for a systematic understanding of the economic and political dimensions of the crisis. Although both approaches have the capacity to deal within asymmetries and uneven development, the heterogeneity in Europe has been an often largely neglected dimension of analysis. However, this recent crisis has shown that this is an essential dimension which has to be addressed in order to better understand the dynamics of European development and integration. Hence, the book aims to deal with asymmetries in Europe and to bridge the gap between the two perspectives.

At the surface the economic crisis appeared in Europe in 2008. It was not just a crisis of the Eurozone but a crisis which affects the European Union as a whole. In 2013 gross domestic product (GDP) in the European Union (28 member states) was 1.5% (and 1.9% in the Eurozone) lower compared to the pre-crisis level. Despite frequent optimistic forecasts, dynamic and cohesive development has not been on Europe's horizon yet. In addition, the development and the impact of the crisis have been very uneven. While for economic core countries of the European Union such as Germany the crisis 'only' manifested in a long-term period of deep stagnation with a poor 2.9% accumulated growth since the beginning of the crisis, most peripheral economies in Europe (with the important exception of Poland) suffered a deep recession. This was not just the case for 'old' Eurozone member countries such as Greece (with a negative record of 23.4% of economic decline) but also for 'new' Eurozone member countries (e.g. Slovenia -10.1%) and non-Eurozone member countries such as Latvia (-8.8%) or Romania (-3.5%) (for an overview of the data see EuroMemoGroup 2014: Table 1.1). What started out as a banking crisis further developed as a Eurozone crisis and was reframed in dominant discourses as a public debt crisis. As the contributions in this volume show, European crisis management in 2009/2010 was inspired by rescuing the financial sector and by Keynesian 'deficit spending' in the core countries of the EU. This helped to avoid a complete meltdown. In the following years the crisis has been used to implement austerity and to deepen authoritarian neoliberalism at the level of the EU (cf. Bruff 2014). Although several years of European crisis management have helped to prevent a total economic and political collapse, it has been far from successful – even in its own terms – namely in restoring solid economic growth. This remains an unresolved puzzle in mainstream economics and dominant approaches in political science. However, if the aim was to take advantage of the crisis in order to deepen neoliberalism and class power, it was successful. In general, it is still not clear what the final outcome of the crisis will be because hitherto implemented measures have tended to increase contradictions. This lack of a clear trajectory is a typical feature of a big structural crisis. The present volume investigates the uneven nature of the European crisis and distinguishes possible scenarios regarding future developments by combining two very promising critical perspectives.

The need for alternatives: critical political economy and post-Keynesian perspectives

The flaws of mainstream European integration literature have been documented very well (Van Apeldoorn, Drahokoupil and Horu 2009; Nousios, Overbeek and Tsolakis 2012b: 9ff.). Also, the problems and shortcomings of economic mainstream theory to explain the European integration and crisis have been analysed in detail (see Revue de la Régulation, Euromemo, Post-Keynesian Economic Study Group, Real World Economics). Whilst since the 1970s European integration has increasingly adopted a neoliberal form which was justified by neo-classical economic theory, it has suffered from constantly declining growth rates since the 1970s (see Cafruny and Ryner 2007). Even in its own terms, namely with regards to economic growth, neoliberal European integration has been no success. In addition, the decades before the crisis were already characterized by a tendency towards a declining share of labour income and a rising share of profits, contributing to increasing inequality (OECD 2011). With regards to the crisis, neo-classical economic theory and conventional European integration scholars as well as Varieties of Capitalism approaches lack convincing explanations (Bruff 2011; Ryner 2012). The highly orthodox nature of European integration scholarship has failed to even recognize that there exists the possibility of a crisis (see Ryner in Chapter 1 of this volume). This is not the place to criticize in detail mainstream theory, but the intention of this volume is to show how alternative approaches help to assess European integration, its crisis and future developments.

Both, critical political economy (CPE) and post-Keynesian (PK) perspectives represent important strands of alternative, heterodox, traditions in the social sciences, and provide a more adequate basis for systematically reflecting on possible paths of future European development. Mainstream or orthodox scholarship tends to reproduce power structures. As Robert Cox has argued, it is concerned with problem solving within a given societal structure rather than with overcoming or transforming this structure (Cox 1981: 128). This is different in the case of critical or heterodox scholarship. Heterodox approaches are at the margins of established academic disciplines and tend to be close to less powerful or subaltern groups in society such as social movements, trade unions, etc. CPE is considered to be an important strand of thought within a heterodox scholarship. PK economics – despite the fact that it often shows a problem solving tendency – is part of heterodox traditions too. Its conviction that capitalist economies do not tend towards full employment but to stagnation, and that this hurts and weakens workers, totally contradicts mainstream approaches in economics. CPE stands in the tradition of political economy, includes the insights of Marx, and analyses the society as a whole by providing an integrated framework for the analysis of economy, society and the state. It can therefore be considered a pre-disciplinary but also a post-disciplinary perspective (Jessop and Sum 2001) which overcomes today's prevailing disciplinary divisions. At the core of CPE is the abstract concept of social relations of production, and hence, a class-based framework of economy and society (for an overview of the Critical International Political Economy debates, see Shields, Bruff and Macartney 2011). In general, CPE tries to understand, explain, and critique given societal structures and developments. It aims at contributing to emancipatory struggles and to overcome exploitation and power relations. Related to the crisis it investigates its causes, dynamics and implications. This approach searches for conditions which allow for alternative developments which overcome specific historical modes of capitalism such as neoliberalism. However, against the background of the multiple contradictions of capitalism, ultimately CPE seeks to overcome a capitalist mode of production. Within CPE there are numerous more specific theories which address different aspects. This is also the case with regards to the analysis of European integration. PK approaches stand in the tradition of Keynes but also combine elements of classical political economy, Marx, and institutionalist approaches and often explicitly criticize neo-classical approaches.

The first post-Keynesians, though not named as such but joined in their economic beliefs, emerged with the publication of the *General Theory* in 1936 and framed the opposition to the equilibrium modelling of Hicks in his interpretation of the *General Theory*. Despite the fact that exactly this influential work of J.R. Hicks (1937) can be seen as the birth of Neoclassical Synthesis and led to the so called *bastard Keynesianism* – a term coined by Joan Robinson (1962: 690) – to sharpen the distinction between equilibrium or so called mainstream economists and alternative economic approaches within the wider Keynesian tradition (see e.g. Snowdon and Vane 2005: Chapter 2), Hicks' work can also be interpreted as important for opening the discussion of Keynes' work to a broader audience. Early post-Keynesians were united in their opposition to the existing economic mainstream, which also manifested in the Cambridge Controversies (e.g. King 2002: Chapter 4), and it becomes evident that their economic thinking was also influenced by their own economic experiences and connectivity to classical economists as Marx. Main proponents in the Cambridge Controversies like Joan Robinson and Sraffa, as well as the works of Kalecki, that substantially influence post-Keynesian economics, account for the economic plurality in PK thinking. This approach usually criticizes economic mainstream approaches and neo-liberal economic policies. It provides an alternative perspective to explain economic growth and unemployment. Already Keynes (1930) had expected, in his famous essay 'Economic Possibilities for our Grandchildren', that a liberal capitalism would end up in stagnation. The key addressee of PK work is 'the State', which is expected to implement adequate institutions and policies to ensure growth and full employment. Besides government spending, a more equal income distribution (including a strong welfare state), and an adequate monetary policy and regulation of the financial sector are considered crucial to ensure stable and high economic growth and full employment. Hence, it aims at better living conditions for workers within a reformed capitalism. In order to rescue capitalism as a social mode of production, a specific configuration of economic institutions and policies is considered indispensable. To avoid or to quickly overcome economic crisis is considered crucial.

Hence, with regards to the ultimate goal there is an important difference between CPE and PK perspectives. While CPE aspires to radical reformism in the short run and the overcoming of capitalism and the implementation of solidary and rational society (Demirovic 2005) in the long run, the overall goal in PK approaches is a well-functioning capitalism characterized by full employment and a well-developed welfare state. With regards to its philosophical roots, CPE relies on critical realism or philosophies which are relatively close to it such as historical materialism, and PK work is based on critical realism, too. Hence, CPE and PK perspectives do stand on a similar philosophical ground (Lawson 1999; Brown, Fleetwood and Roberts 2002; Nousios, Overbeek and Tsolakis 2012a: 258ff). From a CPE position, PK contributions can be seen as a more concrete approach to the analysis of economic processes at the surface or price level. The analysis of the role of money, the financial sector and central banking tend to be less developed in CPE, but there are important links and both perspectives are complementary in this regard (Evans 2004). PK work has drawn special attention on the topic of endogenous money (Davidson 2002) and its results for actors in capitalist economies. While this leads, in a first step, to a split in PK scholarship into different points of view on endogenous money (for an overview, see Lavoie 2006; Dow 2006) and the partial marginalization of especially one part, the *circuit money* approach (e.g. Gnos 2006; Realfonzo 2006), discussion and research opened up again more recently. The concept of financialization (Epstein 2005; Erturk et al. 2008; Lapavitsas 2013) and also the regulation approach (Clévenot 2011) turned out to provide important links which combined insights from PK and CPE. Financialized, finance-led, or finance-dominated capitalism were terms used to describe pre-crisis modes of development (Stockhammer 2008). Also, both approaches point to the importance of the global economic and financial structures and the Euro in explaining dynamics of European integration (Cafruny and Ryner 2007; see Flassbeck and Lapavitsas in Chapter 8 in this volume). Moreover, there is a further link between a specific strand of PK economies – especially the monetary economists of the French and Italian *circuitist approach* – going back to Michal Kalecki and CPE. In his famous article, Kalecki (1943) explains why capitalists have a structural interest in at least a minimum level of unemployment and why they prefer military Keynesianism to welfare spending.

To sum up, whilst CPE understands the economy as part of society, which means that economics and politics are intrinsically linked and the 'economic' is considered to be part of a broader social relation, PK approaches focus on the analysis of economic relations, thereby abstracting from the societal basis of the economy and in so doing from political processes. Thereby, PK work focuses on specific economic mechanisms, the impact of institutions and economic policies. It shows how problems – which in CPE are called economic contradictions (such as a lack of demand in PK terminology, or over-accumulation in CPE language) – can be overcome by adequate institutional arrangements. In general, PK approaches tend to be more optimistic that the correct policies and institutions – and not the wrong neo-classical policies – can be implemented by benevolent politicians and economic policy makers. Contrary to this, CPE approaches tend to argue that it is not a question of the correct economic ideas and policies but of the configuration of social forces which have the power to implement desired structures, hence economic policy and economic development in the end it is a political question.

Crisis and uneven development

In general, there are two different ways how critical political economists and post-Keynesians deal with the economic crisis. When the crisis broke out as a banking crisis first, many scholars focused on the problems in the financial sector in order to deal with the roots of the crisis. However, this has changed since then. Today, many scholars point to problems in the productive economy and to the links between production and finance. In the present volume, most contributions adopt, with a varying emphasis, this more integrative perspective for analysing the crisis. In addition, it has to be clarified what one refers to when talking about crisis, because the term is used differently.

Post-Keynesians usually refer to an economic crisis in terms of the lack of economic growth. In general, growth is considered to be endogenous, path-dependent and mainly driven by investment as a substantial factor of aggregate demand (Setterfield 2001). When explaining crisis, PK scholars point to falling investment, a development which may have different origins. One important cause is the inherent instability of financial structures (Minsky 1992). The outbreak of the global economic crisis in the financial sector underlines the importance of this aspect and drew again more attention towards Minsky, who focused on increasing financial fragility in boom phases and pointed out that the financial structures of developed economies were unstable even in these times, for example in the 1960s (Minsky 1982). However, a lack of aggregate demand may also be caused by defective institutional configurations which lead to economic imbalances such as those from which Europe is suffering. Hence, PK analysis provides a very specific account of the concrete 'mechanisms' of economic crisis. In addition, it provides instruments for analysing the medium-term implications of overall economic policy measures such as increasing wages, government expenditure, taxes or interest rates. Parts of these economic policy recommendations are directly influenced by Minsky (2008: Chapter 13), such as the discussion of the importance of the state as employer or the argument for strong and stable institutional settings in the financial markets that offset overly strong economic upswings and downturns (e.g. Palley 2003; Auerback, McCulley and Parenteau 2010). Other PK proposals reflect on the underlying theoretical incapabilities of mainstream economics and provide more general propositions as a *Keynesian New Deal*, which in turn should lead to a shift in overall economic policy adjustment from neoliberal proposals to Keynesian policies (e.g. Hein and Truger 2012/2013). Strong institutional settings are manifested in the demand for international macroeconomic coordination, combined with a reregulation of financial markets and stronger Keynesian macroeconomic policies. More concretely, the latter part cumulates into a third strand of proposals focusing on the inadequacy of austerity measures in times of economic crisis (e.g. Kitromilides 2011). At the centre of their attention are the effects of austerity measures in times of economic distress.

In CPE, the term crisis is used more broadly. Firstly, it refers to an economic crisis in the sense of the absence of dynamic economic accumulation. The lack of accumulation of capital and economic growth are addressed in particular by the regulation school (Boyer and Saillard 2002; Jessop and Sum 2006), but also by the social structures of accumulation approach (Kotz 1994; McDonough, Reich and Kotz 2010), which both represent important strands in CPE. While the social structures of accumulation approach focuses very much on a global level and tries to distinguish different types of capitalism (state capitalism, neoliberal capitalism), the regulation school traditionally focuses on the national level while also seeking to address accumulation and regulation at different inter-related spatial scales. The starting point for the regulation approach was the question why in capitalism, despite its multiple contradictions, stable periods of economic growth can be observed. This is explained by the coherence of a regime of accumulation with a specific mode of regulation based on structurally stable institutional forms. Small and big crises are distinguished. While small crises are solved within a given mode of regulation, in order to overcome a big crisis a new regime of accumulation and a substantial change in the mode of regulation is required. Already when the crisis broke out, regulationist scholars considered it to be a systemic or big crisis (Guttmann 2008). Secondly, the term crisis is used to refer to other types of crisis such as political crisis, ideological crisis, social crisis, ecological crisis, etc. CPE scholars point to multiple crises in the current conjuncture and to the interconnectedness of different types of crises. Hence, in a CPE tradition a broad variety of explanations for the crisis which focus on different and interconnected causalities exists, and complexity is reduced in different ways. At a very abstract level, overaccumulation is considered to be the ultimate cause of crisis (Overbeek 2012). Other authors point to different types of structures or adopt agency-oriented approaches, such as neo-Gramscian perspectives, and focus on different dimensions of the crisis (e.g. Bieling 2013). CPE analyses how discourses emerge and which role they play in political struggles. It analyses the role of state apparatuses, policy making, and social struggles, etc., in normal times and also in periods of crisis. Overall, CPE is characterized by a high degree of heterogeneity, which is less a weakness and more an expression of the fact that it tries to address complexity in different ways. To some extent, this broad variety of CPE approaches to the European crisis and its futures is also mirrored in this book.

CPE and PK perspectives traditionally take uneven development and associated asymmetries seriously. However, PK work often tends to focus on the nation-state and the links between nation-states, although the role of nation-states within a larger framework such as the Eurozone is also addressed. In a PK tradition, uneven development has been discussed by mainly Myrdal, Hirschmann and Thirlwall. The spatial dimension of the crisis is mainly discussed when referring to economic imbalances within Europe, and this analysis mainly applies to Thirlwall's (2003: 41) work stating that growth might be restrained by the balance of payments (e.g. Soukiazis, Cerqueira and Antunes 2013/2014). Permanent current account deficits serve as the crucial factor for growth repression, and surpluses in the European North have mirrored the current account deficits in the European South. The flow of funds from the European North to the European South had led to substantial imbalances, and diverging unit labour costs are emphasized when searching for the reason for persisting imbalances (see Niechoj, Chapter 9 and Flassbeck and Lapavitsas, Chapter 8 in this volume). The importance of reshaping labour costs, increasing wage levels in the European North and strengthening wage bargaining coordination across Europe becomes even more important when taking the results from empirical studies on a European level into account (Ederer and Reschenhofer 2013). Hence, PK approaches demand structural change in the sense of stronger macroeconomic coordination combined with proposals to diminish European imbalances and to stabilize global financial markets.

CPE has a long-standing tradition of dealing with uneven development. It often focuses on the globally uneven dimensions of capitalist development and the perspectives for less developed or dependent countries and regions (Cardoso and Faletto 1979; Kay 1989; Smith 2008; Harvey 2006; Petras and Veltmeyer 2013). However, uneven development in Europe has also been addressed (Becker and Jäger 2012; Drahokoupil and Myant 2012). The concepts of core and periphery are crucial for the understanding of uneven development. Generally speaking, core and periphery interact in an asymmetric way. This leads to the emergence of different economic and political structures in the core and periphery. According to critical political economy, developments in the core should not be understood without including the analysis of the periphery and vice versa. Core and periphery are not just concepts to be applied to the global scale but are also useful for discussing inner-European developments, because of the huge disparities, structural differences and very asymmetrical links between different European political economies.

In general, there are apparent links between CPE and PK perspectives with regards to the understanding of the crisis, even if the focus and the specific explanations are different. For example, the understanding of the tendency in capitalism towards crisis and stagnation is similar in CPE and PK work. What is called a crisis of over-exploitation – in the specific expression of an overaccumulation, overproduction or underconsumption – in CPE scholarship is considered to be a crisis due to the lack of effective demand in PK work. Both approaches provide important but different concepts which help to address the uneven nature of capitalist development and its crisis, as the different contributions in this volume show.

Structure of the book

The contributions in the book investigate central aspects of the European crisis. Thereby, they do not focus on isolated country cases but address the general structure of uneven development between core and periphery in Europe. The Eurozone crisis – despite its specific features – is considered to be part of the broader European crises, and this has to be investigated. The individual chapters do not in all cases adopt either a CPE perspective or a PK perspective, and in some papers both perspectives are combined. Overall, the analysis of the genealogy of the crisis provides a framework for investigating possible European futures.

I: The European crisis in a global perspective

The first part explicitly deals with the European crisis in a global perspective. It starts with a chapter by Magnus Ryner, who investigates the failures and blind spots of mainstream European integration theories and economy orthodoxy. Building on the classical work by Thomas Kuhn, he argues that the intrinsic problems in the 'paradigm' prevailing in orthodox European integration studies are founded upon on the separation between politics and economics. He explains why heterodox approaches are needed in order to understand the European crisis. In particular, Ryner suggests regulation theory which combines elements of PK and CPE to be used as an alternative framework for the analysis of European integration and its crisis.

The following chapter considers in detail how CPE and PK approaches can be linked, and what this implies for the analysis of the European crisis. On the one hand, Engelbert Stockhammer and Karsten Köhler show that PK analysis points to imbalances in Europe as cause for the European crisis, and they see European-wide wage coordination and inflationary adjustment as the way out of crisis. On the other hand, they argue that CPE, with its understanding of neoliberalism as a strategy of capitalist class interests, helps to understand the deeper roots of crisis. Hence, they show very clearly how both approaches complement each other and how they can be used to understand the crisis.

Jan Toporowski deals with global finance, the banking crisis and the role of macroeconomic regulation in the EU crisis. Focusing on PK arguments in line with Minsky regarding financial fragility in the global financial structure, he argues that macroeconomic coordination in the field of banking regulation on a European level is missing. This destabilizes not only the financial sector – primarily the banking sector – but also hampers the channelling of existing imbalances to find a way out of the global crisis, via investments. He states that appropriate imbalances in the financial sector can be used to promote investment but simultaneously fiscal deficits or imbalances are part of the situation. Fiscal deficits on their own will not manage to overcome the crisis, when financial management in terms for banking regulation is missing.

The final chapter in this section deals with Europe in a broader historical and global perspective in order to provide a firm understanding of the nature of European integration, its crisis, and its future course against the background of the development of the global political economy. European integration is analysed within the context of global US hegemony. Alan Cafruny argues that uneven development and German geoeconomic orientation are crucial for understanding European dynamics. In the crisis, the logic of power has become entirely intergovernmental and the centre of gravity has shifted from a Franco-German directorate to Berlin. Given the mercantilist export structure of German big business, Cafruny argues that it seems extremely unlikely that Germany will transform itself into a 'benevolent' European hegemon exerting power as leadership and not domination. This has severe implications for future European integration and potential solutions to the crisis.

II: The uneven nature of European integration and of crisis management

The second part deals with central aspects of the uneven structure of European integration, the crises and its management by bringing different perspectives together. It starts with a chapter on uneven and dependent development in Europe, building mainly on the insights of regulation theory and the dependency approach. Joachim Becker, Johannes Jäger and Rudy Weissenbacher show how different regimes of accumulation were asymmetrically linked and what this implied for the crisis and uneven nature of European development and crisis management. They argue that centrifugal tendencies have become stronger, and that due to asymmetric and dependent structures within Europe the periphery will have to rely more strongly on its own strategies in order to open up the perspective for progressive development.

The next chapter outlines a neo-Gramscian perspective for understanding uneven European development and political and economic struggles, and the implications for the future of Europe. Hans-Jürgen Bieling explicitly addresses the transnational and supranational dynamics of European crisis management against the background of uneven development. He argues that crisis management can be understood as a revolution from above which is aimed at restoring power relations under new constitutional conditions of the European Union.

This is followed by a paper dealing with responses to the crisis which can be summarized under the heading of 'enhancing competitiveness'. Angela Wigger shows how transnational capitalist interests at the European level have been able to deepen the neoliberal 'competitiveness' agenda which was a main reason for the economic crisis in Europe and which has its roots in overaccumulation. This focus on competition together with austerity policy weakens labour and puts workers in different member states into even stronger direct competition.

A further chapter explains economic imbalances in Europe and shows their consequences and implications for future developments. Heiner Flassbeck and Costas Lapavitsas build their argument mainly on a post-Keynesian analysis but also on critical political economy perspectives. Thereby, they focus in particular on the specific problems and asymmetries within the Eurozone. They analyse the dramatic consequences of economic implications of crisis management in Europe and provide a proposal for alternative economic policies in the Eurozone.

III: Possible futures

Given the uneven and dependent structure of European development, the final part of the book seeks to investigate different possible European futures. This starts with a chapter by Torsten Niechoj. He adopts a post-Keynesian perspective. Based on this, he develops three different scenarios for sketching out future European developments. In the following chapter John Grahl puts the more recent crisis and its management into a historical perspective. He shows how former progressive elements in terms of social policies have slowly disappeared in the EU. This long-run tendency has speeded up during the recent crisis and seems very unlikely to be reversed soon.

Lukas Oberndorfer discusses the management of the economic crisis by adopting a critical legal perspective. In a detailed way, he shows why

European economic governance has become more authoritarian during the crisis. This analysis shows the limits for progressive scenarios within authoritarian constitutionalism. He asks to what extent a deepening of democracy is necessary and possible in order to allow for alternative development trajectories.

The next chapter in this section, by Mònica Clua-Losada and Laura Horn, deals with the role of labour in Europe. Contrary to the previous chapters, this contribution focuses less on the specific European conditions and more on the role of labour as a protagonist in pushing for progressive developments in general. In so doing, the authors provide a more long-run perspective for potential future developments which, due to the complexity of social struggles, cannot be derived directly from the given specific historical configuration.

Finally, some general conclusions based on the contributions in the book are presented. This concluding chapter attempts to discuss systematically possible futures in an integrative way and to give an overview for the preconditions necessary for them to materialize.

References

Auerback, M., McCulley, P. and Parenteau, R.W. (2010) What Would Minsky Do? In Papadimitriou, D. and Wray, R. (eds) *The Elgar Companion to Hyman Minsky*. Cheltenham/Northampton: Edward Elgar, pp. 117–133.

Becker, J. and Jäger, J. (2012) Integration in Crisis: A Regulationist Perspective on the Interaction of European Varieties of Capitalism. *Competition & Change* 16(3), pp. 169–187.

Bieling, H.-J. (2013) European Financial Capitalism and the Politics of (De-)financialization. *Competition & Change* 17(3), pp. 283–298.

Boyer, R. and Saillard, Y. (eds) (2002) *Régulation Theory. The State of the Art*. London: Routledge.

Brown, A., Fleetwood, S. and Roberts, J.M. (eds) (2002) *Critical Realism and Marxism*. London: Routledge.

Bruff, I. (2011) What about the Elephant in the Room? Varieties of Capitalism, Varieties in Capitalism. *New Political Economy* 16(4), pp. 481–500.

Bruff, I. (2014) The Rise of Authoritarian Neoliberalism. *Rethinking Marxism* 26(1), pp. 113–129.

Cafruny, A.W. and Ryner, J.M. (2007) *Europa at Bay. In the Shadow of US Hegemony*. London: Lynne Rienner Publishers.

Cardoso, F.H. and Faletto, E. (1979 [1971]) *Dependency and Development in Latin America*. Berkeley: University of California Press.

Clévenot, M. (2011) Post-keynésianisme et théorie de la régulation: des perspectives communes. *Revue de la Régulation* 10(2).

Cox, R. (1981) Social Forces, States, and World Orders. *Millennium – Journal of International Studies* 10(2), pp. 126–155.

Davidson, P. (2002) *Financial Markets, Money and the Real World*. Cheltenham and Northampton: Edward Elgar.

Demirovic, A. (2005) Die Perspektive der vernünftigen Gesellschaft. *PROKLA. Zeitschrift für Kritische Sozialwissenschaft* 35(4), pp. 479–496.

Dow, S. (2006) Endogenous Money: Structuralist. In Arestis, P. and Sawyer, M. (eds) *A Handbook of Alternative Monetary Economics*. Cheltenham and Northampton: Edward Elgar, pp. 35–51.

Drahokoupil, J. and Myant, M. (2012) The European Sub-prime? Financial Crisis and the East-European Periphery. In Petros N., Overbeek, H. and Tsolakis A. (eds) *Globalisation and European Integration. Critical Approaches to Regional Order and International Relations*. Abingdon: Routledge.

Eckhard, H. and Truger, A. (2012/2013) Finance-dominated Capitalism in Crisis – The Case for a Global Keynesian New Deal. *Journal of Post Keynesian Economics* 35(2), pp. 187–213.

Ederer, S.T. and Reschenhofer, P. (2013) Macroeconomic Imbalances in the EU. *Working Paper* No 42. WWW for Europe. [Online] Available from http://www.foreurope.eu/fileadmin/documents/pdf/Workingpapers/WWWforEurope_WPS_no042_MS71.pdf [Accessed 1 June 2014].

Epstein, G.A. (ed.) (2005) *Financialization and the World Economy*. Cheltenham: Edward Elgar.

Erturk, I., Froud, J., Johal, S., Leaver, A. and Williams, K. (2008) *Financialization at Work*. London: Routledge.

EuroMemoGroup (2014) *EuroMemorandum 2014. The Deepening Divisions in Europe and the Need for a Radical Alternative to EU Policies*. [Online] Available from http://www2.euromemorandum.eu/uploads/euromemorandum_2014.pdf [Accessed 1 June 2014].

Evans, T. (2004) Marxian and Post-Keynesian Theories of Finance and the Business Cycle. *Capital & Class* (83), pp. 47–100.

Gnos, C. (2006) French Circuit Theory. In Arestis, P. and Sawyer, M. (eds) *A Handbook of Alternative Monetary Economics*. Cheltenham and Northampton: Edward Elgar, pp. 87–104.

Guttmann, R. (2008) A Primer on Finance-led Capitalism and its Crisis. *Revue de la Régulation* (3/4).

Harvey, D. (2006) *Spaces of Global Capitalism. Towards a Theory of Uneven Geographical Development*. London: Verso.

Hein, E. and Truger, A. (2012/2013) Finance-dominated Capitalism in Crisis – The Case for a Global Keynesian New Deal. *Journal of Post Keynesian Economics* 35 (2), pp. 187–213.

Hicks, J.R. (1937) Mr. Keynes and the 'Classics': A Suggested Interpretation. *Econometrica* 5(2), pp. 147–159.

Jessop, B. and Sum, N.-L. (2001) Pre-Disciplinary and Post-Disciplinary Perspectives in Political Economy. *New Political Economy* 6(1), pp. 89–101.

Jessop, B. and Sum, N.-L. (2006) *Beyond the Regulation Approach. Putting Capitalist Economies in their Place*. Cheltenham: Edward Elgar.

Kalecki, M. (1943) Political Aspects of Full Employment. *Political Quarterly* 14, pp. 322–331.

Kay, C. (1989) *Latin American Theories of Development and Underdevelopment*. London: Routledge.

Keynes, J.M. (1930) Economic Possibilities for our Grandchildren. In Keynes J.M. [1963] *Essays in Persuasion*, New York: W.W. Norton & Co., pp. 358–373.

King, J.E. (2002). *A History of Post Keynesian Economics Since 1936*. Cheltenham andNorthampton: Edward Elgar.

Kitromilides, Y. (2011) Deficit Reduction, the Age of Austerity, and the Paradox of Insolvency. *Journal of Post Keynesian Economics* 33(3), pp. 517–535.

Kotz, D.M. (1994) The Regulation Theory and the Social Structure of Accumulation Approach. In Kotz, D.M., McDonough, T. and Reich, M. (eds) *Social Structures of Accumulation. The Political Economy of Growth and Crisis*. Cambridge, MA: Cambridge University Press, pp. 85–98.

Lapavitsas, C. (ed.) (2013) *Financialization in Crisis*. Chicago, IL: Haymarket Books.

Lavoie, M. (2006) Endogenous Money: Accommodationist. In Arestis, P. and Sawyer, M. (eds) *A Handbook of Alternative Monetary Economics*. Cheltenham and Northampton: Edward Elgar, pp. 17–34.

Lawson, T. (1999) Connections and Distinctions. Post Keynesianism and Critical Realism. *Journal of Post Keynesian Economics* 22(1), pp. 3–14.

McDonough, T., Reich, M. and Kotz, D.M. (eds) (2010) *Contemporary Capitalism and Its Crises. Social Structure of Accumulation Theory for the 21st Century*. Cambridge, MA: Cambridge University Press.

Minsky, H. (1982) Can 'It' Happen Again? In Minsky, H. *Can 'It' Happen Again? Essays on Instability and Finance*. New York: M.E. Sharpe, pp. 3–13. [Reprint from Carson, D. (ed.) (1963) Banking and Monetary Studies. Homewood: Irwin, pp. 101–111.]

Minsky, H. (1992) The Financial Instability Hypothesis. *Working Paper* No. 74. The Jerome Levy Institute.

Minsky, H. (2008 [1986]) *Stabilizing an Unstable Economy*. New York: McGraw Hill.

Nousios, P., Overbeek, H. and Tsolakis, A. (eds) (2012) *Globalization and European Integration. Critical Approaches to Regional Order and International Relations*. Abingdon: Routledge.

Nousios, P., Overbeek, H. and Tsolakis, A. (2012) Globalisation and European Integration. The Nature of the Beast. In Nousios, P., Overbeek, H. and Tsolakis, A. (eds) *Globalization and European Integration. Critical Approaches to Regional Order and International Relations*. Abingdon: Routledge, pp. 3–32.

OECD (2011) *Divided We Stand: Why Inequality Keeps Rising*. Paris: OECD.

Overbeek, H. (2012) Sovereign Debt Crisis in Euroland: Root, Causes and Implications for European Integration. *The International Spectator: Italian Journal of International Affairs* 47(1), pp. 30–48.

Palley, Th. (2003) Asset Price Bubbles and the Case for Asset Based Reserve Requirements. *Challenge* 46(3), pp. 53–72.

Petras, J. and Veltmeyer, H. (2013) *Imperialism and Capitalism in the Twenty-First Century. A System in Crisis*. Farnham: Ashgate.

Realfonzo, R. (2006) The Italian Circuitist Approach. In Arestis, P. and Sawyer, M. (eds) *A Handbook of Alternative Monetary Economics*. Cheltenham and Northampton: Edward Elgar, pp. 105–120.

Robinson, J. (1962) Review: *Money, Trade and Economic Growth* by J.G. Johnson. *The Economic Journal* 72(287), pp. 690–692.

Ryner, M. (2012) Financial Crisis, Orthodoxy and Heterodoxy in the Production of Knowledge about the EU. *Millennium – Journal of International Studies* 40(3), pp. 647–673.

Setterfield, M. (2001) Macrodynamics. In Holt, R.P.F. and Pressman, S. (eds) *A New Guide to Post Keynesian Economics*. London: Routledge.

Shields, S., Bruff, I. and Macartney, H. (eds) (2011) *Critical International Political Economy. Dialogue, Debate and Dissensus.* Basingstoke: Palgrave Macmillan.

Smith, N. (2008) *Uneven Development. Nature, Capital, and the Production of Space.* Athens: The University of Georgia Press, 3rd edition.

Snowdon, B. and Vane, H. (2005) *Modern Macroeconomics, Its Origins, Development and Current State.* Cheltenham/Northampton: Edward Elgar.

Soukiazis, E., Cerqueira, P.A. and Antunes, M. (2013/2014) Growth Rates Constrained by Internal and External Imbalances and the Role of Relative Prices: Empirical Evidence from Portugal. *Journal of Post Keynesian Economics.* 36(2), pp. 275–298.

Stockhammer, E. (2008) Some Stylized Facts on the Finance-Dominated Accumulation Regime. *Competition and Change* 12(2), pp. 184–202.

Thirlwall, A.P. (2003) *Trade, the Balance of Payments and Exchange Rate Policy in Developing Countries.* Cheltenham and Northampton: Edward Elgar.

Van Apeldoorn, B., Drahokoupil, J. and Laura, H. (eds) (2009) *Contradictions and Limits of Neoliberal European Governance. From Lisbon to Lisbon.* Houndmills: Palgrave Macmillan.

Part I

The European crisis in a global perspective

1 The crisis of European integration and economic reason

Orthodoxy versus heterodoxy[1]

Magnus Ryner

This chapter has two objectives. Firstly, it offers an explanation why orthodox European integration scholarship failed to identify, let alone predict, the factors that generated the crisis in Europe.[2] Secondly, it identifies the ontological foundation of a heterodox recasting of the production of knowledge about the EU that faces the full implication of the anomaly that the financial crisis represents for integration scholarship, which with variations forms the basis of subsequent chapters in this book.

Concerning the first aim, I cut through variations in the complex ecosystem of integration theory to identify their common code that is 'prior to any theoretical rule' (Kuhn 1962: 24, 66–67), and which owes its success primarily to instrumental reasons. Instrumentality is not in and of itself a problem, and the capacity of European integration scholarship to address certain particular questions is not in doubt. Anxious to shroud itself in the aura of science, however, European integration scholarship conflates the particularity of its instrumentalism with general knowledge about the EU. It thereby constitutes itself as an *orthodoxy* that is unduly intolerant towards forms of research on the EU that do not conform. Hence, there are important questions and issues pertaining to the EU that fall outside the borders of admissibility as defined by the code of European integration orthodoxy, and which it cannot address. These could be called 'blind-spots'. It is the argument of this article that the emergent properties of the financial crisis are located exactly at such a blind-spot of European integration orthodoxy. To invoke Puchala's (1971) oft-cited metaphor about the blind and elephants, one could say that the financial crisis points to a central part of the proverbial beast – perhaps the trunk – that European integration orthodoxy does not touch at all.

Concerning second aim of the article, I suggest that a more productive *heterodoxy* can be discerned from Post-Keynesian and Critical Political Economy. These approaches have the distinct advantage over the European integration orthodoxy in that they conceive production, power and hence a significant element of arbitrariness as *co-constitutive of 'integration' itself.* Hence, they are better placed to discern the arbitrary elements that generated the financial crisis, with attendant implications for Europe.

Orthodoxy, heterodoxy and European integration

The terms orthodoxy and heterodoxy are derived from the concept of *doxa*. Doxa refers to unconscious, taken-for-granted, and habitual assumptions of the world that define the universe of possible discourse in a social meaning system. Related to the concept of *habitus,* doxa determines what resonates and what is recognizable or 'sensible'. Orthodoxy arises when these assumptions are questioned by heterodox challenges to this universality and taken-for-grantedness (heterodoxy is defined simply by way of these terms of negation). In such situations, orthodoxy defends *doxa* by postulating the taken-for-granted assumptions as 'reified abstractions', which deem heterodox challenges as inadmissible and nonsensical. As such, doxa and orthodoxy are intimately wound up in the tendency of social orders to naturalize their own arbitrariness (Bourdieu 1977: 164).

Thomas Kuhn can be invoked to defend the proposition that orthodoxy does not only exist in traditional societies or in religious world views, but also – as Bourdieu insisted – in the social scientific field (Kuhn 1962). Whilst, according to the scientific method, all hypothetical proposition should in principle be subject to falsification, as Kuhn's work on paradigms suggests this is not the case. It is not even possible to describe the world scientifically without resort to certain concepts. As a result, the structure of scientific reasoning remains trapped in certain foundational *a priori* assumptions – or reified abstractions – that mediate between empirical research and causal claims in a complex reality (for more on this, see van Apeldoorn, Bruff and Ryner 2010).

Whilst it might be one step too far to suggest that EU scholarship constitutes a Kuhnian scientific paradigm, it is justified to suggest that EU scholarship has orthodox codes. As Rosamond's sociology of knowledge of the field suggests, social scientific knowledge production on the EU has not developed simply as a natural-rational response to external events. Whilst not denying that European integration scholarship constitutes a progressive research programme that has developed in response to such events, Rosamond (2007) shows that the *particularity* of these responses is due to a 'disciplinary politics' internal to European integration scholarship itself. This disciplinary politics is power-laden and determines what counts as legitimate research and how it should be conducted. Taking this cue from Rosamond, and relating Kuhn to Bourdieu, it can be argued that the orthodox codes of this disciplinary politics shape the habitus of the scientific field and set the terms for what is considered to be serious debate. As such, they prescribe the rules of performance in institutions through which one may project symbolic power of scientific knowledge (Bourdieu 1991: 8). Crucially, Kuhn (1962: 23) suggests that these central codes become successful because they answer questions that are considered 'acute'. Acute for whom, one might ask.

In this vein, Alan Milward and Viebeke Sørensen (1993; see also van der Pijl 1996: 263–90) trace the origins of the success of European integration orthodoxy to its appeal to American Atlanticist grand strategy after the

Second World War. It was concerned with consolidating the transatlantic alliance by rendering it organic and enduring through the reconstruction of Europe in the image of America's particular variant of modernization. This Atlanticist concept permeated the European Commission, where it has remained ideologically central in no little measure because of the importance assigned to this bureaucracy in the process. Foundational works such as those of Karl Deutsch (1957) and Ernst Haas (1968) on the politics of integration and Jacob Viner (1950) and Bela Balassa (1962) on the economics of integration, themselves based respectively on pluralist systems-theory (Parsons 1951; Easton 1953) and the neoclassical synthesis (Hicks 1937), addressed acute questions for this grand strategy and lent it intellectual credibility.

Two closely interrelated attributes of the basic and enduring code of European integration orthodoxy can be discerned from the foundational works. The first may be referred to as the *disciplinary split*, which, in contrast to IR in general, has made European integration scholarship reticent towards political economy. Classical political economy, which enjoyed a century-long golden age following the publication of Adam Smith's *The Wealth of Nations*, had rested on a unified conception of social science where production and power were seen as co-constitutive in and by social relations. Classical liberal, mercantilist and Marxist political economists had in different ways adopted such a unified conception to explore the foundations of production and distribution of surplus required to make civilization materially possible. However, with the disciplinary split in the late nineteenth century into sociology and economics, the social sciences fragmented. Neoclassical economics severed the link between production and power by summarily abandoning conundrums of value theory and their attendant concerns with classes and surplus. Identifying its concern rather with opportunity costs of 'individuals' and the allocation of scarce resources, economics restricted its view to exchange relations between 'households' and 'firms' abstracted from social structure. Sociology, by contrast, abstracted social relations from both production and power. It came to refer to something that existed in the interaction between individuals whose social existence as such was taken for granted, in contradistinction to economic and political relations. The *density* of these interactions determined the degree of orderliness, that is 'integration', of society and the potential for 'social concensus'. Political science was defined in narrow terms as 'power in government' – an abstraction that displaced social and economic relations to 'the environment' without asking how the 'environment' constrains 'government' (Wolf 1997: 8–10).

Continuing to hold on to this disciplinary split, European integration orthodoxy is based on a division of labour between the 'economics' of integration and the 'political sociology' of integration. Drawing in particular on international trade theory, the first postulates *a priori* that free-market price formation results in Pareto-optimal integration (equilibrium) between supply and demand. Taking this at face value, political sociology reduces the question of integration to one of the density of interaction required to ensure the prevalence of administrative-managerial rationality, as required to ensure social and political equilibrium.

This was a central thread of thought to Robert Cox (1976: 177–81), who in his critique of neo-functionalism came very close to the mark indeed in specifying the second attribute of the orthodox code, which may be called *the integration telos.* It is the product of an amalgam of what he calls the 'natural-rational' approach of liberal idealism and the 'positivist evolutionary' approach of functionalist systems theory. This amalgam conceives a reified-abstract telos, where it is assumed *a priori* that 'economic integration' (the realm of economics) and 'social and political integration' (the realm of political sociology) are expressions of the 'rational' and 'general' potentials that inhere in human nature. These can be distinguished from the arbitrary irrational special interests, and the realm of power politics that were associated with the old European (inter-) state system, and which poses the external constraint to the realisation of this potential. The central question *shared by all theories* of the European integration orthodoxy becomes one of whether it is warranted to be 'optimistic' or 'pessimistic' about the prospects of the integration process transcending such old-European (inter-) state politics. Hence, Stanley Hoffman's emblematic 'realist' and 'pessimistic' critique of neo-functionalism did not challenge the terms of the question as he gloomily observed the resurgence of nationalism in Gaullist guise after the Empty Chair Crisis (1966: 862–63, 872–73, 889–901). It is not difficult to see how subsequent debates between 'supranationalists' (Sandholtz and Zysman 1989; Burley and Mattli 1993; Mattli and Slaughter 1995; Jabko 1999; Fliegstein and Stone Sweet 2002) and 'intergovernmentalists' (Moravcsik 1998; 1999; Garrett 1995) on the causes and consequences of the Single Market plot onto the register of this debate, framed as they are by the regime theory of 'complex interdependence', which itself sought a middle position (Keohane and Nye 1977; Keohane 1984). 'Political science' theories of 'multilevel governance' that are supposed to break the mould of IR are strikingly caught up in the same terms of debate, based as they are on the aforementioned conventional systems theory and as such only bring the idea of a 'middle position' between the 'pessimists' and 'optimists' to its ultimate conclusion (Marks, Hooghe and Blank 1996; Hix 1999; Alesina, Angeloni and Schuknecht 2005). Similarly, contrary to what one might suppose, most constructivist scholarship does not challenge this basic code either, as questions of subjectivity tend to be reduced to more or less dense socialisation phenomena that were present in Haas' original work. These are *engrenages* that pertains to the cementing of transnational elite consensus and *politicization* that pertains to the transfer of mass loyalty and legitimate representative politics to the EU level (Risse-Kappen 1996; Risse *et al.* 1999: 147–87; 2005; Marcussen 1999; Haas 2001; Haas and Haas 2002; Checkel 2003; Zürn and Checkel 2005).

Money and finance in European integration orthodoxy

It is with reference to this code, then, that the European integration orthodoxy has made sense of money and finance in Europe, such as the formation and implication of the Economic and Monetary Union (EMU) and the creation of a single market in financial services. Consequently, this orthodoxy has departed from *a priori* assumptions that made it unable to see the signs of the developing of the crisis at the outset.

Following the intellectual division of labour of the disciplinary split and the neoclassical synthesis, the economics of integration has made excessive *a priori* assumptions about the stability of monetary and financial integration, departing as it does from equilibrium models. As such, the economics of integration offers in large measure highly specialized elaborations on one aspect or the other of the two key neoclassical theories of money and finance, namely the efficient market hypothesis and the theory of sound money. Both of these see integration of financial and money markets as no different from, and as a logical extension of, the Pareto-optimal case for free trade.

This line of reasoning is clear in the Cecchini, Padoa-Schioppa and Sapir Expert Reports, which the European Commission established to provide the intellectual point of reference for, respectively, the 'Europe 1992' Single Market, monetary integration based on 'sound money' (ultimately leading to the Maastricht design of the EMU), and the Financial Services Action Plan (FSAP) of the Lisbon Agenda (European Commission 1988; Padoa-Shioppa 1987; Sapir *et al.* 2004).

These depart from the analytical model initially developed by Bela Balassa to justify the elimination of tariff and non-tariff barriers (based on the principle of 'mutual recognition') to create an integrated European market. According to these, the economies promised by the Single Market – to be realized *inter alia* through optimal allocation of factors of production, economies of scale, technological development, competition and learning – would be facilitated by the sturdy macroeconomic framework of a monetary union. The common currency would reduce exchange rate uncertainties and transaction costs. A macroeconomic framework based on maintaining price stability and fiscal balance – as institutionalized by an independent European Central Bank (ECB) and the Growth and Stability Pact (GSP) – would increase credibility in free and therefore efficient financial markets. Such markets would minimize costs of capital and allocate resources according to their optimal utilization, especially clearing up lock-in effects in existing industries and providing resources for high-tech investments (Hartmann, Maddaloni and Manganelli 2003: 7). Lower rates of interest and transaction costs, in a context of increased competition, would provide higher rates of welfare-generating investments and innovation. These would be further induced by the liberalization of labour markets, welfare systems and taxation regimes that in part would be the result of the discipline exerted by the strict macroeconomic regime and in part induced by Lisbon Process Best Practice (the Open Method of Coordination). The outcome, as stated in the Lisbon Agenda, would be a more flexible and mobile labour force, which can be better deployed with the new investments. The overall result would be faster growth, better profitability, more employment and in time higher wages. The USA is explicitly seen as the role model with its flexible labour markets and highly capitalized and sophisticated 'deep' and liquid financial markets, which are seen as explaining the growing 'productivity-gap' between the USA and Europe.

Of course, the economics of integration currently insists that it is possible and desirable to accommodate the financial crisis in a much more parsimonious way within its framework rather than through the wholesale heterodox recasting that I suggest here. Indeed, whilst it may be conceded that attention was primarily elsewhere, it may even be claimed that the relevant warnings were there all along. Such analysis departs from a neoclassical macroeconomic (neo-Keynesian) workhorse model, where the assumption of spontaneous compulsion of the market towards balance and equilibrium is relaxed because of 'sticky' prices in rigid oligopolistic markets and imperfect information in the short run. It focuses its attention on the influx of monetary and financial resources that followed when the monetary union eliminated exchange rate risks, especially into member states in the European periphery, where stability culture was less entrenched than in the Eurozone core and most notably Germany. The attendant reduction of domestic savings, widening of indebtedness and current account deficits should have been, according to this school of thought, countered with much more stringent and precautionary fiscal policy and possibly ECB monetary policy. A prominent advocate of this view is the former Research Director of the ECB and current Minister of Finance of Portugal, Vitor Gaspar, and it provides intellectual context to the emphasis of current crisis management on the reassertion of fiscal austerity norms (Detken, Gaspar and Winkler 2004; Fagan and Gaspar 2007; Gaspar, Smets and Vestin 2007).

But the extent to which such arguments are compelling is very limited, and indeed disturbingly symptomatic of paradigm catastrophic developments. First, it does not account for the marginal status of these elements in the overall analysis. Even in 2008, the Pareto-optimal macroeconomic effects of EMU were stressed (Fagan and Gaspar 2008). Second, indebtedness and current account deficits are seen exclusively as short-term adjustment problems caused by the regime shift to monetary union. Third, the fact that the financial resources are going to consumption rather than high-tech investments in supposedly more efficient financial services markets is noted, but no attempt is made to explain it. The two latter points do not address the fact that the financial crisis started as a massive misallocation of investments in the highly developed monetary and financial market systems of the USA, which, qua the Sapir Report, was the role model to be emulated. Of course, it could be argued that the root of the problem resided in overly expansionary macroeconomic policies in the USA as well as in the PIIGs (Portugal, Italy, Ireland, Greece). But then one must entertain the possibility that it was this much more expansionary policy that explains the output and productivity gap between the USA and the EU in the first place, and not the supply-side institutional differences of labour and capital markets that the Sapir Report sought to eliminate (Crouch 2009). Finally, European economic growth would have been even more anaemic without US expansionary policies and with a tighter fiscal policy stance in the PIIGS prior to the financial crisis.

Political sociology of monetary and financial integration in Europe defers to the economics of integration with regards to economic growth and stability, and then abstracts its object of analysis altogether from economic dynamics to concern itself with the density of socio-political relations at different levels of the Euro-polity. Unremarkably then, there is little evidence of ability or interest in addressing questions that pertain to the build-up, breakout and development of the financial crisis. Moravcsik (2006), for instance, argued that the credible commitments in the Maastricht agreements had made the EU 'institutionally stable'.

The few knowledgeable analyses on the matter at hand subscribe to a very thin 'states and markets' conception of political economy. Rather than seeking an integral analysis of production and power, this variant of political economy maintains the disciplinary split and then simply treats economics and politics as externally interactive realms. As such the market equilibrium bias is retained, leading to complacent conclusions. The states and markets approach departs from a workhorse neo-Keynesian macroeconomic model to derive political implications from wedges created by sticky oligopolistic prices and imperfect short-run information. These create spaces in which interest-maximizing political actors, such as states and interest groups, can act and affect outcomes. Just as in the case of the political sociology approach in general, the question becomes one of whether it is warranted to be optimistic that the density of the webs of interdependence are sufficiently strong to credibly maintain Pareto-optimal commitments and hence political harmony.

The conclusions remained affirmative even after the outbreak of the financial crisis. Enderlein and Verdun (2009: 492) have drawn on endogenous optimum currency area theory and an old favourite concept from neo-functionalism – spillover – to remarkably conclude that none of the 'negative scenarios on the future of the EMU predicted what really happened'. In stark contrast to developments at the time of publication, they continued to assert that bond markets integration was reducing debt-servicing costs, and they suggested that 'actual empirical studies' showed that welfare state expenditure was increasing in the Eurozone and thus engendering social cohesion (ibid.: 496).[3] In the midst of escalating crisis, Enderlein and Verdun viewed the EMU as a success.

To be fair, these authors at least acknowledge that the EMU is wound up in a force-field of transnational power and we can at least begin to discern moves away from *a priori* assumptions that integration as such inherently expresses rationality-in-general. Jones (2002: 121–81; 2003: 211–18) recognizes that the EMU was motivated in part to minimize constraints on European policy-makers in global financial markets, where the US dollar is the key currency. Whilst he does not take this argument far, it is the starting point of one of the few international political economy pieces in mainstream European integration outlets which begins to identify the problems wound up with the financial crisis. Like Jones, Benjamin Cohen sees the EMU as a mechanism to adjust to the vagaries of US policy priorities and to mitigate European sensitivity and vulnerability (Cohen 2003; see also Henning 1998; 2006). Cohen's argument also rests on an analytical framework derived from the aforementioned wedges identified by the workhorse neo-Keynesian macroeconomic model, and argues that states are endowed with differential power resources to delay and deflect balance of payment adjustments (Cohen 2006). He argues that EMU has made the EU as a whole less vulnerable to the US deflection of adjustment externalities. But in the absence of a fully integrated bond market, the lack of anything equivalent to the US Treasury Bill, political fragmentation in the fiscal policy field, and an 'anti-growth bias' in its institutional setup, the Euro is no serious contender to US hegemony in the monetary and financial field (Cohen 2007; 2009). The question is, though, whether the Euro offers enough of an alternative vehicle for investment to deprive the USA of power to delay and deflect. Invoking hegemonic stability theory with its root in the work of Kindleberger, Cohen's argument suggests that this could be a profound source of instability in the world economy. This is a potentially appropriate context in which to consider the weak regime of international financial and monetary management, characterised by US passivity and unilateralism, in which the financial crisis emerged. It is also a potentially appropriate context in which to consider the inability of the USA to avoid the contagion of the financial crisis and the difficulties of managing it, especially considering that the surplus pools now reside in potential geopolitical rivals to the USA, such as China (Cohen 2009; see also Kirshner 2008; Helleiner 2008; Otero-Iglesias 2012).

On the other hand, Cohen's analysis ultimately rests on a neoclassical economic conception. Consequently, he is sanguine about the merits and stability of the international monetary regime (Cohen 2008). He has very little to say about the generative mechanisms and destabilizing dynamics behind the crisis, including those within Europe itself. More can be discerned from two of the other exceptions in mainstream integration sources, namely a piece by Jean Dermine (2000; see also Mügge 2010) on bank mergers that followed in the wake of the FSAP and one by Antoine Rebérioux (2002) on corporate governance. Dermine issued warnings that the mergers could be a source of financial instability, raising questions about bank supervision and regulation. Rebérioux raised questions about the complementarity of the reforms behind these mergers and the institutions of corporate governance in Europe.

Heterodox openings

It may not be a coincidence that both of these authors are active in France, since according to Milward and Sørensen (1993: 4), this is the centre of an intellectual alternative to European integration orthodoxy. According to them, there was a distinctive European policy concept in the post-Second World War period, which coexisted with Atlanticist grand strategy but which also offered an alternative to it. From this perspective, European 'integration' was not about dissolving nation-states through the supposedly equilibrating force of markets and managerial pluralism. It was rather about 'rescuing' the state and recasting it towards new social purposes after a war where the very being of European states as functional units were in question. US assistance and the transferring of certain functions to the Community level played an important and even enduring role in this regard. However, such transfers were also circumscribed and were pursued only to the extent that it was possible to maintain the priority of the national interest. This was a successful enterprise, since west European states in many respects became *more* powerful than they had ever been. They embarked on 'unprecedented programmes of intervention in economic and social life with the express purpose of shaping and controlling their national destinies. Concepts such as 'the mixed economy' and 'the welfare state' reflect the recognition of this 'historical reality' (ibid.: p. 5). This conjures up the image of 'social settlement' between different classes and social groups, which is quite different from the image of equilibrium that besets the European integration orthodoxy.

Heterodox tendencies emerged against this backdrop, and it has formed a liminal realm where works of relevance to the EU have been produced for some time. Two French industrialist-intellectuals, writing in the social-mercantilist tradition, have been important catalysts in this regard. Being convinced that the common and single market was necessary for economies of scale, they were nevertheless concerned with the design of the common and single market and its effects on the capacity of Europe to be able to extract relative gains in the form of high value added products and production processes as required to maintain positive-sum social bargains between labour and capital (Servan-Shreiber 1969; Albert 1993). They gave impetus to the literature on 'models' or 'varieties' of capitalism, which contra neoclassical equilibrium asserts a distinct economic rationale on European (or 'Rhenish') economic institutions based on corporatist coordination, monopolistic 'voice-based' financial relationships between banks and firms, producing social stability in the context of long-term time horizon in the service of technological change, which creates 'fruits of progress' that can be distributed. This in turn provoked an alter-ego literature by neo-Marxists, who engaged with Albert and above all Servan-Shreiber (Mandel 1967; Poulantzas 1974).

Post-Keynesian and critical political economy perspectives

These tendencies, as well as anti-neoclassical and non-equilibrium based post-Keynesianism, are brought together in the so-called Parisian regulation school (Lipietz 1987) (see also Chapter 2 by Stockhammer and Köhler and Chapter 5 by Becker *et al.* in this volume). With Post-Keynesianism and

Marxism, the regulation school sees capitalist market relations as inherently unstable and even contradictory, because of the constitutive properties in the power relation between the factors of production of capital and labour. Marx famously suggested that capitalism inherently tends towards over-accumulation. On the one hand capitalists act on the basis of the profit motive that requires the expansion of markets, but on the other surplus augmentation depends on the containment of wages which in the last instance holds back the expansion of consumption and final demand relative to the accumulation of capital. When the total mass of capital cannot be profitably deployed, this generates crisis tendencies. To be sure, technological change can contain this, but intensified competition will generate uneven effects that compound general crisis-tendencies. Drawing on the position advocated by Joan Robinson and Piero Sraffa in the Cambridge capital controversy, post-Keynesians agree that capitalist dynamics cannot be separated from power relations between capital and labour (indeed, the very measurement of capital cannot be abstracted from them), and market dynamics as such are prone to generate under-consumption (e.g. Robinson 1973).

Regulation theory agrees that such a general generative mechanism inheres in capitalism. However, it can never be fully actualized because the homogenizing force of market exchange (or commodification) cannot be fully actualized. Concrete capitalism is dependent on 'necessary impurities' which are not subject to market exchange, such as family relations, hierarchical formations in production units such as corporation. That means, as the varieties of capitalism literature stress, that capitalism depends on the heterogeneous embedding of institutions, which relate commodification to these necessary impurities (Hodgson 1996).

> In a world in which information is an issue and in which externalities are laden with significance, there is no such thing as general equilibrium or perfect competition. Nor is there any reason why maximum competition should be the best possible form of relationship between economic agents, for competition in these contexts entails the adoption of behavioural strategies, the effects of which could be socially and even individually disadvantageous. This is the environment in which the problems of regulation arise. Regulation theory is concerned with heterogeneous economic processes in which necessity and contingency, the constraint of the past and the creation of the new are intertwined. It deals with the processes that emerge, are reproduced then wither away under the effects of the unequal development inherent in capitalism.
>
> (Aglietta 1998: 44)

On the basis of this theoretical synthesis that does not presuppose a priori the stability for capitalist markets but rather tries to explain the particular institutional configurations that may stabilize them, regulation theory developed a concrete, historical-conjunctural analysis of the post-war 'Fordist' phase of capitalism. Phases of capitalism are characterized by particular 'regimes of capital accumulation', defined by specific production technologies that enable particular 'solutions' to the contradictions of capitalism. Semi-automation and mechanics, applied through the conveyor belt, provided the Fordist basis for productivity growth, enabling the expanded reproduction of capital. At the same time, this highly scale-dependent system solved its 'realization problem', or avoided overaccumulation, through the *ex ante* integration of mass consumption with mass production. Particularly important was a historic compromise between capitalist managers and labour, allowing collective bargaining in exchange for acquiescence to managerial change at the workplace, even if this implied an increased tempo and deskilling of work. Pioneered in the USA in the 1920s, Fordism was 'exported' to western Europe as part and parcel of US post-war hegemony and it was adapted with institutional variations in European mixed market economy welfare states after 1945. Here, Atlanticism and European integration played a significant role. In order to stabilize, regimes of accumulation require enabling institutional frameworks or 'modes of regulation'. Keynesian demand management, welfare state expansion, collective bargaining regimes, and practices designed to deepen and extend consumer market relations such as advertisement were essential components of the Fordist mode of regulation. All of these practices served to integrate mass production and mass consumption. In short, all the practices and developments associated with modified liberalism, including European integration, balanced the requisites of openness for the expansion of mass production and national closure required for interventionist economic policy. From such a perspective, the Treaty of Rome, facilitating the creation of a Common Market compatible with economies of scale, and the 1965 Luxembourg Compromise that confirmed policy discretion by interventionist nation-states, were two sides of the same coin.

According to regulation theory, the crises of the Bretton Woods system and European integration in the 1960s and 1970s expressed a deeper crisis in Fordism. By the late 1960s, Fordism had reached its frontier of productivity expansion as the scope for conveyor-belt rationalization was exhausted. Productivity growth declined and price-setting, macroeconomic policy, and raw material price-increases resulted in stagflation as the attention of policy makers increasingly shifted to price stability. Disintegrative conflicts over economic management in Europe and across the Atlantic reflected a disjuncture between accumulation regimes and regulation modes in crisis, and uncertainties with how one might deal with these (Aglietta 1982). Nevertheless, this crisis opened up new economic possibilities deriving from computer-based cybernetic automation and information technologies. Regulation theorists do not subscribe to a determinist reading of this situation. In principle, a variety of 'post-Fordist' strategies designed to break down information bottlenecks and deploy cybernetic general purpose machines in order to adjust production to demand without productivity losses were possible. Following the variety of capitalism literature, regulation theory argues that diversified quality production on the basis of social-democratic, labour-inclusive, co-determination practices provided the basis of a viable post-Fordist future (compare Streeck 1992 and Leborgne and Lipietz 1988). However, the particular mode of regulation that was promoted by a Single Market was based on negative integration, and a monetarist EMU biased developments in favour of a neo-liberal post-Fordism (Lipietz 1989; Grahl and Teague 1989; 1990; Boyer 1990; 2000).

On the basis of this, regulation theory offers a sustained account capable of making sense of the financial crisis. In production, despite advanced technological change, neoliberal post-Fordism returned to a more classical capitalist mode of exploitation as profitability became based on the containment of wage costs and *ex post* market determination of wages. Overaccumulation is an inherent problem in such a situation. The lack of ex ante integration of consumption renders problematic the profitable deployment of accumulated capital. But it is exactly here that modern financial markets, centred around the USA and to an extent the UK, came to serve a crucial function for capital accumulation over the last two decades. Financial intermediation facilitated expansion of demand among the middle classes and corporations through an extension of credit, underwritten by the increased exchange value of assets, such as real estate and shares through what David Harvey has called 'temporal displacement' (Harvey 1990). The breakdown of information bottlenecks, facilitated by technological change, have been used to innovate financial services in the direction of ever more sophisticated structures of hedging and spread betting through derivatives and other forms of securitization. However, this system is not without its contradictions. In their efforts to boost stock values of their shares in the here and now, corporations tend to undermine their capacities to engage research and development, technological innovation and productivity growth, and ultimately wage earners with flexible wages and precarious jobs provide a slim foundation for sustainable consumption (Aglietta 2000; Aglietta and Breton 2001; Aglietta and Reberioux 2005; Watson 2009). When financial capital sought profitable deployment in increasingly risky subprime segments of the market, the bubble burst in 2007, putting the future of this accumulation regime in question. The Eurozone crisis is in the last instance a concrete manifestation of this crisis (Aglietta 2012), and subsequent chapters of this book explore this manifestation and assess the limitations of contemporary European crisis-management.

Notes

1 This chapter is an abridged and edited version of 'The Financial Crisis, Orthodoxy, Heterodoxy and the Production of Knowledge about the EU', *Millennium: Journal of International Studies* 40(3) (2012), pp. 647–73, DOI 10.1177/03058298124423000, and is republished here with the kind permission of SAGE.

2 A survey of the discipline-leading *Journal of Common Market Studies* from the time of the inception of the Single Market in 1993 to mid-2009 revealed that, at a

generous interpretation, only 5 of 732 articles (0.7 per cent) had anything of pertinence to say on the topic.

3 With regards to the latter point they commit the fallacy that is well known in welfare state research to conflate actual expenditure with welfare state standards. Research demonstrates unequivocally that effective welfare entitlements have been retrenched in Europe (Korpi 2003). This is corrosive on the so-called 'equivalence principle' of incomes replacement, which is crucial to the logic of appropriateness in Christian Democratic welfare settlements (Cafruny and Ryner 2007). Even Martin Rhodes' (2002) rather upbeat assessment of the positive effect of the Euro on the welfare state concedes that increased expenditure is due to automatic stabilizers paying out unemployment insurance and disintegration of the nuclear family as a reproductive unit, which requires higher expenditure on childcare.

References

Aglietta, M. (1982) World Capitalism in the Eighties. *New Left Review* 136 (old series), pp. 1–41.

Aglietta, M. (1998) Capitalism at the Turn of the Century: Regulation Theory and the Challenge of Social Change. *New Left Review* 232 (old series), pp. 40–90.

Aglietta, M. (2000) Shareholder Value and Corporate Governance: Some Tricky Questions. *Economy and Society*. 29(1), pp. 146–159.

Aglietta, M. (2012) The European Vortex. *New Left Review* 74 (new series), pp. 15–36.

Aglietta, M. and Breton, R. (2001) Financial Systems, Corporate Control and Capital Accumulation. *Economy and Society* 30(4), pp. 433–466.

Aglietta, M. and Rebérioux, A. (2005) *Corporate Governance Adrift: A Critique of Shareholder Value*. Cheltenham: Edward Elgar.

Albert, M. (1993) *Capitalism against Capitalism*. Oxford: Wiley Blackwell.

Alesina, A., Angeloni, I. and Schuknecht, L. (2005) What Does the European Union Do? *Public Choice* 123(3/4), pp. 275–319.

Balassa, B. (1962) *The Theory of Economic Integration*. London: Allen and Unwin.

Bourdieu, P. (1977) *Outline of a Theory of Practice*. Cambridge: Cambridge University Press.

Bourdieu, P. (1991) *Language and Symbolic Power*. Cambridge: Polity.

Boyer, R. (1990) The Impact of the Single Market on Labour and Employment: A Discussion of Macroeconomic Approaches in Light of Research in Labour Economics. *Labour and Society* 15(2), pp. 109–142.

Boyer, R. (2000) The Unanticipated Fallout of European Monetary Union: The Political and Institutional Deficits of the Euro. In Crouch, C. (ed.) *After the Euro*. Oxford: Oxford University Press, pp. 24–88.

Burley, A.-M. and Mattli, W. (1993) Europe Before the Court: A Political Theory of Legal Integration. *International Organization* 47(1), pp. 41–76.

Cafruny, A. and Ryner, M. (2007) Monetary Union and the Transatlantic and Social Dimensions of Europe's Crisis. *New Political Economy* 12(2), pp. 141–165.

Checkel, J. (2003) 'Going Native' in Europe? Theorizing Social Interaction in European Institutions. *Comparative Political Studies* 36(1/2), pp. 209–231.

Cohen, B. (2003) Global Currency Rivalry: Can the Euro Ever Challenge the Dollar. *Journal of Common Market Studies* 41(4), pp. 575–595.

Cohen, B. (2006) The Macrofoundation of Monetary Power. In Andrews, D. (ed.) *International Monetary Power*. Ithaca, NY: Cornell University Press, pp. 31–50.

Cohen, B. (2007) Enlargement and the International Role of the Euro. *Review of International Political Economy* 14(5), pp. 746–733.
Cohen, B. (2008) The International Monetary System: Diffusion and Ambiguity. *International Affairs* 84(3), pp. 455–470.
Cohen, B. (2009) Global Currency Rivalry; Dollar Dominance, Euro Aspirations: Recipe for Discord? *Journal of Common Market Studies* 47(4), pp. 741–766.
Cox, R. (1976) On Thinking about Future World Order. *World Politics* 28(2), pp. 175–196.
Crouch, C. (2009) Privatised Keynesianism: An Unacknowledged Policy Regime. *British Journal of Politics and International Relations* 11(3), pp. 382–399.
Dermine, J. (2000) Bank Mergers in Europe: The Public Policy Issues. *Journal of Common Market Studies* 38(3), pp. 409–425.
Detken, C., Gaspar, V. and Winkler, B. (2004) On Prosperity and Posterity: The Need for Fiscal Discipline in a Monetary Union. *ECB Working Paper* 420.
Deutsch, K. et al. (1957) *Political Community and the North Atlantic Area: International Organization in the Light of Historical Experience.* Princeton, NJ: Princeton University Press.
Easton, D. (1953) *The Political System: An Inquiry into the State of Political Science.* New York: Alan A. Knopf.
Enderlein, H. and Verdun, A. (2009) EMU's Teenage Challenge: What Have We Learned and Can We Predict from Political Science. *Journal of European Public Policy* 16(4), pp. 490–507.
European Commission (1988) *Europe 1992: The Overall Challenge* SEC 88(524) Final, 13 April, Brussels: The Commission of the European Communities.
Fagan, G. and Gaspar, V. (2007) Adjusting to the Euro. *ECB Working Paper* 716.
Fagan, G. and Gaspar, V. (2008) Macroeconomic Adjustment to Monetary Union. *ECB Working Paper* 946.
Fliegstein, N. and Stone Sweet, A. (2002) Constructing Politics and Markets: An Institutional Account of European Integration. *American Journal of Sociology* 105 (5), pp. 1206–1243.
Garrett, G. (1995) The Politics of Legal Integration in the European Union. *International Organization* 49(1), pp. 171–181.
Gaspar, V., Smets, F. and Vestin, D. (2007) Is Time Ripe for Price Level Stability? *ECB Working Paper* 818.
Grahl, J. and Teague, P. (1989) The Cost of Neo-Liberal Europe. *New Left Review* 174 (old series), pp. 33–50.
Grahl, J. and Teague, P. (1990) *1992: The Big Market.* London: Lawrence and Wishart.
Haas, E. (1968) *The Uniting of Europe: Political, Economic and Social Forces.* 2nd edition. Stanford, CA: Stanford University Press.
Haas, E. (2001) Does Constructivism Subsume Neo-functionalism? In Christensen, T., Jørgensen, K.-E. and Wiener, A. (eds) *The Social Construction of Europe.* London: Sage, pp. 22–31.
Haas, E. and Haas, P. (2002) Pragmatic Constructivism and the Study of International Institutions. *Millennium: Journal of International Studies* 31(3), pp. 573–601.
Hartmann, P., Maddaloni, A. and Manganelli, S. (2003) The Euro Area Financial System: Structure, Integration and Policy Initiatives. *ECB Working Paper* 230.
Harvey, D. (1990) *The Condition of Postmodernity.* Oxford: Blackwell.
Helleiner, E. (2008) Political Determinants of International Currencies: What Future for the US Dollar? *Review of International Political Economy* 15(3), pp. 354–378.

Henning, R. (1998) Systemic Conflict and Regional Monetary Integration: The Case of Europe. *International Organization* 52(3), pp. 537–573.

Henning, R. (2006) The Exchange Rate Weapon and Macroeconomic Conflict. In Andrews, D. (ed.) *International Monetary Power*. Ithaca, NY: Cornell University Press, pp. 117–138.

Hicks, J. (1937) Mr Keynes and the 'Classics': A Suggested Interpretation. *Econometrica* 5(2), pp. 147–159.

Hix, S. (1999) *The Political System of the European Union*. Basingstoke: Macmillan.

Hodgson, G. (1996) Variety of Capitalism, Variety of Economic Theory. *Review of International Political Economy* 3(3), pp. 380–433.

Hoffman, S. (1966) Obstinate or Obsolete? The Fate of the Nation-State and the Case of Western Europe. *Daedalus* 95(3), pp. 862–915.

Jabko, N. (1999) In the Name of the Market: How the European Commission Paved the Way for Monetary Union. *Journal of European Public Policy* 6(3), pp. 475–495.

Jones, E. (2002) *The Politics of Economic and Monetary Union*. Lanham, MD: Rowman & Littlefield.

Jones, E. (2003) Liberalized Capital Markets, State Autonomy, and European Monetary Union. *European Journal of Political Research* 42(2), pp. 111–136.

Keohane, R. (1984) *After Hegemony: Cooperation and Discord in the World Political Economy*. Princeton, NJ: Princeton University Press.

Keohane, R. and Nye, J. (1977) *Power and Interdependence: World Politics in Transition*. Boston, MA: Little, Brown.

Kirshner, J. (2008) Dollar Primacy and American Power: What's at Stake? *Review of International Political Economy* 15(3), pp. 418–438.

Korpi, W. (2003) Welfare State Regress in Western Europe: Politics, Institutions, Globalization and Regionalization. *Annual Review of Sociology* 29, pp. 589–609.

Kuhn, T. (1962) *The Structure of Scientific Revolutions*. Chicago, IL: University of Chicago Press.

Leborgne, D. and Lipietz, A. (1988) New Technologies, New Modes of Regulation: Some Spatial Implications. *Environment and Planning D* 6(3), pp. 263–280.

Lipietz, A. (1987) Rebel Sons: The Regulation School. *French Politics and Society* 5, pp. 3–7.

Lipietz, A. (1989) The Debt Problem, European Integration and the New Phase of World Crisis. *New Left Review* 178 (old series), pp. 37–49.

Mandel, E. (1967) International Capitalism and 'Supra-Nationality'. In Miliband, R. and Saville, J. (eds) *The Socialist Register 1967*. London: Merlin Press, pp. 27–41.

Marcussen, M. (1999) The Dynamics of EMU Ideas. *Cooperation & Conflict* 34(4), pp. 383–411.

Marks, G., Hooghe, L. and Blank, K. (1996) European Integration from the 1980s: State Centric v. Multilevel Governance. *Journal of Common Market Studies* 34(3), pp. 341–378.

Mattli, W. and Slaughter, A.-M. (1995) Law and Politics in the European Union: A Reply to Garrett. *International Organization* 49(1), pp. 183–190.

Milward, A. and Sørensen, V. (1993) Interdependence or Integration? A National Choice. In Milward, A. *et al.* (eds) *The Frontier of National Sovereignty: History and Theory 1945–1992*. London: Routledge, pp. 1–32.

Moravcsik, A. (1998) *The Choice for Europe: Social Purpose and State Power from Messina to Maastricht*. London: UCL Press.

Moravcsik, A. (1999) A New Statecraft? Supranational Entrepreneurs and International Cooperation. *International Organization* 53(2), pp. 267–306.

Moravcsik, A. (2006) What Can We Learn from the Collapse of the European Constitutional Project? *Politische Vierteljahresschrift* 47(2), pp. 219–241.

Mügge, D. (2010) *Widen the Market, Narrow the Competition: Banker Interests and the Making of a European Capital Market.* Colchester: ECPR Press.

Otero-Iglesias, M. (2012) The (In-)tangible Euro Challenge to the Dollar: Insights from the Financial Elites in Brazil and China. *Cambridge Review of International Affairs* 25(1), pp. 123–142.

Padoa-Schioppa, T. (1987) *Efficiency, Stability and Equity: A Strategy for the Evolution of the Economic System of the European Community.* Oxford: Oxford University Press.

Parsons, T. (1951) *The Social System.* London: Routledge & Kegan Paul.

Pijl, K.V.D. (1996) *Vordenker der Weltpolitik.* Opladen: Leske & Budrich.

Poulantzas, N. (1974) Internationalisation of Capitalist Relations and the Nation State. *Economy and Society* 2(1), pp. 145–179.

Puchala, D. (1971) Of Blind Men, Elephants and International Integration. *Journal of Common Market Studies* 10(3), pp. 267–284.

Rebérioux, A. (2002) European Style Corporate Governance at the Crossroads. *Journal of Common Market Studies* 40(1), pp. 111–134.

Rhodes, M. (2002) Why EMU Is – Or May Be – Good for European Welfare States. In Dyson, K. (ed.) *European States and the Euro.* Oxford: Oxford University Press, Chapter 13.

Risse, T. (2005) Neofunctionalism, European Identity, and the Puzzles of European Integration. *Journal of European Public Policy* 12(2), pp. 291–331.

Risse, T. et al. (1999) To Euro or Not to Euro? The EMU and Identity Politics in the European Union. *European Journal of International Relations* 5(2), pp. 147–187.

Risse-Kappen, T. (1996) Exploring the Nature of the Beast: International Relations Theory and Comparative Policy Analysis Meet the European Union. *Journal of Common Market Studies* 34(1), pp. 53–80.

Robinson, J. (1973) *Economic Heresies: Some Old Fashioned Questions in Economic Theory.* New York: Basic Books.

Rosamond, B. (2007) European Integration and the Social Science of EU Studies: The Disciplinary Politics of a Subfield. *International Affairs* 83(1), pp. 231–252.

Sandholtz, W. and Zysman, J. (1989) 1992: Recasting the European Bargain. *World Politics* 42(1), pp. 95–128.

Sapir, A. et al. (2004) *An Agenda for a Growing Europe: The Sapir Report.* Oxford: Oxford University Press.

Servan-Shreiber, J.-J. (1969) *The American Challenge.* New York: Antheneum.

Streeck, W. (1992) *Social Institutions and Economic Performance.* London: Sage.

Van Apeldoorn, B., Bruff, I. and Ryner, M. (2010) The Richness and Diversity of Critical IPE Perspectives: Moving Beyond the Debate on the 'British School'. In Phillips, N. and C. Weaver (eds) *International Political Economy: Debating the Past, Present and Future.* Abingdon: Routledge, pp. 215–222.

Viner, J. (1950) *The Customs Union Issue.* New York: Carnegie Endowment for International Peace.

Watson, M. (2009) Investigating the Potentially Contradictory Microfoundations of Financialization. *Economy and Society* 38(2), pp. 255–277.

Wolf, E. (1997) *Europe and the People without History*. Berkeley: University of California Press.

Zürn, M. and Checkel, J. (2005) Getting Socialized to Build Bridges: Constructivism and Rationalism, Europe and the Nation State. *International Organization* 59(4), pp. 1045–1079.

2 Linking a post-Keynesian approach to critical political economy

Debt-driven growth, export-driven growth and the crisis in Europe[1]

Engelbert Stockhammer and Karsten Köhler

The financial crisis began in the market for derivatives of US subprime mortgages and translated into the worst recession since the 1930s in all advanced economies. However, five years after the crisis began the experience differs dramatically across countries. Only in Europe has the crisis mutated into a sovereign debt crisis. This chapter offers an analysis that puts neoliberalism at the very heart of the crisis in Europe – both as a cause of the imbalances at the root of the crisis and, specific to the EMU (Economic and Monetary Union), and as an economic policy regime that has turned the financial crisis into a sovereign debt crisis. Neoliberalism has given rise to an unstable finance-dominated accumulation regime. It has not led to a sustained profit-led growth process, but to two complementary growth models that rely either on financial bubbles and rising household debt ('debt-driven growth') or on rising export surpluses ('export-driven growth'). European neoliberalism fostered financial deregulation and, as a consequence, financial flows that fuelled the housing bubbles in Spain and Ireland. European neoliberalism is also at the root of the uniquely dysfunctional economic policy reaction to the crisis. The EMU came with an economic policy package that has downward flexible wages (or 'internal devaluation') as the preferred adjustment mechanism, which creates a deflationary bias and puts the adjustment burden on the deficit countries. It also has constrained national fiscal policies from counteracting the recession and, by trying not to play the lender of last resort (LOLR) for governments, but only for private banks, it has paved the way for sovereign debt crises.

This article will offer an analysis that is founded in post-Keynesian economics (PKE), but also incorporates insights from critical political economy (CPE). We will argue in line with CPE approaches that the policy package of the EMU is in part due to the strategy of (national) European capitalist classes which have aimed at curtailing the relatively corporatist nation-states by imposing fiscal and monetary policy constraints. These constraints have become binding in the crisis, putting welfare state arrangements in question and proving counterproductive as they impose pro-cyclical austerity policies on the countries in crisis. By separating money (and central banks) from governments they have created a highly unstable situation that undermines nation-states' ability to underwrite social compromises.

The chapter is structured as follows. Section 2 introduces post-Keynesian economics, Marxian and critical political economy. Section 3 discusses neoliberalism and the EMU's economic policy regime. Section 4 analyses the export-driven and debt-driven growth models in Europe. Section 5 highlights how the neoliberal European economic policy regime has amplified the crisis and discusses the dialectics of public and private debt. Section 6 concludes by outlining a Keynesian alternative for Europe and evaluating the relation between PKE and CPE.

Marxist economic theory, post-Keynesian economics and critical political economy

Critical political economy is an ambitious project that seeks to unveil the exploitative nature of the capitalist mode of production (Sweezy 1942; Foley 1986). In the three volumes of *Capital* Marx attempts to analyse the capitalist mode of production based on the labour theory of value, which claims that living labour potentially creates value in production which is then realized (or not) in exchange relations. Profits are thus based on surplus labour of the working class. Exploitation is at the very heart of the system, but it is concealed by the fact that labour power becomes a commodity itself and the wage contract appears to be voluntary. However, given that workers do not have independent access to the means of production they need to sell their labour power in order to survive. This system creates social tensions based on class conflict that intensify in times of the periodic crisis which the system generates. Marxist explanations of crisis include the rising organic composition of capital, profit squeeze through the strengthening of bargaining power of workers, as well as profit realization problems due to underconsumption (Weisskopf 1979). In these crises it becomes apparent that capitalist relations of production are backed by a state that will ultimately resort to suppression in order to maintain the class structure of society.

Classical Marxism was organically linked to the socialist movement. However, with the split of the movement into a social democratic and communist wing and the expansion of the university sector in the post-Second World War period, Marxian theories began to develop increasingly in line with academic disciplines. In economics Marxism was barely visible until the late 1960s and 1970s, when the graduates of the student movement contributed to a short blooming of Marxian economics. In the 1980s this ebbed off during the period of a sharp rightward shift of the discipline under the Monetarists. While there are several Marxist academic journals (such as the *Review of Radical Political Economics*) and associations in economics, they remain deeply divided over basic issues such as the labour theory of value.

PKE was developed in the aftermath of the Great Depression and was based on Keynes' argument that demand formation is the key for understanding crises. Post-Keynesians developed Keynes' theory further and opposed its assimilation into mainstream economics in the form of the neoclassical synthesis (King 2002; Lavoie 2009). PKE emphasizes fundamental uncertainty about the future as a pervasive feature of a capitalist economy and the importance of social conflict in determining inflation and income distribution. Market economies will in general not lead to full employment and the growth performance will critically depend on 'animal spirits', i.e. non-rational behaviour shaped by social conventions and institutions. Investment is never constrained by the availability of savings, but it can be constrained by the availability of finance. Thus Keynes and Minsky highlight the role of financial factors in creating or amplifying crises. In the Sraffian and Kaleckian streams of PKE class conflict plays a prominent role using a surplus approach, but without regarding labour as the sole source of the surplus (as the labour theory of value does). PKE is marginalized within the economics discipline, but it has a high degree of coherence and has been able to develop an academically productive research paradigm.

CPE scholars mainly operate within the academic disciplines of political science, international relations and sociology (Pistor 2005; Ryner and Cafruny 2009). These disciplines have shown more tolerance to the existence of different theoretical paradigms. With the narrowing of economics as a discipline many of the issues previously at home in economics departments have moved into neighbouring social sciences. The emergence of international political economy (IPE) is an illustration of this. Within IPE nationalist, liberal and Marxist or critical approaches are usually distinguished. The latter have a Marxist inspiration in that they highlight power relations as well as class conflicts, but they have typically moved away from classical Marxism. For example, there is little use of the labour theory of value in IPE. Rather, in many cases the role of the state as mediator and instrument in social conflicts is highlighted.

How do PKE and CPE compare? The two come out of two different academic disciplines, which impacts on the type of research questions investigated as well as on the methodologies applied. PKE is a critical paradigm in economics with a macroeconomic focus. It uses mathematical modelling and in its empirical research standard econometric methods. Its distinguishing feature within economics is the role of effective demand as the driving factor for economic growth and the emphasis on fundamental uncertainty, financial structures, social conflict and institutions in determining demand. PKE has a normative theory of government policies which is oriented towards full employment. Consequently, European integration is analysed in terms of its economic policy architecture and its influence on income distribution and aggregate demand.

CPE has a much richer social ontology and analyses state behaviour as the outcome of (domestic) class struggles and organization on the one hand, and international power relations on the other hand. CPE is by its very nature concerned with a theory of the state and how different class agents influence state policies, making use of a theory of ideology and discourse analysis which is certainly a hallmark of CPE. Apparently, both approaches take a different focus on European integration. In the following analysis, we will try to synthesize both perspectives.

This chapter will use the concepts of the mode of regulation and regime of accumulation as a bridge between a post-Keynesian analysis and a critical political economy approach. These concepts stem from the French Regulation School (see also Ryner, Chapter 1, and Becker, Jäger and Weissenbacher, Chapter 5, in this volume), which developed in the 1970s from a Marxist approach (Aglietta 1979). It highlighted that capitalist relations have to be regulated in historically specific institutional arrangements (the mode of regulation) which would give rise to different macroeconomic regularities (the regime of accumulation). From the beginning this approach emphasized the need for complementarities in the institutional forms, such as labour relations and the monetary regime, as well as the link between income distribution and aggregate demand. In the 1980s the Regulation School was developed further as a theory that explicitly merged Marxist, Keynesian and Institutionalist elements in order to analyse historically contingent macroeconomic and socioeconomic systems (Boyer 1990). While it was very successful in analysing the post-war formation under the heading of Fordism, it never developed a similarly effective analysis of neoliberalism and has lost momentum as an economic paradigm. At the same time its key concepts have become widely used in the social sciences.

Neoliberalism in Europe as a mode of regulation

There is an extensive debate on the nature of neoliberalism (Harvey 2005; Glyn 2006; Foucault 2008; Brenner, Peck and Theodore 2010), which has highlighted that it is characterized by active market building rather than simple laissez-faire policies. While neoliberalism is often associated with free market rhetoric even at the macro level, it is not necessarily opposed to government intervention on *economic* grounds. It is the political (and ultimately democratic) nature of the interventions that worries neoliberals. Government intervention is then pursued in rule-based and technocratic form (to counteract populist and opportunistic impulses of politicians and the electorate). In this chapter we take a regulationist approach and regard neoliberalism as a key factor in reconfiguring the mode of regulation. By identifying neoliberalism as a political project, we are giving up the well-defined utopian or theoretical template to which it aspires and opening it up for an analysis of the specific interests that shape neoliberal interventions (see also Fourcade-Gourinchas and Babb 2002). The key macroeconomic characteristics of the 'neoliberal mode of regulation' are the weakening of labour, internal and external financial deregulation and the EMU economic policy regime (Stockhammer 2008).

In continental Europe the organizational strength of labour was eroded by two decades of high unemployment, welfare state retrenchment and globalization. The effects of these events on income distribution have been profound (see Atkinson, Piketty and Saez 2011 on top incomes and Stockhammer 2013 on wage shares). Financial deregulation has domestic as well as international dimensions: at the international level, capital flows have been liberalized; domestically, changes in the financial framework have given rise to a rapid pace of financial innovation, eventually increasing the scope for speculation. Both developments have strengthened the influence of the financial sector. Real interest rates have risen well above the growth rates of real GDP. Financial ratios such as stock market capitalization, derivatives turnover or cross-border lending have grown faster than real output. Overall, the income shares of financial capital have increased considerably (Duménil and Lévy 2001; Power, Epstein and Abrena 2003). Moreover, the influence of financial investors on non-financial businesses has increased substantially under the so-called shareholder value revolution (Lazonick and O'Sullivan 2000).

In continental Europe neoliberalism came, at least as far as economic policy is concerned, often in the guise of European integration and EU policies. In particular the Single European Act, competition policy, and, later, the services directive reflect the liberal creed. The Maastricht Treaty and the Stability and Growth Pact (SGP) combined an anti-inflation priority with a restriction on fiscal policy without offering adjustment mechanisms for the imbalances that it gave rise to. The economic policy regime in the Euro area is enshrined in the Maastricht Treaty, the Stability and Growth Pact, and the Lisbon Treaty. The basic structure can be summarized as follows: first, fiscal policy is essentially national policy. The EU budget, restricted to 2% of GDP, is too small and too inflexible to serve a macroeconomic function. It is simply not designed to provide a counter-cyclical stimulus in case of crisis. Second, national fiscal policies are restricted in the short-term as the budget deficit must not exceed 3% of GDP (except in severe recessions) and they must aim for a balanced budget in the medium-term. Third, monetary policy is centralized at the EU level and it is effectively inflation targeting, with the independent European Central Bank (ECB) having set the inflation target close to or below 2%. Fourth, financial markets are liberalized, internally as well as externally. Thus the EU forgoes instruments of controlling credit growth or allocating credit. Fifth, there was a no bail-out clause, stating that neither other national governments nor the ECB will support individual countries which are facing financial problems (this is the only area where we will see fundamental changes in the policy setup). Sixth, labour markets are supposed to be flexible. The European Commission (EC) and the ECB regard wage flexibility as the cure for economic imbalances. By this they mean *downward* wage flexibility (they have not called for higher wages in Germany). But this anti-labour bias should not hide the fact that within the economic policy regime of EMU there is an economic logic to the argument: with fiscal policy restrained, exchange rate policy abolished and monetary policy centralized, the standard economic policy tools are all paralyzed. The burden of adjustment has thus to be carried by the labour market and wage policy.

Why was such a policy package adopted? The reasons are complex. First, and this is the factor we want to highlight, it was the political strategy of many national capitalist classes to pursue European integration as a means to curtail corporatist national states that proved resilient domestically (see Bonefeld 2002 for a similar argument). Second, the historical situation in the aftermath of the 1992/3 European Monetary System crisis had made clear that the previous monetary regime was unsustainable. Monetary integration, or so it was widely perceived, either had to go all the way or national currencies had to be re-established. It was the southern European countries that wanted monetary integration, not Germany, as the high inflation countries had been burnt by the experience of the 1980s when they had to follow German interest rates without having a say in the determination of these rates. However, it was Germany (or the Bundesbank) who wrote the rules for the new currency. Third, for important actors, most especially the Bundesbank, monetarist ideology played a major role. Fourth, on the part of some actors (namely Jacques Delors) there was an attempt to instrumentalize monetary integration for the project of European political integration. A common currency was regarded as a first step towards political integration (Delors 1994: 237–243).

The EU policy regime is clearly a form of neoliberalism. It is characterized by a strong belief in the efficiency of the market, a distrust of state activity and an anti-labour bias. This was criticized sharply by post-Keynesian economists (Arestis, McCauley and Sawyer 2001; Hein and Truger 2005; Huffschmid 2005; Euromemo 2010; Stockhammer 2011): first, they predicted, reliance on labour market flexibility in the adjustment will not generate full employment. Keynes (1936: chapter 19) had argued in the *General Theory* that wage flexibility in a crisis is likely to make things worse: wage cuts will lead to shrinking consumption demand and to deflation, which may depress demand further in a debt-burdened economy as the real (inflation-adjusted) value of debt increases. Second, the EU policy system would create a deflationary bias. In the case of imbalances within the EU, with some countries running trade deficits and others running trade surpluses, the burden of adjustment would effectively fall on the country with trade deficits. This creates a deflationary bias. The adjustment of the surplus countries would be inflationary and growth-oriented, whereas the adjustment of the deficit countries is deflationary. They have to dampen demand (to decrease imports) and lower their prices and wages (to restore competitiveness).

We argue that the form of the crisis in Europe is due to the specific neoliberal policy regime which has been established in the European Union. The policy regime is, to a significant extent, the outcome of the peculiar strategy in Europe whereby the elites of various countries sought to implement policies at the European level for which they could not gain popular acceptance at the national level. This transnational class strategy has interacted in complex ways with different national interests and strategies. Much of what the EU has done has been about imposing constraints on the scope of economic activity of nation-states. The aim here was not to abolish the nation-state, but to change it. In the process nation-states were systematically weakened. The fiscal rules have restricted their abilities to react in the face of a crisis. And the loss of monetary sovereignty has meant that national governments have lost the capacity to be national lenders of last resort. In times of sovereign debt crises this can lead to a fundamental weakening of the state. Together these two measures undermine the ability of nation-states to stabilize economic activity and, indeed, to survive. They thereby also lose the ability to forge social compromise and to create stability. Of course, this was partly intended by the ruling classes. The SGP and the ECB charter were meant to circumscribe the capacities of nation-states. However, this policy regime also proves profoundly dysfunctional as it effectively worsens the economic crisis.

Imbalances in Europe: export-driven growth in Germany and debt-driven growth in the periphery

Stockhammer (2008, 2012) argues that neoliberalism has given rise to a finance-dominated accumulation regime which does not match the neoliberal utopia and is characterized by profound dysfunctionalities. Neoliberalism has led to a polarization of income distribution expressed in rising profits and top incomes, but has nowhere translated into an investment boom. One might think that capitalists invest their profits (indeed in Marx's *Capital* they are forced to do so by competitive pressures). Keynesians have long questioned this. In their view, the investment decisions of capitalists are a category sui generis (often interpreted as driven by animal spirits). Rather than generating a profit-led growth regime, neoliberalism has had to rely on other means of stimulating demand. It has resulted in two distinct growth models, which are both unstable: debt-driven growth and export-driven growth. It is the interaction of these processes that gave rise to the imbalances that erupted in the crisis. The crisis is thus a crisis of neoliberalism in the sense that neoliberalism is at the very roots of the crisis.

While traditional Marxist accumulation models mostly assume a profit-led regime and Kaleckian (or underconsumptionist) models assume a wage-led regime, the modern post-Keynesian model allows for both (Bhaduri and Marglin 1990). Simply put, in a wage-led economy higher wages will have expansionary effects as workers have a higher consumption propensity than capitalists. In a profit-led economy, profits get re-invested and thus drive the growth process. More technically, a rise in the wage share has a negative effect on investment (higher profits do lead to higher investment), a positive effect on consumption because capitalists save more than workers, and a negative effect on net exports because the higher wage share implies a loss of competitiveness. The net effect will depend on the relative size of the partial effects and determines whether an economy is wage-led or profit-led.

This model has given rise to a substantial empirical literature (Bowles and Boyer 1995; Stockhammer and Onaran 2004; Naastepad and Storm 2006/7; Hein and Vogel 2008; Stockhammer and Stehrer 2011). The majority of empirical studies find that private domestic demand is wage-led. The size of the export effects will critically depend on the geographical unit that is analysed: for individual countries, in particular for small open economies, they will be substantial, whereas for the world economy overall they play no role. This is important for our context because while individual European countries may well be profit-led due to exports, the Euro area overall is a relatively closed economy and empirical evidence suggests that demand is wage-led (Stockhammer, Onaran and Ederer 2009; Onaran and Galanis 2012).

So if the world economy is in a wage-led demand regime, how have economies grown at all? It is important to realize that in the neoliberal era, growth has nowhere been driven by business investment. Growth has not been the result of a profit-led growth regime. Rather, two different growth models have emerged: the Anglo-Saxon countries developed a debt-driven growth model, which was underpinned by increasing household debt, strong consumption demand and, in some cases, a residential investment boom (Lavoie and Stockhammer 2012). Other countries, namely Germany, China and Japan, adopted an export-driven growth model, where domestic demand is weak and growth relies on export surpluses. Germany pursued this strategy particularly aggressively, with average real wages stagnating in the decade prior to the crisis and the sharpest increase in wage inequality among advanced economies (OECD 2008).[2]

The peripheral European countries also followed a debt-driven growth model. While the level of household debt has been traditionally low, the increase in household debt, which is the variable relevant for consumption expenditures, has grown rapidly. Indeed, Table 2.1 shows that the increase in household debt in southern European countries was not only above the increase in northern European countries (with the exception of the Netherlands), but it also exceeded that of the USA and the UK. The rapid expansion of credit was made possible to a significant extent by European financial integration. The European Financial Services Action Plan aimed at creating a single financial market for Europe (Grahl 2009). In theory this means uniform interest rates across Europe and in practice it meant massive capital flows from Germany, France and the UK to the peripheral European

Table 2.1 Increase in household debt (in % GDP), 2000–08

Northern European countries		*Anglo-Saxon countries*	
Germany	-11.3	USA	26
Netherlands	32.8	United Kingdom	28.1
Austria	7.9	**Southern European Countries**	
France	15.8	Ireland	62.7
		Greece	35.5
		Spain	33.8
		Portugal	27.4

Eurostat, except USA: Flows of Funds

countries. While this initially fostered manufacturing investment (as in the case of Spain and Ireland), it soon fuelled an unsustainable property boom.

At the same time, southern European countries experienced substantially higher price and wage inflation. As a consequence the south lost competitiveness. This is illustrated in Table 2.2, which gives the growth in unit labour costs (ULC), a standard measure of cost competitiveness, from 2000–08. Southern European countries all had a growth of more than 24%, compared to a Euro area average of 16% and Germany at 3%. Together with fast growth in many southern countries, this resulted in substantial current account deficits, which were mirrored by export surpluses in the north. These surpluses were recycled as private credit flows back to the southern European countries, where they financed property bubbles and rising household debt. In fact the situation differed by country, but a massive increase in *private* household debt (in southern European countries) is the hallmark of this growth. With the exception of Greece, public debt was declining (see also de Grauwe 2010).

The crisis, the EU policy regime and the role of money

The underlying factors of the crisis include financial deregulation, the rise in inequality and the international imbalances that had built up. These are directly tied to neoliberalism and the two growth models in the finance-dominated accumulation regime. Initially the crisis hit debt-driven and export-driven economies equally hard. However the export-driven economies were quicker to recover as they were not suffering from a debt overhang. In the USA the crisis was countered by counter-cyclical fiscal policy[3] and by aggressive monetary policy in the form of quantitative easing.[4] In the USA the crisis turned into a weak recovery. Economic policy in Europe was less anti-cyclical. While many countries adopted stimulus packages in the first year of the crisis, fiscal policy turned to austerity more quickly and, worse, it became restrictive in those countries hit hardest by the crisis after 2010. Monetary policy in the EU tried to avoid what is now known as unconventional monetary policy or quantitative easing as long as it could, but as the

Table 2.2 Increase in unit labour costs (ULC), 2000–08

Northern European countries		*Southern European countries*	
Germany	3%	Ireland	33%
Netherlands	19%	Greece	26%
Austria	9%	Spain	30%
		Italy	27%
Euro Area (12)	16%	Portugal	24%

AMECO (http://ec.europa.eu/economy_finance/db_indicators/ameco/index_en.htm)

Euro crisis deepened, the ECB did expand its balance sheet. From Spring 2009 the US Federal Reserve and the Bank of England increasingly bought government bonds, i.e. they supported government spending. The ECB was, in the early phase of the financial crisis, much more hesitant. It started quantitative easing later, expanded its balance sheet less, and has hardly bought government bonds. In short, the ECB is playing the role of lender of last resort for the financial sector, but – different from the US Federal Reserve and the Bank of England – not for the government sector. Only in August 2012, when the Greek sovereign debt crisis threatened to engulf the other Euro member states, did the ECB commit to buying government bonds (under the condition that those countries submitted to the conditionality of the bailout packages – the so-called Outright Monetary Transactions, OMT, programme). Given the different growth models and differences in economic policy, the crisis led to sharply different performances across Europe: a fragile recovery in the north and a depression in the southern European countries.

While recent developments have vindicated Keynesian criticisms, the EU's policy package has not changed direction, but become, as of today, more rigid and doctrinaire (see Oberndorfer, Chapter 11, and Grahl, Chapter 10, in this volume). The Treaty for Stability, Coordination and Governance in the Economic and Monetary Union (TSCG) has tightened the grip on fiscal policy (Grahl 2012). Constitutional debt brakes are to be introduced in the Euro member states; there will be an automatic obligation to austerity if public debt exceeds the 60% target (the 1/20 rule) and the European Commission will be involved in the national budget process (the European Semester). The one area where there has been a change in direction is with respect to the no bail-out clause. The EU has, belatedly, set up a collective fund for member states that have lost access to market finance (European Financial Stability Facility—EFSF, and European Monetary Fund—EMF). This fund gives loans to the countries that are misleadingly referred to as 'rescue packages' and imposes conditionality that is similar in spirit as International Monetary Fund (IMF) adjustment programmes, but without nominal devaluation.[5]

The crisis has illustrated the strong interdependence of the government sector and the financial system. The crisis thus raises interesting questions about the nature of money and the state. Economic theory is divided on the theory of money. Mainstream economics (and indeed parts of Marxian theory) regard money as emerging from private transactions. In classical economics (and Marx) gold can become money because it has value as a commodity. By contrast, post-Keynesian theory and other heterodox traditions stress that debt relations and in particular government debt and the ability of governments to collect taxes in their own currency are the foundation of money (Goodhart 1998; see also Graeber 2011: Chapters 2 and 3). Ingham (2004) stresses the state origin of money, but highlights that the social mode of production of credit money is through private banks. Money thus is a contested field that has sovereign power as a constituent element, but private institutions are critically involved. This is also reflected in central banks.

Most central banks were originally founded in order to strengthen state finances and later acquired bank supervision functions. Central banks were first LOLR for the state and only later became LOLR for private banks. However, in the process of EMU, central bank independence was strengthened and the ECB was forbidden to fund governments directly. That is, by design it was meant to be a LOLR for the private sector only. Money and monetary policy was to be insulated from the political process.

Public debt is a private asset. Most government bonds are held by private banks and pension funds. Public debt is essential for the working of the private financial sector. It forms the most important collateral used on money markets and repo markets (Gabor 2014; Mehrling 2011). The credibility of public debt is thus essential for the functioning of private debt markets. A sovereign debt crisis also poses a mortal threat to the respective country's banks, as they usually lose access to the private financial markets. In the Euro area this is amplified by contagion effects as the credibility of one country's sovereign debt calls into question the quality of another country's assets. But this dialectic between private and public debt goes further. The credibility of public debt depends, in many cases, on the assessment of private financial institutions. In the case of Spain and Italy, debt levels were clearly sustainable at the interest levels prior to the crisis. After the financial crisis, interest spreads on southern European countries increased sharply; essentially, the banks started speculating against the governments that had rescued them (Weeks 2013).

Conclusions

The escalation of the crisis in Europe is, in our view, due to the fact that political forces have built half a European state, while they have seriously damaged the ability of nation-states to counter an economic crisis (and by implication) to underwrite social compromises. This is not an accident. In our analysis, this particular form of European integration is the outcome of a strategy of European national capital classes that have used European integration to undermine the, in their view, excessively corporatist and Keynesian (national) states.

So, how have the national bourgeoisies fared? In the south, they got many of the reforms they wanted (in particular with respect to the labour market and the welfare state), but under conditions that they did not want. By this we mean the recession, but also the increasing influence of the German government as well as of German capital. In the north, capital could push further desired changes in policy regimes, but they are in danger of paying for substantial parts of the costs either in the form of inter-country transfers or in the form of debt restructuring in which their countries would have to shoulder (some of) the costs of the crisis. Meanwhile, European labour is divided, with their experience of the crisis differing sharply between themselves: for example, Germany has a lower unemployment rate than before the crisis and southern countries have the unemployment rates comparable to the Great Depression.

Europe now faces several challenges. It has to re-balance its trade flows and cost and price levels. And it has to deal with high private and public debt. In principle, the cost imbalances can be dealt with by inflationary adjustment (that is adjustment in the surplus countries to increase prices and output) or by deflationary adjustment in the deficit countries.[6] The latter is presently being pursued under the name of 'internal devaluation'.

A Keynesian economic strategy aims for an inflationary adjustment strategy with higher wage growth and expansionary fiscal policy in surplus countries, namely Germany. This would simplify adjustment across Europe. For short-term crisis management, ECB intervention on public debt markets is essential, but Europe needs a complete overhaul of its economic policy mix, one that thoroughly breaks with neoliberalism. This would require a system of transnationally coordinated wage bargaining that takes into consideration issues of equity and trade balances. The macroeconomic aim of European wage coordination ought to be higher wage growth in the trade surplus countries, which would help prevent imbalances (see also Flassbeck and Lapavitsas, Chapter 8, and Niechoj, Chapter 9, in this volume). Furthermore, an inflationary environment would greatly facilitate reducing the debt level. To counteract the regressive distributional effects of bank rescues, a substantial wealth tax would have to be introduced. At the same time the bail-out of financial institutions would have to come with proper socialization to ensure change in management practices. Finally, there needs to be a European social security system (see also Grahl, Chapter 10, in this volume). A European tax on profits that finances social expenditures, say unemployment benefits, would redistribute income from prosperous to depressed regions without increasing debt levels. This would build what Europe needs: a system of funding financial flows to deficit units that does not create rising liabilities for either the private or the public sector.

The post-Keynesian approach has the advantage of offering an analytical framework that allows for an economic evaluation of economic policy regimes. However, its suggestions have strong normative elements with little regard for the political preconditions of its implementation. Nor does it offer, by itself, much of an explanation of why these measures have not been implemented. It is here where we see the main complementarity between PKE and CPE perspectives. We suggested to combine them by building mainly on the regulationist concept of the mode of regulation. The CPE approach has made important contributions by documenting how capitalist classes have shaped European economic integration (van Apeldoorn 2000; Macartney 2009). Indeed, our analysis of the origins of the economic policy regime draw inspiration from these approaches and we regard them as complementary with PKE.

Based on CPE we understand neoliberal policies as the outcome of capitalist class interests and strategies.[7] PKE helps to highlight the macroeconomic dysfunctionality of a neoliberal mode of regulation in terms of creating a viable growth regime; moreover, with regard to the process of European integration this might lead to different appraisals of the results of neoliberal policies.

From a PKE perspective the separation of fiscal and monetary policy, the categorical commitment to price stability and the suppression of real wages have created a regime of slow growth due to a lack of aggregate demand. Furthermore, the institutional structure of EMU sets considerable constraints for stabilizing the economy in case of a recession. As we have shown, these policies have led to a weak economic performance of the EMU, especially in the south. Incorporating PKE insights may help CPE to understand that profits not only have to be extracted in production, they also have to be realized by sufficiently high and stable aggregate demand. It is here where the neoliberal regime runs into trouble.

Notes

1 Sections 3, 4 and 5 of this article are based on Stockhammer (2014).
2 Hein and Mundt (2012) offer a more in detailed classification the growth models of G20 countries.
3 Fiscal policy was moderate in the sense that given the extent of the recession it was far from sufficient to ensure full employment. However, by historical standards it was indeed substantial. The budget deficit (in the USA) peaked at 10% of GDP and stayed above 7% for four years.
4 The increase in the balance sheet of the US Federal Reserve corresponds to some 15% of GDP since 2008.
5 The 'rescue packages' have in no case led to a decline in public debt. For example, in the case of Greece public debt has increased from 113% (2008) to 160.6% (2012), in Ireland from 44.2% to 116.2% (according to the EC's 2012 spring forecast). Greece has not received financial aid, but rather public loans at rates well above the market rates of Germany. These loans are used to repay private lenders. Essentially the 'rescue packages' have been gigantic machineries for transforming private debt into public debt. Credit Suisse estimates that the second Greek rescue package reduced the private sector share in the holding of Greek government debt from 62% to 30% (Credit Suisse Economics Research 2012).
6 Stockhammer and Sotiropoulos (2012) find that the internal devaluation strategy presently pursued would require a reduction of 23–47% of GDP in the southern European countries in order to eliminate the current account imbalances.
7 It is difficult to define capitalist *interests* independently of what capitalist political organization demands. Their class instincts or short-term interests will typically be about deregulation or the suppression of labour. However, PKE points out that in the long-term, social democratic reforms will often be consistent with high growth and high profitability. CPE is not unified on the extent to which class interests are about profitability or just power relations.

References

Aglietta, M. (1979) *A Theory of Capitalist Regulation. The US Experience*. London: Verso.

Arestis, P., McCauley, C. and Sawyer, M. (2001) An Alternative Stability Pact for the European Union. *Cambridge Journal of Economics* 25, pp. 113–130.

Atkinson, A., Piketty, T. and Saez, E. (2011) Top Incomes in the Long Run of History. *Journal of Economic Literature* 49(1), pp. 3–71.

Bhaduri, A. and Marglin, S. (1990) Unemployment and the Real Wage: The Economic Basis for Contesting Political Ideologies. *Cambridge Journal of Economics* 14, pp. 375–393.

Bonefeld, W. (2002) European Integration: The Market, the Political and Class. *Capital and Class* 77, pp. 117–142.

Bowles, S. and Boyer, R. (1995) Wages, Aggregate Demand, and Employment in an Open Economy: An Empirical Investigation. In Epstein, G. and Gintis, H. (eds) *Macroeconomic Policy after the Conservative Era. Studies in Investment, Saving and Finance*. Cambridge: Cambridge University Press, pp. 143–173.

Boyer, R. (1990) *The Regulation School: A Critical Introduction*. New York: Columbia University Press.

Brenner, N., Peck, J. and Theodore, N. (2010) Variegated Neoliberalization: Geographies, Modalities, Pathways. *Global Networks* 10(2), pp. 182–222.

Credit Suisse Economics Research (2012) *European Economics. Assessing Debt Sustainability and Financing Needs in Greece ahead of the PSI.* [Online] Available from: https://doc.research-and-analytics.csfb.com/docView?language=ENG&source=ulg&format=PDF&document_id=948097251&serialid=IjiUHEvdB6unRmTlYr3p6Dv6YM8Upex%2FTeRbVrcgI6U%3D [Accessed 6 September 2013].

de Grauwe, P. (2010) The Financial Crisis and the Future of the Eurozone. *Bruges European Economic Policy Briefings*. 21.

Delors, J. (1994) *L'unité d'un homme: entretiens avec Dominique Wolton*, Paris: Odile Jacob.

Duménil, G. and Lévy, D. (2001) Costs and Benefits of Neoliberalism: A Class Analysis. *Review of International Political Economy* 8(4), pp. 578–607.

EuroMemo Group (2010) Confronting the Crisis: Austerity or Solidarity. *EuroMemorandum 2010/11*. [Online] Available from http://www2.euromemorandum.eu/uploa-ds/euromemorandum_2010_2011_english.pdf [Accessed 10 July 2013].

Foley, D. (1986) *Understanding Capital. Marx's Economic Theory*. Cambridge, MA: Harvard University Press.

Foucault, M. (2008) *The Birth of Biopolitics: Lectures at the College de France, 1978–1979*. Houndsmills: Palgrave MacMillan.

Fourcade-Gourinchas, M. and Babb, S. (2002) The Rebirth of the Liberal Creed: Paths to Neoliberalism in Four Countries. *American Journal of Sociology* 108(3), pp. 533–579.

Gabor, D. (2014) Learning from Japan: The European Central Bank and the European Sovereign Debt Crisis. *Review of Political Economy* 26(2), pp. 190–209.

Glyn, A. (2006) *Capitalism Unleashed: Finance, Globalization and Welfare*. Oxford: Oxford University Press.

Goodhart, C. (1998) The Two Concepts of Money: Implications for the Analysis of Optimal Currency Areas. *European Journal of Political Economy* 14(3), pp. 407–432.

Graeber, D. (2011) *Debt. The First 5000 Years*. New York: Melville House.

Grahl, J. (2009) *Global Finance and Social Europe*. Aldershot: Edward Elgar.

Grahl, J. (2012) The First European Semester: An Incoherent Strategy. Paper presented at the PERG Workshop *Europe in Crisis*, April 2012, Kingston University.

Harvey, D. (2005) *A Short History of Neoliberalism*. Oxford: Oxford University Press.

Hein, E. and Truger, A. (2005) European Monetary Union: Nominal Convergence, Real Divergence and Slow Growth? *Structural Change and Economic Dynamics* 16 (1), pp. 7–33.

Hein, E. and Mundt, M. (2012) Financialisation and the Requirements and Potentials for Wage-led Recovery – A Review Focussing on the G20. *ILO Working Papers, Conditions of Work and Employment Series* No. 37, Geneva.

Hein, E. and Vogel, L. (2008) Distribution and Growth Reconsidered – Empirical Results for Austria, France, Germany, the Netherlands, the UK and the USA. *Cambridge Journal of Economics* 32(3), pp. 479–511.

Huffschmid, J. (2005) *Economic Policy for a Social Europe: A Critique of Neo-liberalism and Proposals for Alternatives.* Basingstoke: Palgrave Macmillan.

Ingham, G. (2004) *The Nature of Money.* Cambridge: Polity Press.

Keynes, J. ([1936] 1973) *The General Theory of Employment, Interest and Money. The Collected Writings of John Maynard Keynes*, Volume VII. Cambridge: Macmillan.

King, J. (2002) *A History of Post-Keynesian Economics since 1936*. Aldershot: Edward Elgar.

Lavoie, M. (2009) *Introduction to Post-Keynesian Economics.* New York: Palgrave Macmillan.

Lavoie, M. and Stockhammer, E. (2012) Wage-led Growth: Concept, Theories and Policies. *ILO Working Papers*, Conditions of Work and Employment Series No. 41.

Lazonick, W. and O'Sullivan, M. (2000) Maximizing Shareholder Value: A New Ideology for Corporate Governance. *Economy and Society* 29(1), pp. 13–35.

Macartney, H. (2009) Variegated Neo-liberalism: Transnationally Oriented Fractions of Capital in EU Financial Market Integration. *Review of International Studies* 35 (2), pp. 451–480.

Mehrling, P. (2011) *The New Lombard Street, How the Fed Became the Dealer of Last Resort*. Princeton, NJ: Princeton University Press.

Naastepad, C.W.M. and Storm, S. (2006/7) OECD Demand Regimes (1960–2000) *Journal of Post-Keynesian Economics* 29(2), pp. 213–248.

OECD (2008) *Growing Unequal? Income Distribution and Poverty in OECD Countries.* Paris: OECD.

Onaran, O. and Galanis, G. (2012) Is Aggregate Demand Wage-led or Profit-led? National and Global Effects. *ILO Working Papers, Conditions of Work and Employment Series* No. 40. Geneva.

Pistor, M. (2005) Agency, Structure and European Integration. Critical Political Economy and the New Regionalism in Europe. In Jones, E. and Verdun, A. (eds) *The Political Economy of European Integration. Theory and Analysis.* New York: Routledge, pp. 109–127.

Power, D., Epstein, G. and Abrena, M. (2003) Trends in the Rentier Income Share in OECD Countries 1960–2000. *PERI Working Paper* 58a.

Ryner, M. and Cafruny, A. (2009) Critical Political Economy. In Wiener, A. and Diez, T. (eds) *European Integration Theory.* 2nd edition. Oxford: Oxford University Press, pp. 221–240.Stockhammer, E. (2008) Some Stylized Facts on the Finance-Dominated Accumulation Regime. *Competition and Change* 12(2), pp. 189–207.

Stockhammer, E. (2011) Peripheral Europe's Debt and German Wages. *International Journal for Public Policy* 7(1–3), pp. 83–96.

Stockhammer, E. (2012) Financialization, Income Distribution and the Crisis. *Investigación Económica* 71(279), pp. 39–70.

Stockhammer, E. (2013) Why Have Wage Shares Fallen? A Panel Analysis of the Determinants of Functional Income Distribution. *ILO Working Paper, Conditions of Work and Employment Series* No. 35.

Stockhammer, E. (2014) The Euro Crisis and Contradictions of Neoliberalism in Europe. *PKSG Working Paper* No. 1401.

Stockhammer, E. and Onaran, Ö. (2004) Accumulation, Distribution and Employment: A Structural VAR Approach to a Kaleckian Macro-model. *Structural Change and Economic Dynamics* 15, pp. 421–447.

Stockhammer, E., Onaran, Ö. and Ederer, S. (2009) Functional Income Distribution and Aggregate Demand in the Euro Area. *Cambridge Journal of Economics* 33(1), pp. 139–159.

Stockhammer, E. and Sotiropoulos, D. (2012) The Costs of Internal Devaluation. *PKSG Working Paper* No. 1206.

Stockhammer, E. and Stehrer, R. (2011) Goodwin or Kalecki in Demand? Functional Income Distribution and Aggregate Demand in the Short Run. *Review of Radical Political Economics* 43(4), pp. 506–522.

Sweezy, P. (1942) *Theory of Capitalist Development*. New York: Modern Reader.

van Apeldoorn, B. (2000) Transnational Class Agency and European Governance: the Case of the European Round Table of Industrialists. *New Political Economy* 5(2), pp. 157–181.

Weeks, J. (2013) Euro Crises and Euro Scams: Trade not Debt and Deficits Tell the Tale. *Review of Political Economy.*

Weisskopf, T. (1979) Marxist Crises Theory and the Post-war US Economy. *Cambridge Journal of Economics* 3(4), pp. 341–378.

3 Banking or macroeconomic regulation?

Cross-border issues in the EU crisis

Jan Toporowski

The thinking and policy on financial regulation since the 1980s has been resolutely focused on the notion that credit is a commodity exchanged on a voluntary basis between a financial intermediary and a 'consumer' of credit services. At the high point of financial deregulation (around the middle to end of the 1980s) it was widely believed that the only pretext for regulation could be consumer protection (because by the time a consumer discovered the true value of a pension or life assurance contract, it was too late) or contract enforcement. In the wake of the 2008 financial crisis, we know better. Threats of insolvency or illiquidity in the financial system were supposed to be dealt with by encouraging the 'prudent' management of balance sheets, so that banks and financial institutions limited the 'risks' of their assets or liabilities. Foremost among the instruments that are supposed to constrain bank managers to limit their risks are supposed to be capital requirements, enshrined since 1988 in the banking rules recommended by the Bank for International Settlements in Basel. Forcing banks to hold more capital is supposed to make 'risky' assets more costly, and provide shareholders' funds to meet the costs of balance sheet losses.

The crisis of 2008, and its predecessors in the emerging market crises of the 1990s, and the Third World Debt crisis in 1982, changed the discourse on financial regulation by introducing a new concept of risk. In addition to the well-known incidental risks associated with changes in the prices of assets, exchange rates, or interest rates, a new concept of risk was introduced; that of 'systemic risk'. In the terminology of finance theory, risk was now divided up into idiosyncratic risk, deemed to be an intrinsic property of particular assets, and 'systemic' risk, that is the risk that all, or a large number of, markets may experience declines in prices, or all, or a significant number of, financial institutions may become insolvent. Idiosyncratic 'risk' is supposed to be the result of portfolio choices; that is, the choices made by fund managers to hold particular assets, and not others, in a given portfolio. Systemic 'risk' is now most commonly attributed to interlocking balance sheets; that is, the tendency of financial firms to hold as assets the liabilities of other financial firms or banks. This is the foundation of the 'network' theory approach to financial risk that is now widely accepted by central banks and financial regulators

(European Central Bank 2010). This approach to 'risk' then reinforces balance sheet regulation as a way of eliminating risk.

In the chapter that follows, it is argued that this approach to banking regulation fetishizes risk and the role of balance sheet decisions in financial outcomes, at the expense of the macroeconomic imbalances that drive cash flows around the economy. A section on methodological considerations discusses the role of risk and uncertainty in the financial system. This is followed by a section that discusses the current European context for banking regulation, in which 'macroeconomic' imbalances are treated as the cause of the crisis, but somehow separate from issues of banking regulation. A third section considers banking regulation in the European Monetary Union. A final section concludes by pointing out that macroeconomic imbalances are essential for eliminating banking risk.

Methodological considerations

The most common approach to banking regulation is founded upon a conviction so widespread that it is virtually never questioned: that bank balance sheets are the results of voluntary individual 'saving' decisions and fund or bank managers' portfolio and funding choices. These are all supposed to be 'rational' choices using risk-return considerations of venerable lineage, even if some of the mathematical formalization dates back to merely the last half-century (see Poitras 2007). There is of course the problem of unintended consequences, a problem that is especially acute in the case of financial contracts. Such contracts, like fixed capital investment, require certain financial commitments now, in exchange for returns whose value, in real or nominal terms, may be unknown. When those returns are negative and involve some kind of a loss, this is attributed to 'risk'. Most of finance theory consists of learned discussions on the statistical distribution of such 'risk'.

This is of course how the matter appears to an individual investor or fund or bank manager. But this cannot be a systematic approach to the way in which the economy functions, because the key economic activities that create and distribute income take place outside banking and financial markets, even if using existing bank liabilities (deposits) as means of payment. Somewhere in that economy lie the roots of financial gains and losses. But not being visible to an individual investor or bank manager, these inexplicable events appear as 'risks'. The assumption of such learned ignorance by economists with serious pretensions was nicely expressed by Marx:

> How insipid the economists are who, when they are no longer able to explain away the phenomenon of over-production and crisis are content to say that these forms contain the possibility of *crises*, that it is therefore *accidental* whether or not crises occur and consequently their occurrence is merely a *matter of chance*.
>
> (Marx 1974: 512)

If it is not abstracted 'risk' that causes outcomes to deviate from expectations, then what does cause unexpected losses in the economy? There is a particular business cycle tradition which explains those losses by attributing them to shifts in macroeconomic 'fundamentals': specifically, the effect of business investment on income and cash flow. In this business cycle analysis profits do not 'automatically' accrue, subject to some abstracted 'risk' factor. Capital does not naturally expand to give a return: it is naïve to believe that the lending of my money to someone else makes that money expand in value. Instead that return has to be generated by some kind of production and market process that brings about the return as a money flow in the form of a surplus of sales over costs. By simply assuming that the return occurs naturally, but is subject to risk, economists, bankers and financial regulators are evading the necessity of finding out the causes of financial returns or losses in favour of a generalized statement of ignorance ('risk'). Faced with darkness they prefer to talk about disconnected things that happen in darkness, rather than seeking means of illumination. This is especially true of those 'experts' who regard the whole financial system as a system for managing risk, much as they might regard lighting as a system for managing darkness rather than for illumination.

This is of course an oversimplification. There are plenty of theorists who, for example, classify 'risk' according to the circumstances under which particular losses may arise – exchange rate risk, counter-party risk, market risk, etc. There are even theorists who will expatiate learnedly about the skewed distributions, fat and thin 'tails' in which crises may happen with unexpected frequency, and so on. A particular kind of mystification has been the outcome of much New-Keynesian scholarship around the idea of 'asymmetric information' (the notion that financial contracts are between parties whose access to information is unequal), and 'adverse selection' (the notion that particular arrangements give rise to riskier contracts). The flaws in the analysis are usually two-fold. In the first place it is assumed that bank or financial contracts have some kind of inherently 'objective' but unknown risk, whose realization causes the problem. Yet we know from common observation that this 'risk', that is supposed to be inherent in a financial or monetary instrument, is not independent of what happens to other financial or banking institutions that are not parties to that instrument. This is the 'contagion' that was widely noted in the wake of the emerging market crises of the 1990s.

The second weakness of this kind of analysis is its dependence on the credulity of the practitioner, regulator, or theorist. Because key variables in the analysis cannot be observed ('risk', 'adverse selection', 'contagion', 'information') but must be inferred from the data provided as evidence of these variables, the analysis becomes circular. If you believe that categories of 'risk', 'adverse selection', 'contagion', and 'asymmetric information' explain the incidence of bank asset deterioration, then you will find the data to support your explanation in those categories. All of them may explain the statistical frequency of losses or defaults in the financial system.

But the process by which bank asset deterioration arises in a modern capitalist economy is essentially a monetary process, rather than a statistical one. This process can only be investigated by examining monetary circulation in the economy, because it is that monetary circulation that provides the cash flow which settles the financial or credit obligations that are bank assets. There are two levels of abstraction in this analysis. On the sectoral level (that is, taking as aggregates households, firms and the government, whose financial obligations are the assets, net of inter-bank or inter-financial institution claims, of the financial system) it was shown a long time ago by Kalecki and Keynes that the cash flows which constitute the income of these sectors is principally determined by the investment expenditure of firms ('capitalists earn what they spend'), plus the fiscal deficit, plus the trade surplus (Kalecki 1942; Keynes 1931).

Steindl developed this analysis to show how it explains financial risk, in the sense that for expected profits to be realized in the economy, the sum of investment, plus the fiscal deficit, plus the trade surplus, must reach a certain threshold set by saving behaviour in the economy. If that threshold is not reached, then expected profits are not realized and firms fall into difficulties with their financial obligations (Steindl 1941, 1945a). Steindl went further and showed that the respective distributions, of profits and debt, among firms concentrates financial risk among smaller borrowers (Steindl 1945b: Chapter IV). Minsky was later to express this as debt structures and cash flows. Following Irving Fisher, Minsky argued that a modern credit economy consists of a system of production and distribution, well-known from economics textbooks, and, alongside that system, a system of debt contracts summarized in balance sheets. Minsky showed, in a similar way to Kalecki, that the risk of financial intermediaries is essentially determined by the cash flows generated from business investment, the fiscal deficit, and the trade surplus (Minsky 1986: 141–157). In this analysis, the price system is not merely the vector that brings supply and demand into equilibrium throughout the economy. The price system also sets the parameters by which cash flows are distributed around the economy. Precisely because that price system is determined by supply and demand, it is not integrated with debt structures in such a way as to ensure that existing financial obligations are adequately serviced.

There are therefore two alternative views on financial risk. One ascribes the failure of financial or banking assets to generate expected returns to nebulous factors (information asymmetries, moral hazard, adverse selection, contagion) affecting the *statistical* distribution of such risk. The other view, derived from Kalecki, Keynes, Steindl and Minsky, points to the inconsistencies that arise in a modern credit economy between monetary or cash flows, and debt structures in that economy. The first view derives from the perceptions of finance practitioners. For them, indeed, risk is something 'out there'. The individual bank manager, creating a bank deposit by issuing a loan to a customer, has no way of knowing how that bank deposit will circulate further in the economy (this is the foundation of theories of asymmetric information – Stiglitz and Weiss 1981). The second view derives from a careful examination of how those bank deposits will circulate in the economy, and the incomes that will be created in that process.

These alternative views affect crucially the scope and possibilities of banking regulation. If the first view is correct, then it should be possible, by a combination of statistical research and prudential regulation, to determine the distribution of financial risk and restrict its appearance in bank balance sheets *independently* of what happens in the rest of the economy. Indeed, it may even be possible, by means of prudent financial regulation, to stabilize the capitalist economy through restricting the financing of *risky* activities. Herein lies that notion that risk is inherent in particular activities or particular balance sheet combinations – maturity transformation, investment banking, hedge funds or private equity are the usual suspects today. In the alternative view, financial risk is an outcome of particular macroeconomic conjunctures affecting the circulation of money and the incomes generated through that circulation given debt structures inherited from the past. At the margin, these debt structures may be altered by financial operations (refinancing on different terms with different maturities). But the risk arises in the gap between cash flows and those refinancing possibilities.

The European context

International banking adds particular complications to the questions of financial stability and the distribution of risk. In the old international portfolio analysis from the 1950s to the 1970s, cross-border lending offered opportunities for diversifying portfolios and stabilizing balance sheets in this way. With the crises of the 1980s, a whole range of new risks were discovered, exchange rate risk, political risk, and so on. For the information-theoretic New Keynesians, the obvious source of the difficulty is the absence of reliable information on conditions and future returns in foreign countries. In other words, the difficulty arises because financial intermediaries do not know the distribution of future returns. Such returns in foreign countries are held to be more opaque because 'agents' are assumed to have knowledge that is geographically localized. Hence it is supposed to be more difficult to 'know' the true risks of financial assets issued abroad.

There are numerous flaws in this kind of reasoning. While it may appear plausible, in fact the absence of information on conditions abroad may be overcome by institutional techniques, such as having a partner in the country where an investment is undertaken. This then reduces the information problem to a 'principal-agent' problem of trust and concordant incentives between the partners. But even if such inconsistencies could be eliminated, and all information were known, there is a much more fundamental logical flaw in the information-theoretic approach to financial risk. Financial contracts are long-term, in relation to the current period. That is, they are claims on future income, or obligations to pay out of future gross (before interest and dividends) income. Can that future income be known? No. Because future income is not just derived from natural endowments whose amount and productivity may be known today. One of those endowments, or factors of production, capital is a produced good. The return on that capital depends on how much capital is produced today. And the day after tomorrow, the amount and productivity of capital will depend on how much capital investment is undertaken between today and then. In other words, future returns, and the distribution of financial risk, is contingent upon decisions taken in the future as well as today. And even if it were possible to know those future cash flows, the assumption that debt structures can be aligned to those cash flows fails precisely because financial contracts are not reconstructed every day to match future cash flows. If financial commitments match future cash flows then, logically, today's debts match today's cash or income flows, and the problem of asset failure disappears. In this sense the information-theoretic approach is an argument that assumes away the problem.

In this regard the analysis of debt structures and the cash flows validating them stands on weaker ground. There is, with minor exceptions (Minsky 1989; Steindl 1989), no literature on international debt structures and cash flows. This is substituted by a very Ricardian kind of analysis that examines foreign borrowing against trade balances. (I refer to it as Ricardian, because like David Ricardo it assumes that money is an imported commodity and that, therefore, the only way to service foreign debt is through a trade surplus). Nevertheless, although undeveloped, this approach of analysing international cash flows and debt structures is crucial for understanding bank failure on an international level. Its implications for macroeconomic management in the European Union remain largely undeveloped, with the signal exception of authors both on the left and the right who consider that the financial crisis in Europe must have something to do with the trade imbalances of the member countries (on the left, Uxó, Paúl and Febrero 2011; on the right Mayer 2012).

In the absence of analysis and instruments of macroeconomic management as ways of stabilizing bank balance sheets, the European Union is turning more towards bank regulation as a way of dealing with the consequences, in those bank balance sheets, of what are perceived to be macroeconomic imbalances. However, the question of financial regulation in the European Union presents a unique set of regulatory dilemmas. On the one hand, it has superficial similarities to the fragmented system of regulation in the United States of America, where states have their own regulatory institutions enforcing regulations within particular states, but there also exists a federal regulatory superstructure in the form of the Federal Reserve, the Securities and Exchange Commission, and so on. But Europe does not yet have any federal regulatory superstructure.

This lack of federal regulation has far-reaching consequences for the structure of banking in Europe. Because of this, banks in Europe, even international banks like Deutsche Bank or Unicredit, are overwhelmingly organized in subsidiaries subject to national regulation and national capital requirements as opposed to having cross-border branches. As a result, most cross-border lending is in the form of securities issued in a given country and purchased by a bank abroad.

There is, however, an even more striking absence in the financial system that is being created for the European Union. This is the lender of last resort that is supposed to keep the financial system from collapsing due to temporary illiquidity. Until 2008, it was widely believed in bank regulatory circles that such a facility was unnecessary and constituted a form of 'moral hazard'. Banks were supposed to take responsibility for the liquidity of their balance sheets, making lending decisions on the assumption that loans would stay on bank balance sheets until repaid. Bank illiquidity was best dealt with in inter-bank markets by banks themselves (with the best 'local' information about the causes of any illiquidity). Central bank liquidity should not be provided because central banks cannot distinguish between situations of illiquidity and insolvency. The provision of such liquidity would inevitably end up supporting 'failed bank business models'.

Accordingly, until 2008, the European Union's policy on bank regulation was the orthodox one of standardizing regulation in different countries, to allow for the creation of a true single market in financial services. This has mostly benefited larger banks that have been encouraged to expand, through mergers and acquisitions, into large international banks – for example, Deutsche Bank, Unicredit, Société Générale (Grahl 2009). In this way, the European Union recreated a similar situation to the classic English system under the Bank Charter Act of 1844: the central bank's functions were restricted to guarding the value of money, leaving banks to take the moral and legal responsibility for their debts or, what amounts to the same thing, for the liquidity of their customers. In a moral and political climate that stigmatized 'excessive' debt and which was created by, or perhaps reflected in, the Maastricht Treaty of 1992, a crisis of illiquidity was inevitable precisely because such a crisis can only be overcome by more lending and more debt, not less.

Regulatory innovation

The inevitable crisis occurred in 2008, not so much because of 'contagion' in the wake of the collapse of Lehman Brothers in September 2008, as due to the freezing of the inter-bank market since earlier that year and the congestion in the capital market as banks lined up to raise additional capital. This left financially exposed a number of large multinational companies (Tata Brothers, GEC, Arcelor Mittal, Rio Tinto Zinc) that had financed major corporate acquisitions with short-term borrowing which they now could neither roll over nor refinance into the capital market. The companies responded predictably by cutting back drastically their investment programmes. As economic activity slowed down, so too did income generation and the ability of firms and households to service existing debt commitments. Inevitably this showed up in the deteriorating loan books of banks. In Spain, Portugal and Ireland, banks that had extended loans to speculative construction booms found themselves suddenly illiquid.

As with the 1844 Bank Charter Act, the default provider of liquidity, or lender of last resort, turned out to be the government. Spanish and Irish government finances that, before the crisis, had been well within the Maastricht limits, were now overstretched by the need to support their banks in order to prevent the collapse of their financial systems. The decisions to support their banks and their failing economies were policy decisions, rather than the result of fiscal indiscipline or government profligacy. As a result, the crisis was transformed from a banking or commercial crisis into a crisis of government finances that exposed the structural interdependence between bank balance sheets and cash flows in the rest of the economy.

The crisis of government finances in its turn drained what little liquidity was left in banks, if only because government bonds that cannot be sold at a fair price must be held to maturity in order to preserve their value. It was recognition that a crisis of government finances could not be confined to government borrowing that finally persuaded the European Central Bank (ECB) to emulate belatedly the 'quantitative easing' of the US Federal Reserve and the Bank of England. In December 2011, and in the following March, the European Central Bank allotted a total of just over €1 trillion of three year loans to banks at rates of interest of just under 1 per cent, virtually doubling the size of the ECB's balance sheet. These Long-Term Refinancing Operations (LTROs) were a very effective move. Not only did this relieve the liquidity of banks in Southern Europe; it also offered European governments the next best facility to central bank financing of a fiscal deficit, namely central bank financing of commercial banks' lending to governments. As long as the yield on government bonds exceeded the rate on central bank borrowing, it was going to be profitable for banks to finance governments.

The LTROs came in the wake of the Vienna Initiative of 2009 that showed the limitations of the earlier attempts at regulating banks. The Vienna Initiative was a much less formal arrangement under which European banks engaged in cross-border lending (Italy's Unicredit, France's Société Générale, Austria's Raiffeisen International) were given 'financial support packages' by the World Bank, the European Bank for Reconstruction and Development (EBRD). and the European Investment Bank (EIB) in return for commitments not to reduce their lending in Central and Eastern Europe. Close to €33 billion of public money was lent to the commercial banks. Far from keeping their lending to Europe's new member states constant, the banks reduced their lending and managed to secure a postponement of required capital increases (Toporowski 2012).

In many respects, the Vienna Initiative showed how fatally compromised was the long-standing strategy of standardizing bank regulation in member states of the European Union, in the face of the deflation that was spreading through Europe. The parallels with attempts at international coordination of bank regulation were obvious. In difficulty, banks have to be rescued if a run on the financial system is to be avoided. But bank rescue also makes banks less dependent on regulators, whose inconvenient demands can always be postponed until circumstances improve. The only way out of the dilemma is macroeconomic management to ensure cash and income flows in the economy are adequate to meet debt obligations and that requires management of the business cycle in an open economy, rather than just management of debt.

The next attempt to revive bank regulation as an alternative to countercyclical policy was the European Commission's proposal of a Banking Union. At the beginning of 2012, the European Commission had set up a High Level Expert Group on reforming the structure of the EU banking sector, chaired by Erkki Liikanen. This reported remarkably quickly, in October 2012, advising the usual diet of balance sheet management (higher capital adequacy, separation of investment from commercial banking functions) for stabilizing banks in Europe (High Level Expert Group 2012). But it also endorsed the European Commission's Directive on a common recovery and resolution procedure for troubled European banks, subsequently passed by the European Parliament (European Parliament 2014). This was part of a European Commission proposal for establishing a Banking Union within the European Monetary Union with a common regulator, to be developed within the European Central Bank, and a common way of dealing with failing banks (European Commission 2014).

In principle the European Banking Union is supposed to 'domesticate' the problem of cross-border lending in Europe, reinforcing the single market. A lender of last resort is proposed in the form of a 'recovery and resolution' mechanism, under the control of the ECB, which will offer necessary liquidity to banks facing liquidity problems. But, apart from the poor condition of European banks, these latest initiatives are motivated implicitly by an urgent desire to 'depoliticize' bank rescues. The practical necessity for this arises out of the European Commission's and European Central Bank's desire to take bank resolution (as rescues are called in banking circles) out of the hands of national governments in order to stop such resolutions from derailing government finances, as they clearly did in the cases of Spain and Ireland. But behind this is also a desire to prevent governments from backing the 'failed business models' of their national banks. Underlying this is the thinking described above, that the 'risk' associated with bank assets is exogenous and outside the control of governments.

Much as military coups to 'depoliticize' government end up politicizing the military, this latest effort to remove government as a lender of last resort can only end up politicizing the European Central Bank even further through its proposed bank resolution mechanism. Two aspects of this proposed system are deeply political. First of all, the allocation of costs of bank rescues between bank shareholders and bondholders, depositors, and public funds has to be a political decision, negotiated between all concerned. This is already exemplified in the rescue of Cyprus in 2013. In the second aspect, costs imposed on residents in any one country will inevitably be seen as reflecting the standing of that country's government within the European Union. There is no purely 'technical' way of resolving bank difficulties.

Conclusion

In the international monetary system, and its European sub-system, the 'natural' way of strengthening banks is through an investment boom, redistributed to neighbouring countries' economies through appropriate trade and fiscal imbalances. As has been argued above, business investment (rather than monetary policy) is the key way of putting into circulation the financial resources of business corporations. In an international setting, such an investment needs to be accompanied by a trade deficit to distribute internationally those financial resources. Europe is handicapped by deflation because the countries where investment is concentrated, around Germany and Scandinavia, have trade surpluses with countries in Southern Europe. Failing such a combination of investment and trade imbalances, debt problems arise which cannot be alleviated by fiscal deficits. Europe needs effective mechanisms of macroeconomic management to create the macroeconomic imbalances (fiscal and trade imbalances) and investment activity that will generate the cash and income necessary to support debt structures. In such a system, government debt is a necessary instrument of banking regulation in order to control the level of liquidity in banking and financial markets. The present approach of providing liquidity to banks and regulating balance sheet proportions (capital adequacy) can provide the means of survival, but cannot strengthen a banking system weakened by deflation in Europe.

References

European Central Bank (2010) *Recent Advances in Modelling Systemic Risk using Network Analysis.* Frankfurt: European Central Bank.

European Commission (2014) *Memo on Banking Stability: Restoring Financial Stability in the Eurozone.* Brussels 14 April.

European Parliament (2014) *Directive of the European Parliament and of the Council establishing a framework for the recovery and resolution of credit institutions and investment firms and amending Council Directives* 77/91/EEC and 82/891/EC, Directives 2001/24/EC, 2002/47/EC, 2004/25/EC, 2005/56/EC, 2007/36/EC and 2011/35/EC and Regulation (EU) No 1093/2010.

Grahl, J. (ed.) (2009) *Global Finance and Social Europe.* Cheltenham: Edward Elgar.

High Level Expert Group on Reforming the Structure of the EU Banking Sector (2012) *Final Report*. Brussels, 2 October.

Kalecki, M. (1942) A Theory of Profits. *Economic Journal* 52(2), pp. 258–267.

Keynes, J.M. (1931) An Economic Analysis of Unemployment. The Harris Lectures. In Moggridge, D. (ed).*The Collected Writings of John Maynard Keynes. Volume*

XIII. The General Theory and After. Part 1 Preparation. London: Macmillan for the Royal Economic Society.

Marx, K.H. (1974) *Capital, a Critique of Political Economy. Volume II. The Process of Circulation of Capital* edited by F. Engels, Moscow: Progress Publishers.

Mayer, T. (2012) *Europe's Unfinished Currency.* London: Anthem Press.

Minsky, H.P. (1986) *Stabilizing an Unstable Economy.* New Haven, CT: Yale University Press.

Minsky, H.P. (1989) Financial Structures, Indebtedness and Credit. In Barrère, A. (ed.) *Money, Credit and Prices in Keynesian Perspective.* London: Macmillan.

Poitras, G. (ed.) (2007) *Pioneers of Financial Economics. Volume 2: Twentieth-Century Contributions.* Cheltenham: Edward Elgar.

Steindl, J. (1941) On Risk. *Oxford Economic Papers*, 5 June, pp. 43–53.

Steindl, J. (1945a) Capitalist Enterprise and Risk. *Oxford Economic Papers*, 7 March, pp. 21–45.

Steindl, J. (1945b) *Small and Big Business: Economic Problems of the Size of Firms.* Institute of Statistics Monograph No. 1. Oxford: Basil Blackwell.

Steindl, J. (1989) Saving and Debt. In Barrère, A. (ed.) *Money, Credit and Prices in Keynesian Perspective.* London: Macmillan.

Stiglitz, J.E. and Weiss, A. (1981) Credit Rationing in Markets with Imperfect Information. *American Economic Review* 71(3), pp. 393–410.

Toporowski, J. (2012) Vienna Initiative: Regulatory Capture and Policy Confusion. *Bankwatch Mail* 52. May, p. 3.

Uxó, J., Paúl, J. and Febrero, E. (2011) Current Account Imbalances in the Monetary Union and the Great Recession: Causes and Policies. *Panoeconomicus* 58(5), pp. 571–592.

4 The European crisis and the rise of German power

Alan Cafruny

The crisis of the eurozone has accelerated processes of uneven development and political fragmentation in Europe. The Franco-German partnership – the motor force of integration for half a century – has shattered amid France's problems with high levels of debt, declining competitiveness, and record unemployment. Notwithstanding a series of bold institutional steps, the EU's security and defence policies remain essentially intergovernmental. German capital and the Federal Republic of Germany (FRG) have ascended to a position of dominance, as evidenced not only by Germany's large trade surplus but also the centrality of German capital within Western European corporate networks (van der Pijl, Holman and Raviv 2011) and central and eastern European production centres (Becker, Jäger and Weissenbacher 2013; Gross 2013). The authority of Berlin in eurozone crisis decision-making is unchallenged. The 'German question' has returned in full force.

This chapter investigates the rise of German power in Europe and the Eurozone. It employs the concept of *geoeconomics*, originally developed by Edward Luttwak (1990) and recently reintroduced by Hans Kundnani (2011), to understand the implications of German policy for European geopolitics. Prior to 1989 West Germany could be considered a *civilian* power because it was engaged in the pursuit of cooperation through multilateral institutions (Maull 1990). Since reunification, however, German policy has evolved in a very different direction. Geoeconomic power refers to 'the admixture of the logic of conflict and the methods of commerce … the harder edge of Germany's pursuit of national interest within Europe and its reluctance to use military force or even to project power in a traditional sense in the wider world' (Luttwak 1990: 17). At the present time Germany pursues a policy of 'selective multilateralism' within a 'logic of conflict' according to which 'methods of commerce' displace 'military methods' with 'disposable capital in lieu of firepower, civilian innovation in lieu of military-technical advancement, and market penetration in lieu of military garrisons and bases' (Luttwak 1990: 22). The rise of geoeconomics is not, of course, limited to Germany, and it has led to a more general renationalization of foreign policy (Martiningui and Youngs 2012) as well as of finance (Alloway and Braithwaite 2012; Sri Kumar 2012) among member states in the EU.

Part I of this chapter describes the relationship between the evolution of German export mercantilism and the emergent European monetary order. The central organizing principle of German (geoeconomic) foreign policy is exports. As Ludwig Erhard wrote 60 years ago, 'Foreign trade is quite simply the core and premise of our economic and social order' (Ash 1994: 244). Throughout the post-Second World War period Germany has pursued mercantilist goals, but the geoeconomic component – the 'logic of conflict' – has become more pronounced in the context of the Eurozone crisis. Part II describes the EU's management of the crisis and the central role played by Germany. Policymakers sought first to rescue their overextended banks and, second, to impose draconian austerity measures on debtor countries whilst preserving the Eurozone that, in its present form, serves as an instrument of German export mercantilism. Eschewing the emphasis on culture and ideology as explanations for Germany's insistence on austerity policies, it suggests that the structural interests of German capital are quite simply inconsistent with the developmental needs of the Eurozone. As Part III shows, Germany is powerful enough to impose austerity, but too weak to adopt a leadership role analogous to that of the USA in the Bretton Woods system. Part IV assesses the implications of this analysis for the European geopolitical space. The dreams of a common European policy have been shattered by the realities of uneven development and German geoeconomic power. Growing geopolitical tensions and fears of US disengagement are forcing the German state to reexamine its 'culture of restraint', but it is unlikely that Germany will fundamentally revise its strategic orientation to Atlanticism and the American superpower.

German state, German capital, and the crisis in the EU

Europe's post-war 'golden age' was greatly dependent on exports to the USA. But the post-Bretton Woods transition to floating exchange rates and the rapid development of mobile transnational financial markets centred on Wall Street made it more difficult to pursue the more or less covert mercantilism that had underpinned the European post-war growth model and concomitant social settlement. Growing monetary instability intensified the problems of uneven development and presented acute problems for West Germany and eventually for the Franco-German relationship. The inability to sustain intergovernmental monetary agreements revealed Europe's collective vulnerability to US monetary unilateralism.

The centrality of the FRG

Prior to Economic and Monetary Union (EMU), the imbalance between the FRG and the rest of the EU meant that the Deutsche Mark was a powerful magnet for international capital seeking a safe and noninflationary haven. The 1992 collapse of the Exchange Rate Mechanism (ERM) exemplified this tendency. As long as European economies were expanding, ERM members could raise their interest rates in order to maintain parity with the rising Deutsche Mark. Reunification, however, precipitated a crisis for Germany and the EU. Then, as now, Germany refused to tolerate inflation to promote European solidarity; when the Bundesbank raised interest rates to unprecedented levels, it ushered in a period of sustained economic stagnation in the fledgling single market, ultimately forcing Italy and the UK to withdraw from the ERM.

The exit from the post-war settlement and entry into a monetary union predicated on austerity was facilitated by the gradual erosion of working class power as a result of growing unemployment, globalization, and the opening up of the former Soviet bloc economies (and later China) with the resultant abundant pools of cheap and unprotected labour. Already in 1985 the highly influential European Round Table (ERT), representing the interests of transnational European capital, had called for a single currency but rejected the Keynesian and fiscal stabilizers inherent in previous plans for monetary union. Its proposal, *Reshaping Europe* (1991), bore remarkable similarities to the Maastricht timetable for EMU (Carchedi 2001; van Apeldoorn 2002). If the decision to adopt EMU was thus a result of many proximate factors operating in both the geopolitical and economic spheres – not least by the time of Maastricht the desire to contain a reunified Germany – it also expressed the strong turn towards finance-led growth and neoliberalism (Gill 1998; van Apeldoorn 2002). EMU thus wrapped neoliberalism in the flag of 'Europe,' legitimizing a turn that had been accomplished in an Anglo-Saxon world that was more susceptible to the calls for 'freedom' from Margaret Thatcher and Ronald Reagan.

Since the late 1990s, German capital has pursued relentless cost-cutting and austerity, which has been closely linked to its foreign direct investment strategy. Crucial stages of German manufacturing and commodity supply chains have been relocated throughout central and eastern Europe (CEE), thereby enabling the German export model to compete globally (Gross 2013). Successive EU enlargements since 2004 have provided a more secure institutional and legal basis for the establishment of an enlarged German manufacturing zone.

Germany's relatively modest record of growth since that time has been achieved largely on the basis of exports. The German economy is 'structurally reliant on foreign demand for its growth' (Tilford 2010: 6) and this is a central factor in the crisis of the Eurozone, as recognized by the US Treasury, the International Monetary Fund (IMF), and perhaps even the European Commission itself (Dalton 2013a; Parkin and Donahue 2013; United States Treasury 2013). A succession of reform programmes and 'employers' offensives' (Kinderman 2005) undertaken by both the CDU/CSU- and SPD-led governments dramatically decreased unit labour costs, especially after 2002 in conjunction with fiscal austerity and the ensuing Hartz IV labour reforms, the latter of which resulted in sweeping changes in unemployment protection and social assistance (see also Flassbeck and Lapavitsas, Chapter 8, and Grahl,

Chapter 10, in this volume). As a consequence, the link between export-led growth, wages, and the expansion of the internal market that characterized Germany's post-war phase has been severed (Hugh 2007; IMF 2007; see also Bibow 2009; Dumas 2010, esp. pp. 162–175). German export mercantilism requires the Eurozone in order to preclude the competitive depreciations that were occurring prior to 1992 and would certainly return in the context of break-up. As Costas Lapavitsas et al. have written, 'The euro is a "beggar-thy-neighbor" policy for Germany, on condition that it beggars its own workers first' (2012: 30). German export mercantilism is thus both a cause and effect of stagnation, as deficit countries are compelled to adjust through internal devaluation. Wage stagnation and growing inequality depress demand and encourage covert forms of mercantilism. Until 2008, moreover, these factors tended to draw European – and especially German – capital into the US financial sector, facilitated by the establishment of a unified market for financial services (Sablowski 2008; Grahl 2011) and thereby exposing the Eurozone more fully to the US crash of 2008.

EU response to the crisis

The onset of the banking crisis in the context of asymmetries that have haunted Europe since the last days of the Bretton Woods system thus posed an enormous challenge to the capacities for European crisis management, and ultimately to Germany. Membership in the EMU initially insulated debtor countries from currency crises even as it kept their borrowing costs artificially low. At the same time, of course, it precluded devaluation as a means of regaining competitiveness. Household debt in Greece, Spain and Portugal skyrocketed to offset the structural current account deficit arising from German export success while German and other core-nation banks became massively over-exposed. Former Bundesbank head Karl Otto Pohl characterized the rescue package for Greece in the following terms (Spiegel 2010):

> It was about protecting German banks, but especially the French banks, from debt write offs. On the day that the rescue package was agreed on, shares of French banks rose by up to 24 per cent … you can see what this was really about – namely, rescuing the banks and the rich Greeks.
>
> (German 'Leadership': EFSF, EMS, the Expanding Role of the ECB)

The successful return of peripheral Eurozone member states to the international bond market in April and May of 2014 has been widely celebrated in the international media and in Brussels. But this optimism is both unwarranted and deceptive. The austerity policies that have accompanied the bail-outs have both deepened the crisis and expanded it beyond the financial sector and into the real economy and society. In March 2014, eight EU countries were experiencing deflation, a further eleven were experiencing what the IMF calls 'lowflation' of less than 0.5% growth, and unemployment in the

Eurozone reached 12% in 2014 (Eurostat 2014; Economist 2014). Unemployment and debt deflation are advancing steadily northward from the periphery into the core.

As European institutions have become more closely involved in austerity, the EU has become engulfed in right-wing populist and anti-EU sentiments. In Germany, fears of a 'transfer union' have engendered a 32% decline in support for the EU since 2007 and influential intellectuals have drawn comparisons between the Maastricht and Versailles treaties (Kundnani 2014). The German Constitutional Court has cast into doubt even relative modest initiatives that have been designed to relieve austerity. European Commission proposals for a 'banking union', under which the European Central Bank (ECB) would become the principal supervisor of large European banks and a Eurozone-wide deposit scheme would be implemented, were vetoed by Germany in an act of 'brutal power politics' (Spiegel 2013).

Options for Germany

As critical political economy scholarship has demonstrated, the construction of the EMU can usefully be understood as an elite project designed to 'constitutionalize' neoliberalism (Gill 1998). Yet, notwithstanding the inherent instability that arises from this project, the 'eurozone crisis' is not simply one of neoliberalism as such, but rather the result of chronic uneven development and the unilateral exercise of overwhelming German power. Indeed, the crisis is also a reflection of the *absence* of a unified European elite or putative 'European transnational capitalist class.' (Cafruny 2003; Cafruny and Ryner 2007). The 'design flaw' (Mahnkopf 2012) in EMU that precludes a Keynesian alternative to austerity survives because it conforms to the interests of German capital. Hence, the paradoxical and unprecedented situation of IMF involvement in the Eurozone crisis management despite the absence of net capital outflows and the fact that the euro has appreciated significantly against the dollar, renminbi and yen since 2009.

In his seminal work, *The World in Depression,* Charles Kindleberger argued that stable monetary orders require a single leader or 'hegemon' powerful enough to resolve collective action problems and extend concessions to subordinate allies (1973). Antonio Gramsci adopts a similar understanding:

> The fact of hegemony presupposes that account be taken of the interests and tendencies of the groups over which hegemony is to be exercised, and that a certain compromise equilibrium should be formed – in other words, that the leading group should make sacrifices of an economic-corporate kind.
>
> (Gramsci 1971: 161)

Many observers propose a role for Germany analogous to that played by the USA after 1945 (Economist 2013; Maier 2012; Matthijs and Blyth 2011;

Soros 2012; Varoufakis 2013). Can Germany abandon geoeconomics and move to a position of *organic* leadership of the eurozone? As noted above, there can be little doubt that, notwithstanding the objections of the Bundesbank and Ordoliberals, German banks and export firms – but not the German working class – have benefited greatly from EMU. The severe downturn experienced by Germany in 2008 and 2009, when Germany's exports were hit hard by the global recession, is a reflection of its extremely high export dependence. Germany's modest 2013 growth rate of 0.5% was a result of the dramatic increase in exports as trade surpluses exceeded 17 billion euros per month (Eurostat 2013a).

The limits of German power

The single currency not only prevented periodic devaluations against Germany within the eurozone, but also served to limit the appreciation of the euro in relation to the dollar, pound, and renminbi. The low interest rate regime allowed German banks to participate in a debt-financed bubble throughout the GIIPs, the necessary counterpart to export surpluses. When the boom ended, as noted above, programmes such as the European Financial Stability Facility (EFSF), European Stability Mechanism (ESM), and various schemes for ECB financing allowed German and other core banks to reduce their own exposure while imposing much of the cost on peripheral countries and core country taxpayers. Finally, the crisis has allowed the German government to issue debt not on the basis of German 'fundamentals', but rather on the basis of 'flight to safety'. Joshua Rosner has calculated that, as a result, German ten-year yields 'should' be twice their current level of 1.2% (Rosner 2012: 17).

To be sure, the costs of even a Greek exit from the Eurozone for Germany would be substantial; it is possible and perhaps even likely that exit and subsequent default would trigger a wholesale collapse of the single currency by increasing pressure on Spain, Portugal and Italy. The loss of the euro would gravely damage the single market. In 2010 German companies sold 218 billion euros of goods to Greece, Italy, Ireland, Portugal and Spain whilst German foreign direct investment in these countries totalled 90 billion euros. Notwithstanding the fact that German exporters have become somewhat less dependent on the Eurozone (see below), the impact would still be very great. German banks and the German state would also suffer severe consequences from a generalized break-up and default. A Greek exit, although involving just 2.3% of eurozone GDP, would involve very high costs for the German and French states (Dor 2012).

The alternative to break-up and default would be to construct a genuine European polity under a 'benevolent' German hegemony including a Treasury and system of common taxation, a banking union under ECB supervision, the establishment of a deposit insurance scheme for banks, the transformation of the ECB into a fully fledged lender of last resort, and the issuance of eurobonds. These policies would provide the institutional basis for a movement away from austerity, led by German reflation. They are advocated almost everywhere but Germany itself, including, as noted above, by the IMF and the US Treasury. Yet, the resources that would need to be expended would be substantial and, arguably, beyond the capacity of the German state.

Here, what is perhaps most salient is the profound vulnerability of Germany under any future scenario. On the one hand, Germany's present incremental strategy of crisis management through bail-outs and austerity has itself become increasingly costly. Between 2008 and 2013 the Bundesbank contributed US $874 billion to the Target2 credit system for which it remains liable.[1] In addition, between May, 2010 and June 2012 the ECB bought more than $250 billion in sovereign bonds. EFSF and ESM support has totalled $500 billion (Glover 2012). The mutualization of debt via the introduction of Eurobonds would represent a significant new liability. The establishment of a debt redemption fund – pooling debt over 60% of GDP – would amount to more than 3 trillion euros, which explains why Germany has categorically rejected joint liability. Germany's financial liability would also have to increase substantially if a European deposit guarantee scheme is introduced. In 2013 Germany's public debt had reached 81.5% of GDP (Eurostat 2013b), and reflation would increase budget deficits and debt, reducing the ability to re-capitalize banks. Higher wages would increase unit labour costs, thereby undermining international competitiveness. The moral hazard implicit in eurobonds would be likely to expand the cost of these programmes, and the growth of anti-austerity parties and movements strengthens German resistance to further bailouts. Germany faces a host of longer-term problems, including extremely low growth rates far into the future, population decline, and the legacy of years of low public investment.

A break-up of the euro in the short-term, then, would certainly impose further massive costs on Germany. Alternatively, Germany could greatly increase its (already implicit) demands for real industrial and commercial assets in return for debt guarantees along the lines of privatization plans for Greece, but this would have enormous political consequences (Michaletos 2012). In sum, whether or not the eurozone breaks up, Germany appears destined to acquire massive liabilities amid growing austerity and resentment. Yet, Germany has already pushed against the outer limits of public opinion in carrying out rescue operations and bailouts. It is extremely unlikely that Germany could fulfil the US Treasury's and IMF's demand that it play a hegemonic Keynesian role throughout the Eurozone. Germany is too weak to exercise 'hegemony' in the Gramscian sense, but strong enough to continue imposing austerity on the rest of the Eurozone.

Geoeconomics and geopolitics

The more forceful exercise of German economic power in the context of the Eurozone crisis raises more fundamental questions about basic European and Euro-Atlantic political-military structures. The management of the crisis has aggravated existing inter-state and inter-capitalist class rivalries that have arisen not only in the form of German mercantilism and the imposition of Europe-wide austerity, but also the abandonment of common industrial projects in the nuclear and military-industrial arenas. The latter includes the failed attempt to merge BAE and EADS in 2012, the deepening subordination of the European military-industrial complex to US firms (Cafruny 2009), and the growing tensions over energy policy and Euro-Russian relations. Notwithstanding the establishment in the Lisbon Treaty of an elaborate EU foreign policy architecture complete with its own diplomatic core, the Common Foreign and Security Policy (CFSP) and Common Security and Defence Policy (CSDP) processes have been virtually irrelevant to major security issues. The re-emergence of the ‘German question’ has gained further urgency in the context of the US’ ‘pivot to Asia’ and growing conflicts with a more assertive and prosperous Russia.

These developments have given rise to much speculation concerning a more assertive German foreign policy, and there is a general consensus within elite foreign policy circles that ‘Germany will have to take the lead more decisively and more often’ (SWP-GMF 2014). Does Germany’s predicament lay the basis for a revival of the ‘second Rapallo’ strategy, as mooted by fractions of German business during the late 1980s and 1990s? (van der Pijl 2006; see also Wallerstein 2009). Is Germany abandoning the ‘culture of restraint’ that has defined its international outlook since 1945 (Sonne 2014)?

The political economy of German–Russian relations

There is a significant mutual interdependence between the EU and Russia. For example, Germany imports approximately 45% of its natural gas and crude oil from Russia, and the dependence on Russian energy greatly affects the competitiveness of German firms not only in Germany itself but also throughout the CEE region. At the same time, Russia has become an increasingly important market for German exports and foreign direct investment, especially in the energy sector. Prior to the crisis Russia was the fastest growing market for German exports, and by 2020 was expected to become Europe’s largest consumer market and the fourth largest consumer market in the world (Sberbank 2014). Within the energy sector, German E.ON and BASF along with French EDF and GDF Suez A.A. have invested heavily in Gazprom but also in pipelines, especially Nordstream, that compete directly with Washington- and Brussels-sponsored initiatives, including the ill-fated Nabucco pipeline, to reduce EU and eastern European dependency on Russian energy. Together with Italian ENI, the key investor in Southstream, they have at least partially ‘dis-intermediated’ (Abdelal 2010: 35) Ukraine whilst bypassing the Baltic States and Poland (Petersen 2010).

More generally, German trade patterns are gradually being transformed. China now receives more German foreign direct investment than France and appears poised to overtake the USA as Germany’s second largest trade partner. It is also the largest market for Germany's machine-tool industry. As Hans Kundnani and Jonas Parello Plesner write, 'the Chinese are increasingly dealing with the EU through Germany rather than through the foreign policy institutions created by the Lisbon Treaty' (Kundnani and Parello-Plesner 2013).

There is a clear relationship between patterns of German trade and interest, on the one hand, and German foreign policy. In 2003 Germany threatened to veto a UN Security Council against US military intervention in Iraq. In March 2011, Germany abstained in the UN Security Council – effectively siding with China and Russia – over the Anglo-French-US proposal (Resolution 1973) to establish a 'no fly' zone in Libya. With the exception of Serbia (1999) and Afghanistan (2001–14), Germany has refused involvement in all actual or proposed NATO military interventions, including most recently Syria. In 2014 the German military budget was 1.3% of GDP and projected to decline in the coming years.

Germany's economic interdependence with Russia and China has led it to form bilateral strategic partnerships that are not mediated through the EU or NATO. Within the G20, Germany has aligned with China against the USA over the issue of global current account imbalances. European Commission efforts to deploy anti-dumping legislation against solar panel manufacturers were blocked by Germany in 2013 following Chinese threats to investigate luxury car dumping (Dalton 2013b). At the same time, however, Germany has recognized that Atlanticism enhances its bargaining position *vis-à-vis* China. Despite the importance of arms exports for Germany, the world's third largest exporter, Germany (and the EU) have maintained the American-initiated arms embargo on China.

Following Georgia's military offensive in the breakaway province of South Ossetia in August 2008, Russian troops invaded and quickly occupied much of Georgian territory. The war opened up divisions within NATO: the USA and former Soviet bloc states favoured some military steps and Germany and France preferred diplomatic settlement. The EU responded in 2009 by offering former Soviet republics the possibility of Eastern Partnership, a form of association with the EU. But the partnerships were essentially initiatives designed to appease Poland, the Baltic States and the Brussels bureaucracy. They were substitutes for rather than pathways to EU membership. German–Russian economic interdependence continued to deepen in the context of a 'modernization partnership' (Adomeit 2012; Libront 2013)

The Eastern Partnership with Ukraine contained political and economic chapters. The latter, the Comprehensive and Deep Free Trade Agreement (CDFTA), would have placed at risk much of the eastern Ukrainian industrial sector. It demanded wholesale neoliberal reforms and the opening up of the Ukraine market to Western exports. It exposed Ukraine to predatory financial speculation and privatization but provided no right to employment or even visa-free travel in the EU. Nevertheless, connection to the EU became identified in the minds of western-oriented Ukrainians with democracy and an end to corruption. Ukrainian President Victor Yanukovych's failure to follow up on his declared intention to sign the CDFTA in November 2013, after having obtained promises of significant financial support from Russia, led to massive popular mobilizations in Kiev's *Maidan* and central and western Ukraine. This in turn provoked a cycle of state repression and increasingly radicalized opposition marked by the increasing activity of violent fascist groups within the *Maidan* followed by a de facto coup d'état by pro-Western politicians in Kiev. The acting government has since signed the political chapter of the Eastern Partnership and declared its intention to sign the CDFTA.

Russia's annexation of the Crimea in March 2014, and violent conflict between nationalist and pro-Russian federalist groups in Ukraine's southern and eastern provinces, have transformed Europe's geopolitical landscape and thereby called into question Germany's existing policy towards Russia. The 'structural adjustment' resulting from the US $18 billion IMF loan negotiated by the acting government in Kiev in May 2014 – and potentially exacerbated by the CDFTA – will lead to greater instability within Ukraine and, hence, potentially serious new tensions between Russia and the West. Despite strong opposition from the pro-Russian business lobby, Chancellor Angel Merkel was aligned with the United States in supporting harsh sanctions against Russia.

Although Germany has thus reaffirmed its geoeconomic stance, it has lent greater support to European integration and independence in the energy sector. The energy disputes between Russia and Ukraine in 2006 and 2009, during which Russia cut off gas exports to Ukraine, impacted on EU member states and thus demonstrated Russia's ability to use gas as a foreign policy instrument. Although initially opposed to a common policy, Germany has now apparently thrown its support behind Commission efforts to reduce the bargaining power of Gazprom, Russia's key gas exporter. The Commission has challenged the potentially monopolistic practices of Southstream, Gazprom's southern counterpart to Nordstream. The Commission's Third Energy Liberalization Package would prevent suppliers from controlling the pipelines used to deliver gas and lead to lower prices. The Commission has also announced that Gazprom contracts with six EU member states contravene EU laws. The shale gas revolution, most advanced in the USA, has been termed a 'geopolitical windfall' (Levi 2013) as US prices for natural gas have declined to one-fifth of the level in Asia and one-third of what Gazprom charges most of its European customers. It has already led to the growth of US coal exports to Western Europe. The transformation of world energy markets as a result of political and technological developments may be reducing Western Europe's dependence on Russian energy.

The end of Gaullism

The rise of German economic primacy throws into sharper relief the fundamental transformation of French policies in both the domestic and international spheres. Having quietly abandoned his campaign calls to establish a 'Latin bloc' against austerity and mired in systemic trade deficits, stagnation, high level of public debt (92% of GDP in 2013) and mass unemployment, President François Hollande has himself proposed harsh austerity measures, including, somewhat ironically, plans to reform French labour laws along German lines.[2] France has correspondingly over the last decade abandoned its distinctive 'Gaullist' stance, expressed since the early 1970s through the commitment to an EU-based foreign and defence policy, in favour of close alignment with the USA. In 2008, then-President Nicholas Sarkozy reintegrated France within the military command structure of NATO. The 50-year Anglo-French Treaty of 2010 stipulated far-reaching political and military cooperation, including the creation of a joint expeditionary task force of 10,000, collaboration on an integrated strike force involving joint use of aircraft carriers, and technology sharing. In 2009 France established a naval base in the United Arab Emirates, enabling its warships to patrol alongside the US Fifth Fleet in the Persian Gulf. France played a leading role in NATO's military and diplomatic operations in Libya. It has pursued an aggressive diplomacy towards Syria and Iran. Although the Lisbon Treaty introduced an elaborate foreign policy bureaucracy, the establishment of close Franco-American ties in the context of German 'selective multilateralism' actually fragmented Europe further and deepened its subordination to the American superpower. Indeed, the Lisbon Summit of 2010 confirmed the centrality of NATO to the EU, when European Council President Herman Van Rompuy expressed a desire to 'break down the remaining walls between NATO and the EU' (European Council 2010).

Transatlantic integration

In July 2013, the EU and USA commenced formal negotiations over the Transatlantic Trade and Investment Partnership (TTIP). The result so far has been a protracted and deeply contentious process. Some of the key issues include French resistance to liberalization of agriculture and media, protectionist pressures in the USA, and the fall-out from revelations concerning NSA surveillance, especially in Germany. Nevertheless, there appears to be substantial momentum among transnational European capital – and German big business in particular – for a further stage in the consolidation of neoliberalism. TTIP signals the further expansion into the transatlantic sphere of processes that started with the Single European Act (SEA), EMU, and North Atlantic Treaty Organization (NAFTA). Called an 'economic NATO' by then-Secretary of State Hillary Clinton (Ignatius 2012), TTIP is also seen to have a geopolitical component insofar as it seeks to establish a 'Western' bloc against China (Rosecrance 2013).

Notwithstanding the significant pull towards Russia and growing trade and investment links with China, the transatlantic economy is crucial to Germany as a destination for exports and foreign direct investment (Hamilton and Quinlan 2013). The conclusions of the recently completed Bertelsman

Stiftung (2013) study provide the most comprehensive guide to the likely impact of the TTIP. The impact of tariff reduction alone would not be substantial. However, the 'deep liberalization' scenario that is the stated goal of both the EU and USA would have far greater impact. The optimistic conclusions of the Report concerning employment and GDP growth in both the USA and Europe should be treated sceptically in view of wildly inaccurate predictions that were made at the times of the SEA, EMU, and NAFTA. However, the study appears on firmer ground in concluding that the TTIP would accelerate the process of transatlantic integration. It predicts a 'strong increase in trade flows between Germany and the USA' (pp. 13, 14, Table 1) and also that Germany's trade with many other countries and regions would decline significantly. This is because trade among EU members is barrier-free, while US–EU trade is subject to both trade and non-trade barriers. Increased transatlantic integration would significantly raise German exports to Japan and the BRICS (Brazil, Russia, India, China and South Africa), because the availability of cheaper intermediate products from the USA would increase the competitiveness of German firms. At the same time, Germany's import from China would decline by 13% and its imports from the other BRICS would also decline significantly. Finally, trade between the member countries of the southern Eurozone and Germany would decrease substantially, accelerating a process that was set in motion by the crisis; in 2012 Greece ranked 44th among German trading partners, just behind Vietnam. In sum, the TTIP might increase Germany's (and the EU's) dependence on the transatlantic economy while actually having disintegrative effects on the EU. Whilst there remain many obstacles to a transatlantic agreement, Germany's strong support for the TTIP is evidence of continuing strategic adherence to Atlanticism regardless of the outcome of negotiations.

Conclusion

Can Germany abandon its geoeconomic orientation and transform itself into a 'benevolent hegemon' exerting power as 'leadership' and not 'domination'? Many observers hoped that Angela Merkel's victory in the September 2013 elections would enable her to abandon her support for austerity. After all, with Merkel's blessing the Commission and the ECB have already pushed up against the limits of German public opinion in carrying out rescue operations and bailouts on a scale that would not have been thought possible when the crisis broke out in 2009. Yet, as this chapter has argued, these policies appear more likely to define the outer limits of the possible for Germany and not the beginning of a new phase. A more sceptical answer to the question does not require cultural explanations grounded in the traditions of Ordoliberalism, Lutheranism (Ozment 2012), Germany's alleged 'fear of history' (Mazower 2013), or the traumatic experience of the Weimar Republic with inflation. Notwithstanding the gains made by German big business as a result of the crisis, Germany lacks the deep resources to abandon its export mercantilism and sponsor a developmental and concessionary European development. This will lead to a deepening of uneven development and political and economic fragmentation in Europe.

Notwithstanding its aforementioned economic diversification, Germany remains highly dependent on European export markets as well as its supply networks and pools of cheap labour in central and Eastern Europe, and it must maintain this latter area as a sphere of influence. In February 2014, FRG President Joachim Gauck asserted that 'The FRG has to be ready to do more for this security which for decades was provided by others for her … To believe that Germany could just continue like before – this does not convince me' (Jones and Vasagar 2014). The desire to exert a stronger political-military presence was indicated most clearly by its willingness to confront Moscow by supporting opposition groups in Ukraine in late 2013 and early 2014.[3] However, neither Germany nor the EU as a whole has the resources or inclination to establish an independent European security order. If Germany does in fact seek to play a more assertive role on the European geopolitical stage it will do so under the umbrella of the American superpower. The implementation of the TTIP would represent a further important step in this direction.

Notes

1 Target2 ('Trans-European Automated Real-time Gross Settlement Express Transfer System') is a payment system that settles cross-border fund flows. The present massive imbalances reflect the need of peripheral countries for external financing, as core country banks have ceased lending. Since 2008 these imbalances have been financed via the ECB.

A Greek importer, for example, might place an order with a German company. Payments to and from the accounts of the buyer and seller are channeled via central banks, so the German exporter's bank gets a credit from the Bundesbank, which in turn has a claim on the ECB. The Greek importer's bank owes its local central bank, leaving the Bank of Greece with a debt at the ECB … The Bundesbank effectively ends up with loans to the other central banks that are reflected in Target2 claims on the Eurosystem.

(Glover 2012).

2 In January 2014 there was widespread speculation in the French media that Peter Hartz, author of the Hartz IV labour reforms, was advising President Hollande (EUobserver 2014).

3 The Stiftung Wissenschaft und Politik-German Marshall Fund of the United States (2014) in its Report advocates a more assertive German foreign policy. Yet, its specific recommendations are still moderate: for example, the need for 'inter-departmental strategic risk analysis', 'a crisis and deployment committee should be established in the Bundesbank', and the FRG 'should regularly submit a report on Germany's security to the Bundestag' (p. 44).

References

Abdelal, R. (2010) The Profits of Power: Commercial Realpolitik in Eurasia. *Harvard Business School, Working Paper* (September).

Adomeit, H. (2012) German-Russian Relations: Balance Sheet Since 2000 and Perspectives until 2025. *Comité d'études des relations Franco-Allemandes*, Institut français des relations internationales.

Ash, T.G. (1994) *In Europe's Name: Germany and the Divided Continent.* New York: Vintage.

Alloway, T. and Braithwaite, T. (2012) Europe's Banks Stage US Retreat. *Financial Times*, 22 July 2012.

Becker, J., Jäger, J. and Weissenbacher, R. (2013) The Political Economy of Dependency and Crisis in the Eurozone. Paper presented at the *European International Studies Association Convention, Warsaw*, 18 September 2013.

Bertelsmannstiftung (2013) *Transatlantic Trade and Investment Partnership: Who Benefits from a Free Trade Deal?* [Online] Global Economic Dynamics Gutersloh. Available from http://www.bfna.org/publication/transatlantic-trade-and-investment-partnership-ttip-who-benefits-from-a-free-trade-deal. [Accessed 23 April 2013].

Bibow, J. (2009) The Euro and its Guardian of Stability: The Fiction and the Reality of the Tenth Anniversary Blast. *Levy Economics Institute, Working Paper* No. 53, New York: Levy Economics Institute.

Cafruny, A. (2003) Europe, the United States, and Neoliberal (Dis)Order: Is There a Coming Crisis of the Euro? In Cafruny, A. and Ryner, M. (eds) *A Ruined Fortress: Neoliberal Hegemony and Transformation in Europe.* Lanham, MD: Rowman and Littlefield, pp. 285–306.

Cafruny, A. (2009) Geopolitics and Neoliberalism: U.S. Power and the Limits of European Autonomy. In van Apeldoorn, B., Drahokoupil, J. and Horn, L. (eds) *Neoliberal European Governance and Beyond – The Contradictions and Limits of a Political Project.* London: Palgrave, pp. 64–83.

Cafruny, A. and Ryner, M. (2007) *Europe at Bay: In the Shadow of US Hegemony.* Boulder, CO: Lynne Rienner.

Carchedi, G. (2001) *For Another Europe: A Class Analysis of European Economic Integration.* London: Verso.

Dalton, M. (2013a) EU Adds to Pressure Over German Exports. *Wall Street Journal.* [Online] Available from http://online.wsj.com/news/articles/SB10001424052702303914304579192181837934694 [Accessed 11 November 2013].

Dalton, M. (2013b) *Solar Panel Dispute Burns Hole in EU Trade Strategy.* [Online] Available from www.google.ru/?gfe_rd=cr&ei=uEsMU5jOLIXK8ge7i4DQAQ#newwindow=1&q=wall+street+journal+luxury+car+dumping+china+germany [Accessed 30 April 2013].

Dor, E. (2012) The Cost of a Greek Euro Exit for Spain. *IESEG School of Management*, Working Paper Series 2012-ECO-09. Lille Catholic University. Lille. France.

Dumas, C. (2010) *Globalisation Fractures: How Major Nation's Interests Are Now in Conflict.* London: Profile Books.

Economist, The (2013) Europe's Reluctant Hegemon. *The Economist.* [Online] Available from www.economist.com/news/special-report/21579140-germany [Accessed 15 June 2013].

Economist, The (2014) Eurozone Lowflation: Getting the Message. *The Economist*, April 3. [Online] Available from www.economist.com/blogs/freeexchange/2014/04/euro-zone-lowflation [Accessed December 2014].

European Council (2010) Remarks by Herman Van Rompuy, President of the European Council, at the NATO Summit in Lisbon. [Online] Available from www.con

silium.europa.eu/uedocs/cms_data/docs/pressdata/en/ec/11890.pdf [Accessed 19 November 2010].

EUObserver (2014) German Labour Reform Mastermind to Advise Holland. [Online] Available from: www.euobserver.com/tickers/122888 [Accessed 28 January 2014].

Eurostat (2013a) *Euroindicators.* [Online] Available from http://epp.eurostat.ec.europa.eu/cache/ITY_PUBLIC/6-18112013-AP/EN/6-18112013-AP-EN.PDF [Accessed 18 November 2013].

Eurostat (2013b) *General Government Gross Debt – Annual Data.* [Online] Available from http://epp.eurostat.ec.europa.eu/tgm/table.do?tab=table&plugin=1&language=en&pcode=teina225 [Accessed 18 November 2013].

Eurostat (2014) Unemployment Statistics, Brussels, October. [Online] Available from http://ec.europa.eu/eurostat/statistics-explained/index.php/Unemployment_statistics [Accessed December 2014].

Gill, S. (1998) European Governance and New Constitutionalism: EMU and Alternatives to Disciplinary Neo-Liberalism in Europe. *New Political Economy* 3(1), pp. 5–26.

Glover, J. (2012) *Soaring Target2 Imbalances Stoke German Risk Angst: Euro Credit.* Bloomberg. [Online] Available from www.bloomberg.com/news/2012-03-13/soaring-target2-imbalances-stoke-german-risk-angst-euro-credit.html [Accessed 13 March 2014].

Grahl, J. (2011) The Subordination of European Finance. In Nousios, P. and Tsokalis, A. (eds) *Competition and Change Special Issue* 15(1), pp. 15–47.

Gramsci, A. (1971) *Selections from the Prison Notebooks.* New York: International Publishers.

Gross, S. (2013) *The German Economy Today: Exports, Foreign Investment, and East-Central Europe.* Center for European and Mediterranean Studies. New York University.

Hamilton, D. and Quinlan, J. (2013) *The Transatlantic Economy 2013: Annual Survey of Jobs, Trade, and Investment between the United States and Europe.* Center for Transatlantic Relations. Johns Hopkins University Paul Nitze School of Advanced International Studies.

Hugh, E. (2007) Structural Aspects of German Export Dependence Part II. [Online] *Edward.Hugh.blog.* Available from www.edward.hugh.blogspot.com/2007 [Accessed 23 June 2014].

Ignatius, D. (2012) An Economic NATO. Atlantic Council, Washington, 6 December.

IMF (2007) Decoupling the Train? Spillovers and Cycles in the Global Economy. *World Economic Outlook*, Chapter 4. Washington, DC. [Online] Available at http://www.imf.org/external/pubs/ft/weo/2007/01/pdf/c4.pdf.

Jones, S. and Vasagar, J. (2014) Germany Must Use Military More, Says President. *Financial Times.* 31 January 2014, p. 3.

Kinderman, D. (2005) Pressure from Without: Subversion from Within: The Two-Pronged German Employer Offensive. *Comparative European Politics* 3(4), pp. 432–462.

Kindleberger, C. (1973) *The World in Depression.* Berkeley: University of California Press.

Kundnani, H. (2011) Germany as Geoeconomic Power. *Washington Quarterly* 34(3), pp. 31–45.

Kundnani, H. (2014) Even Germany's Intellectual Elite is Falling Out of Love with the EU. *EUobserver*, 3 April. [Online] Available at http://euobserver.com/opinion/123673 [Accessed December 2014].

Kundnani, H. and Parello-Plesner, J. (2012) *China and Germany: Why the Emerging Special Relationship Matters for Germany.* London: European Council on Foreign Relations.

Lapavitsas, C. et al. (2012) *Crisis in the Eurozone*. London: Verso.
Levi, M. (2013) *Geopolitical Consequences of U.S. Natural Gas Exports*. Subcommittee on Terrorism, Nonproliferation, and Trade, House Committee on Foreign Affairs, U.S. House of Representatives. 25 April 2013.
Libront, K. (2013) *Economization of German Security Policy: The Case of German-Russian Relations*. Working Paper, 17th Annual International Conference on Economics and Security, SIPRI, Stockholm, 14–15 June.
Luttwak, E. (1990) From Geopolitics to Geo-economics. *The National Interest* 37, Summer.
Mahnkopf, B. (2012) The Euro Crisis: German Politics of Blame and Austerity – A Neoliberal Nightmare. *International Critical Thought* 2(4), pp. 472–485.
Maier, C. (2012) Europe Needs a German Marshall Plan. *New York Times*, 13 June 2012, p. 23.
Martiningui, A. and Youngs, R. (eds) (2012) *Challenges for European Foreign Policy: What Kind of Geoeconomics?* Madrid: FRIDE A European Think Tank for Global Action.
Matthijs, M. and Blyth, M. (2011) Why Only Germany Can Fix the Euro: Reading Kindleberger in Berlin. *Foreign Affairs*. 17 November.
Maull, H. (1990) Germany and Japan: The New Civilian Powers. *Foreign Affairs 69 (5)* Winter, pp. 91–106.
Mazower, M. (2013) German Fear of History Jeopardises Europe's Future. *Financial Times*, 18 July 2013.
Michaletos, I. (2012) Germany's Eurozone Woes. *Worldpress*, 4 July. [Online] Available at http://worldpress.org/print_article.cfm?article_id=4223&dont=yes [Accessed December 2014].
Ozment, S. (2012) German Austerity's Lutheran Core. *New York Times*. 11 August 2012. [Online] Available from www.nytimes.com/2012/08/12/opinion/sunday/in-euro-crisis-germany-looks-to-martin-luther.html [Accessed 23 June 2014].
Parkin, B. and Donahue, P. (2013) IMF Backs U.S. Treasury in Criticizing German Exports. [Online] *Bloomberg*. Available from www.bloomberg.com/news/2013-10-31/germany-strikes-back-at-u-s-criticism-over-economic-policy.html [Accessed 1 November 2013].
Petersen, A. (2010) Russo-German Energy Pincer. *Wall Street Journal*, 8 September. [Online] Available from http://online.wsj.com/news/articles/SB10001424|0527487037 13504575475182399179228 [Accessed 23 June 2014].
Rosecrance, R. (2013) *The Resurgence of the West: How a Transatlantic Union Can Prevent War and Restore the United States and Europe*. New Haven, NC: Yale University Press.
Rosner, J. (2012) *Maastricht: Union that Foresaw its Failure but Closed its Eyes*. New York: Graham Fisher.
Sablowski, T. (2008) Towards the Americanization of European Finance? The Case of Finance-Led Accumulation in Germany. In Panitch, L. and Konings, M. (eds) *American Empire and the Political Economy of Global Finance*. New York: Palgrave, pp. 135–158.
Sberbank (2014) Consumer Speed Kings: Team Russia Leads the World. [Online] *Investment Research*. Available from http://slon.ru/images/doc/sberbank_consumer_speed_kings.pdf [Accessed 23 June 2014].
Sonne, W. (2014) The Culture of Restraint is No More: Germany is Ready for a Larger Role in the World. [Online] *AIGS*. Available from www.aicgs.org/issue/the-culture-of-restraint-is-no-more-germany-is-ready-for-a-larger-role-in-the-world [Accessed 3 February 2014].

Soros, G. (2012) The Tragedy of the EU and How to Resolve It. *The New York Review of Books.* 27 September.

Spiegel (2010) Former Central Bank Head Karl Otto-Pohl. [Online] *Spiegel* 5/18. Available from http://www.spiegel.de/international/germany/former-central-bank-head-karl-otto-poehl-bailout-plan-is-all-about-rescuing-banks-and-rich-greeks-a-695245.html [Accessed 23 June 2014].

Spiegel (2013) Brutal Power Politics: Merkel's Banking Union Policy Under Fire. 16 December 2013. [Online] *Spiegel.* Available from http://www.spiegel.de/international/europe/criticism-in-brussels-german-banking-union-policy-under-fire-a-939314.html [Accessed 23 June 2014].

Sri Kumar, K. (2012) Europe Losing the Battle Against Debt Crisis. *Financial Times.* 23 July 2012, p. 7.

SWP-GMF (2014) *New Power New Responsibility: Elements of a German Foreign and Security Policy for a Changing World.* Washington and Berlin: Stiftung Wissenschaft und Politik (SWP) and The German Marshall Fund of the USA (GMF). [Online] Available at www.swp-berlin.org/fileadmin/contents/products/projekt_papiere/GermanForeignSecurityPolicy_SWP_GMF_2013.pdf [Accessed December 2014].

Tilford, S. (2010) *How to Save the Euro.* Centre for European Reform. September.

United States Treasury (2013) *Report to the Congress on International Economic and Exchange Rate Policies.* October. Washington, DC.

van Apeldoorn, B. (2002) *Transnational Capitalism and the Struggle over European Integration.* London: Routledge.

van der Pijl, K. (2006) *Global Rivalries From the Cold War to Iraq.* London: Pluto Press.

van der Pijl, K., Holman, O. and Raviv, O. (2011) The Resurgence of German Capital in Europe and the Restructuring of the Atlantic Networks of Interlocking Directorates After 1991. *Review of International Political Economy,* 18(3) August, pp. 384–408.

Varoufakis, Y. (2013) Europe Needs a Hegemonic Germany. [Online] *Zed Books blog,* 25 February. Available from http://zed-books.blogspot.com/2013/02/yanis-varoufakis-europe [Accessed 23 June 2014].

Wallerstein, I. (2009) Western Europe and Russia – Coming Together. Commentary No. 270, 1 December. [Online] Available from http://www.iwallerstein.com/western-europe-and-russia-coming-together [Accessed 23 June 2014].

Part II

The uneven nature of European integration, European crisis, and crisis management

5 Uneven and dependent development in Europe

The crisis and its implications[1]

Joachim Becker, Johannes Jäger and Rudy Weissenbacher

The European crisis is not yet over. Austerity policies introduced to counter crisis seem to have had contrary, in many respects devastating effects (Kentikelenis et al. 2014). These 'anti-crisis' policies have put the burden of the crisis above all on lower and middle classes of peripheral countries and deepened the core-periphery divide within the European Union.

The analytical tools we apply in this chapter are taken from the Latin American dependency approach and from regulation theory. During the 1970s and 1980s, critical development studies networks had applied findings from the Latin American dependency approach, polarization theory, and alternative regional development approaches to the European situation of uneven development and the process of integration. Theory building in this tradition seems to have been marginalized by the convergence euphoria during the integration process. In this chapter, we draw on research that attempts to follow up on aspects of this tradition and adapt and apply it to the age of financialization (Becker and Weissenbacher 2014). We combine the Latin American dependency approach with a framework in a political economy tradition based on an adapted version of the regulationist school (Becker and Jäger 2012) in order to analyse the current crisis in Europe. The critical Latin American approaches towards development share with the regulationist approach the focus on historical developments and variations in space. They deal, however, more specifically with uneven development than the regulationist approach. This turns out to be crucial for our conclusions regarding future European developments and political strategies.

Regulation, accumulation and dependency

While regulation theory helps to understand the specific configuration of the asymmetric interaction of regimes of accumulation within Europe and their supporting structural forms (Becker and Jäger 2012), dependency theory allows for grasping more profound dimensions of long-term economic and political dependency and its implications. Since the 1940s, critical Latin American theorists have pointed to the asymmetries between the core and the periphery and the specific configurations of development models in the periphery (Kay 1989). Development and underdevelopment are thus understood as two sides of the same coin. The development processes in the economies of the core dominate and structure the processes of (under-)development in the periphery. As a result, the mode of accumulation and therefore the type of development is different in the core and the periphery. The relatively advanced sector of an economy is the link to the world market and transfers its dynamics to developing countries. Other sectors are dependent on this developed sector but these do not tend to develop. This leads to structural heterogeneity and respective social structures in the periphery.

Typical for the social structures is a so-called *'lumpen bourgeoisie'* (Frank 1979). This class organizes the exploitation of the domestic population to the benefit of the core of the world economy (and to its own benefit). For example, the export of commodities leads to the transfer of a substantial part of the surplus value from the periphery to the core. The dominant class in the periphery imports luxury goods from the core, which allows it to live in wealth in the midst of a plundered country (Saad-Filho 2005: 139). This type of analysis particularly relates to commodity exporting countries. Cardoso and Faletto (1976), however, pointed out that the composition of the ruling bloc can be much more complex depending on the concrete economic structure. External interests are 'internalized' in civil society and the state. The relationship between external and domestic capital can take different forms – from strategic alliance to partial conflict (Cardoso and Faletto 1976: 217; Becker 2008: 16).

Dependency theorists such as Amin (1970: 289) highlight different forms of production in core and periphery, mainly drawing on the existing patterns of accumulation in the post-war decades. In the core countries of the world economy, the link between the industries producing investment goods and mass consumption goods – in regulationist terms a specific coherence of the regime of accumulation – is possible due to an accumulation process which is driven by internal economic activity and thus potentially allows for the coherence of wages and productivity. This allows for a balanced production of consumption goods and investment goods. Differently from the core economies, the periphery is characterized by deformed and export-dependent accumulation. Capitalist and non-capitalist sectors of the economy co-exist and hamper the balance between the growth of productivity and wages. The consequence of this is a limited and deformed internal market in which the production of export goods (often raw materials) and the production of luxury goods remain dominant. An investment goods industry is at best very weak, and internal demand is mainly based on high incomes in the export sector. This favours the import of high income goods from abroad and hampers accumulation based on economic activity internal to the periphery.

As peripheral economies are characterized by the absence or weakness of the investment goods sector, a technological dependency and a worsening trade balance due to increasing imports in periods of economic upturns are caused. Hence, a strong extraversion of the economy is a key element of peripheral economies. Besides the asymmetric trade relation, dependency is also characterized by an asymmetric structure of cross-border capital movements, leaving productive capital and money capital distinguished from each other. Nevertheless, both types of capital, when exported to the periphery, lead to a direct transfer of surplus value in the form of repatriated profits or interest payments to the core (dos Santos 1969: 45). Dependency theorists insist that the importance of different forms of dependency changes historically (dos Santos 1969; Cardoso and Faletto 1976). As dependency theory emerged during the 1960s and 1970s, it was concerned mainly with asymmetric production and trade relations, and direct investment, respectively, but less with the export of money capital to the periphery. Likewise, the literature hardly discussed sectors that were closely related to the import of money capital into the periphery, such as real estate. But especially in phases of high capital imports, the proliferation of sectors that are not exposed to strong international competition, like real estate and construction, can be observed (cf. Becker 2014: 186).

Until 1945 the internationalization of productive capital was rather weak. In the post-war period US direct investment was first directed to Latin America. From 1953 onwards the export of capital to Western Europe became more important (Panitch and Gindin 2012: 114). Direct investment from the core directly influences the productive development in peripheral economies, which makes it a key element of asymmetric relations of dependency. Historically, the internationalization of money capital had started earlier than the internationalization of productive capital. Following the crisis of 1929, a tendency towards a re-nationalization of money capital had started. Also, during the period of Fordism the internationalization of money capital remained relatively restricted and was not focused on by dependency theorists. With the crisis of the 1970s and the following tendencies of financialization in the economies of the core of the world economy, a new period of internationalization of money capital had started. As Arrighi (1994: 221) shows, periods of financialization in the core were usually preceded by the exhaustion of productive accumulation in the core of the world economy. In such a situation, capital was usually searching for new and more flexible forms of capital investment, often in the form of financial investment.

Contemporary dependency: financialization

Financialization can show two forms. On the one hand, it can be based on fictitious capital such as shares, etc.; on the other hand, it may consist of interest bearing capital, i.e. credit (Becker et al. 2010: 229). In the case of fictitious capital and the case of real estate which is treated as financial asset, an inflow of capital leads to strong price increases (Tavares 1983: 234). This can be understood as an inflation of financial assets which allows for profits in the books. Financial institutions pressure in favour of political measures which help to foster such price increases (i.e. by privatizing the old-age pension scheme, by tax exemptions for financial assets, etc.) and at the same time keep inflation low for consumption goods.

This implies a de facto bifurcation of the price system, with low inflation for common commodities and high inflation for financial assets. Prices for financial assets tend to grow faster than profits and a second disproportional development emerges. If the disproportions are recognized by financial investors the trend is reversed, often very abruptly, and the bubble bursts. If financial investments are financed to an important extent by credit the banking system enters into crisis too. In case of a double crisis of fictitious capital and the banking sector in the economies of the core, capital from the periphery is withdrawn. This means that via the financial channel the periphery is affected by the crisis in the core. A policy aiming at high interest rates is crucial for this strategy, because usually interest rates in the periphery are higher than in the core in order to attract capital or to avoid capital outflows. Financializiation is thus being pushed into the periphery by the inflow of capital (Becker 2014: 182), as banks seek to make profits due to the spread between active and passive interest rates.

In the case of extremely high interest rates, the state is often the main debtor because the high level of interest rates does not allow for financing private investment or for consumption by credit. In such an economic situation it is often interest payments for public debts which guarantee a high level of profits (Faria 2007: 95). If the interest rates are more moderate, private households may turn out to be the driving force of financialization as well. This type of financialization tends to gain momentum when it is pushed by capital inflows, and in that sense it is a dependent form of financialization. In many cases open or hidden partial currency substitution, such as euroization or dollarization, tend to boost such developments. Often a rigid exchange rate system and an overvaluation of the currency aim at supporting capital inflows. For those who are indebted in foreign currency, a devaluation of their own currency makes a default more likely. As Heymann and Kosacoff (2000: 17) show, dollarization is the central informal obstacle to abandoning an exchange rate regime which aims at attracting foreign capital. Relevant sectors of a society tend to pressure in such a case in favour of a monetary integration into an informal empire, as Fiori (1999) has shown for the case of Latin America. The subordinate integration into a monetary zone implies serious constraints on economic policies and clearly favours financial interests and capital linked to import activities.

Dependent financialization is contradictory. An overvalued currency leads to soaring imports, a worsening of the current account and escalating foreign debt (Faria 2007: 98). At a certain point the tensions in the external accounts are discovered by financial investors and the capital inflows dry up. A currency crisis, and in the case of dollarization a banking crisis, are the consequence. Hence external debts do not solve the problem of scarcity of foreign exchange but postpone it. Dependent financialization makes crisis more likely (Fiori 1999; Bresser-Pereira 2007).

European integration: dependency and development

As latecomers, capitalist industrialization and closer integration into the West European economy for the countries of the Southern European periphery coincided with such an exhaustion phase. For these countries the expansive phase of Fordism was just peripheral Fordism (Becker and Weissenbacher 2014: 17). Global financial crises (1973–74 and 1980–82) and deregulation in the wake of the end of the post-war global financial system 1971/73 (Bretton Woods-System) provided unfavourable situations for their transition from dictatorships to European integration. In the case of the countries of the Eastern European periphery, the protective shield of state socialist integration (COMECON) did not turn out to be a safe haven against world economic turbulences either (Weissenbacher 2007). The crisis of the capitalist world system led – beginning in the USA (Ronald Reagan) and UK (Margaret Thatcher) – to the global coup that enforced liberal policies. It was the onset of 'debt crisis' in peripheral countries, and the age of 'Washington Consensus' and financialization.

These changes left their marks also in European integration history. A Keynesian model was replaced by a neoliberal integration model (Ziltener 2000: 85). With the end of the Bretton Woods system, West Germany assumed aspects of the political-economic power in Europe that the USA was exercising at a global level. The implementation of the European Monetary System (EMS) was a central element in that. The Deutsche Mark became the anchor currency, and in consequence the monetary policy of the Deutsche Bundesbank – which stood for monetary stability – dominated the EMS hierarchy. In order to attract capital to finance the current account deficit, countries such as Italy and later Spain had to offer relatively high interest rates (Busch 1991: 210). Deficit countries were pressed into restrictive economic policies in order to avoid worsening current account imbalances. Although devaluation was still possible, it bore the immediate danger of refinancing risks on the financial markets. As dependency theorists showed for Latin America, a stronger orientation towards a dominant monetary norm (the Deutsche Mark in Europe) increases spatial and social differences. Even France had to back down from its Keynesian policy of stimulating industrial development in the early 1980s (Steinhilber 2000: 15).

Hence the restrictive monetary norm proved to be an effective mechanism against an alternative economic policy approach. But in addition, the single market project in general had an emphasis towards an uneven structure. The European integration process had been a club of core countries (plus southern Italy) in the beginning. With the accession of peripheral countries came 'cohesion' and 'convergence' policies (and payments), but they never lived up to the actual needs of a balanced integration model (Marsh 2011: 70, 154). Critical Political Economists in the new member countries who were inspired by dependency theory criticized the subordinate incorporation into the European division of labour and the consequent weakening of economic linkages within peripheral economies (see e.g. Romão 1983: 109). The single market project disabled key aspects of progressive economic policy, such as controls on the cross-border movement of capital, which have been considered crucial in Latin American thinking on development. The hope of social democrats such as the President of the European Commission, Jacques Delors, that a social democratic project could be favoured by the dynamics of the internal market turned out to be an illusion. On the contrary, the single market boosted the implementation of a neoliberal currency union. Already in 1988 at a meeting of governors of European central banks, a claim was made for a European central bank based on the model of the Deutsche Bundesbank in combination with a restrictive fiscal stability pact (Panitch and Gindin 2012: 198).

Dependent financialization in the European Monetary Union

The EMU proved to favour both financialization processes and neo-mercantilist strategies of the core states, particularly Germany. Germany applied different strategies to regain the competitiveness it had lost by unifying with and integrating Eastern Germany, and to mould the European structure according to its needs. In the early years of EMU, the government of social democrats and Greens implemented policies which encouraged wage deflation and the growth of a low-wage sector – the latter is today the largest in Western Europe in relative terms. The government also severely cut unemployment benefits, which became infamous as 'Hartz IV reforms'. While the dual wage sector held German imports low (and led to overall real wage cuts), transferring a part of the production towards Central Eastern Europe was a strategy for stimulating the German export sector. Thereby the economies of the Visegrád countries and Slovenia became integrated into the German productive system. (The share of foreign value added in German exports is 37%, as compared to 11% in the case of the USA and to 28% global average, according to UNCTAD [2013: 127, 129]). In addition, there was decreasing integration of Southern European countries (including France) and a bias among these countries towards Germany instead. German current account surpluses increased considerably after the implementation of the Eurozone. Germany also managed to replace imports from Europe with (lower quality) imports from China between 1999 and 2008 (Simonazzi, Ginzburg and Nocella 2013: 666; Lehndorff 2012: 80). German financialization had shown a special trait as it retained a rather strong link to German industrial exports by providing external capital that was crucial for the import capacity of European peripheral countries. Austerity and the current crisis reduced credit and the import capability of Southern European countries, and German export strategy shifted more towards 'third markets' outside the EU (Becker and Weissenbacher 2014: 16, 26). All in all, German financialization has generally been more outward- than inward-looking.

In the Southern European periphery industrialization had started relatively late. These countries lost the possibilities to protect their economy and to support their industry when entering the EU. German export-oriented capital and the German government had obviously no interest in the implementation of countervailing instruments at the European level which would help Southern Europe (López and Rodríguez 2010: 161). As a result, these countries experienced a partial de-industrialization (López and Rodríguez 2010: 161; cf. also Álvarez Peralta, Luengo Escalonilla and Uxó González 2013: 89). Shifts to overvalued exchange rates cemented this tendency. In consequence, Southern European economies started to focus on tourism, services and the construction industry within the context of an emerging growth regime characterized by dependent financialization. This was most pronounced in Spain (López and Rodríguez 2010; Etxezarreta *et al.* 2014; Mota, Lopes and Antunes 2014: 211).

With the introduction of the Euro, Southern European countries lost the possibility to devalue their currency, what had been the last remaining instrument to protect domestic sectors from external competition. Consequently, the pressure on domestic productive sectors increased, and restrictive wage policies in Germany and a temporary significant appreciation of the Euro made the pressure even stronger. As the Latin American experience would have predicted, productive sectors became even more maligned, meaning that de-industrialization took place in two phases – immediately after EU accession, and post-Euro introduction. In the 2000s, current account imbalances continued to rise rapidly. Before the crisis, Portugal and Spain had a current account deficit of around 10% of GDP and Greece showed a deficit of almost 15%. The current account deficit was mainly financed by external debt. In 2010, external debt levels reached 231.5% in Portugal, 179.6% in Greece and 165.3% in Spain (Becker 2012: 469). Indeed, current account deficits and external debt reached far higher levels than in Latin America in the years before the outbreak of a crisis, because of the assumed lower risk of Eurozone member countries.

Surplus liquidity from the European core, mainly from Germany but also from France (Lapavitsas et al. 2012: 83), supported the process of dependent financializiation in the Southern countries of the European periphery. This process consisted of a credit-led real estate boom in Spain and a credit-based expansion of consumption in Greece. The sharply falling interest rates after the implementation of the Euro contributed to the expansion of private credit to households. The inflow of credit to those countries stimulated economic growth: hence, a pseudo-convergence in terms of GDP per capita with the levels of the core countries of the European Union was observed, while simultaneously the gap in the productive structure was widening between the core and the periphery (cf. Becker and Weissenbacher 2014).

In Eastern Europe, dependent financialization was also the cornerstone of the growth models (Becker 2007). During the process of joining the EU, the preconditions were set for Western European capital to take over important economic sectors in all Central and Eastern European countries with the exception of Slovenia. The integration into the German export sector took place via foreign direct investment, especially in Hungary, Slovakia and the

Czech Republic (see Drahokoupil 2009). Again with the exception of Slovenia, the banking sector was taken over by Western European banks (Frangakis 2009: 71). As with Southern Europe after accession, East and Southeast European countries experienced periods of de-industrialization during and after the transformation period (Becker, Ćetković and Weissenbacher forthcoming). The 'growth' model in the Visegrád countries and in Slovenia was based on industrial exports and financialization. With the exception of Hungary, debts for financing consumption and real estate were mainly provided in domestic currency. Growth in Southern Europe and the Baltic countries was above all based on credit expansion, and this exhibited strong parallels with the growth models of Argentina and Uruguay in the second half of the 1970s and in the 1990s (see Becker 2007).

Banks refinanced the strong internal growth of loans by credit from abroad (often at their holding company). The option to refinance abroad proved to be a strong incentive for banks to expand the provision of credit in foreign currency such as the Euro but also the Swiss Franc. The debtors received their income in domestic currency: therefore, a devaluation of the currency that implied the relative increase of the costs for servicing the debt was problematic for debtors. As in Argentina (see Heymann and Kosacoff 2000: 17), indebted middle classes were chained to the exchange rate and the related neoliberal economic policy. Similar again to pre-crisis Argentina, the contradictions and vulnerabilities of the pseudo-boom based on external credit were not discussed in public. In the long run, financialized growth models were not sustainable, as the experience in Latin America at the end of the 1970s and beginning of the 1980s, and also in the 1990s, had already shown (Becker 2007).

The European crisis in core and periphery

Starting in 2008, the crisis has developed unevenly in Europe. The divergent modes of development became visible at the surface. Those economies that were closely related with US financial markets, such as the UK, Ireland, the Benelux countries and to a lesser extent Germany and France, were affected directly by the financial crisis in the USA. The destabilization of the financial sector in especially the Anglo-Saxon countries, and later in the Benelux countries, led to a credit crunch which immediately affected private consumption and investment. The heavily export-oriented economies such as Germany suffered a sharp reduction of their export revenues in 2008 and 2009 (Becker and Weissenbacher 2014: 16). This fall in German exports negatively affected Central and Eastern European countries (mainly the Czech Republic, Slovakia, Slovenia and Hungary) that were closely related to the German export industry (Becker 2011: 271; Dymarski 2014: 100). Export-oriented countries, however, experienced an economic recovery relatively quickly. For example, the German export sector had compensated for the reductions of exports to the European periphery by increasing its exports to China, Brazil, India, and Russia (Becker and Weissenbacher 2014: 26).

In contrast, the heavily financialized periphery of the EU, especially countries with extremely high current account deficits and a high share of foreign currency loans, was mainly affected by the restriction of credit. An economic policy that aimed at maintaining the exchange rate, in combination with an austerity policy that was implemented to reduce current account deficits, drastically deepened the recession. The Baltic countries, characterized by extremely big credit and real estate bubbles and a high degree of Euroization, were hit by a reduction of GDP of more than 14% in 2009 alone (Myant and Drahokoupil 2011: 313). Hence, in accordance with crisis experiences in Latin America in the last three decades (cf. Becker 2007), countries with a high share of foreign currency loans suffered the most from the crisis (Kulikova 2011: 25).

For Southern European Eurozone countries, particularly Greece, the Euro provided only temporary protection. Once international banks and the financial sector noticed the structural vulnerability of those countries, they reduced credit and made it more expensive. For this reason, a new stage of deepening crisis started for the periphery of the Eurozone in the beginning of 2010. The patterns of anti-crisis policy were very similar to those in Central and Eastern Europe and tended to deepen the crisis. In Greece, GDP fell by 23.4% between the pre-crisis peak and 2013 (EuroMemo Group 2014: 12, Table 1.1). Industry suffered heavily across these countries: industrial production in June 2012 was only 73.6% in Greece, 78.4% in Spain and 86% in Portugal of the level reached in 2005 (Becker and Weissenbacher 2014: 71, 23). The recessive impact of the EU/International Monetary Fund (IMF) programmes is much stronger than the original official assumptions that were made to justify the austerity measures, with the IMF belatedly conceding that it had made a serious error of judgement (Blanchard and Leigh 2013). Despite the extreme recession, the Greek current account still shows a deficit, the debt indicators have worsened and the crisis has deepened. There are similar tendencies in other Southern European countries: namely, a deepening of the crisis, a sharp increase in unemployment, only slowly decreasing current account deficits and a more severe debt crisis. The so-called anti-crisis policies are designed to produce a recession in order to reduce internal demand and imports. But at the same time debt/GDP relations continue to worsen (cf. Álvarez Peralta et al. 2013: Chapter 7). Hence the different development patterns in the core and the periphery have become more apparent during the crisis (cf. Álvarez Peralta et al. 2013: 169).

The so-called anti-crisis management was aimed at restoring pre-crisis structures. It was focused on stabilizing banks and the finance sector. This was made possible by substantial government financial support and by offering public guarantees, in particular in the Anglo-Saxon countries but also in the Benelux countries (Álvarez Peralta et al. 2013: 199, Table 6.1). Supporting banks and socializing losses led to a sharp increase in public debt. Likewise, austerity policies in the periphery, aimed at stabilizing the exchange rate and financial conditions, reflect the interests of the finance sector. The same has been the case for Central and Eastern Europe – at least where there were significant outstanding liabilities of Western European banks.

Devaluations deflate the price of financial assets of Western European capital in the periphery. In such a case, a haircut for peripheral economies would be unavoidable because devaluation implies an appreciation of Euro-denominated debts. Western European creditors wanted to postpone a haircut at least to the point at which they have reduced outstanding debts substantially. In addition, export-oriented capitalists in neo-mercantilist countries wanted to preserve the Eurozone because this structurally favoured their export interests. Moreover, the stabilization of the exchange rate or the continued membership in the Eurozone was supported by large groups of the indebted middle classes in the European periphery. Therefore, there has been a heterogeneous coalition of internal and external actors which supports the austerity measures in the periphery. Nevertheless, in Southern Europe the acceptance of austerity policies by the middle classes is eroding, and there are widespread protest movements. Regarding the social basis supporting neoliberal austerity, there are apparent similarities to Argentina in the 1990s. (On Argentina see Castellani and Schorr 2004: 69.)

There was disunity between the European Commission, IMF, European Central Bank (ECB) and various governments (for example the German and French) on how to deal with the situation, with the European Commission appearing to be especially dogmatic (Wehr 2010: 45, 105; Marsh 2011: 248). Nevertheless, the differences were of degree rather than of kind; no serious move has been made to reverse the austerity programmes. Moreover, the IMF's participation in the implementation and monitoring of anti-crisis policies implies an inclusion of US interests in European anti-crisis policies (see also Cafruny, Chapter 4 in this volume). This shows the narrow limits of the autonomy of the European project from broader global processes.

In order to provide emergency loans to the European periphery, first the European Financial Stability Facility (EFSF) and the European Financial Stabilisation Mechanism (EFSM) and then the European Stability Mechanism (ESM) were established. Changes in the EU treaties made sure that access to ESM credits is subject to conditionality. Hence, the ESM in the EU fulfils a similar purpose as the IMF at the global level. Moreover, neoliberal austerity policies are being pushed by liberal and conservative governments and by the European Commission. In particular for the Eurozone, a rules-based economic policy is introduced. The implication is a further institutionalization of an authoritarian neoliberal economic policy at the level of the EU (Heinrich 2012: 401) which stands not just in a Hayekian (Anderson 2012: 56) but also in a German Ordoliberal tradition (Oberndorfer 2012; see also Oberndorfer, Chapter 11 in this volume). These policy measures go hand in hand with the interests of German banks and financial capital as well as with the interests of export-oriented fractions of capital, which have all been strengthened by the crisis (Becker and Jäger 2012; Overbeek 2012: 235).

The crisis management is based on dominance but not hegemony. It causes ruptures on two levels. Firstly, rules-based economic governance is mainly institutionalized with regards to the Eurozone. Countries outside the Eurozone, in particular the UK, tend to be politically marginalized. This is very obvious in the case of the banking union, in which the ECB is playing a key role. This and other developments provided the background for the proposal of a referendum on British membership of the EU. Secondly, there is a deepening rupture in the relation between the core countries and the European periphery. The overwhelming burden of the crisis is shifted onto the working class and parts of the petty bourgeoisie in the periphery. This causes a deepening of social conflict. Social protests are mainly driven by national trade unions and well-educated young people – though there are significant differences with regard to the role of different social actors and the relationship between social protests and (left-wing) political parties (see Gallas, Nowak and Wilde 2012; Becker and Hofmann 2014; Clua-Losada and Horn, Chapter 12 in this volume).

Nevertheless, with some minor exceptions mass protest has not yet prevented austerity policies and wage cuts. But in some cases, the established party system is under heavy pressure. For example, in Slovenia the lack of a leftist political party which could support the strong social protests was recognized as a problem by leftist intellectuals (Krašovec 2013) and, finally, a left-wing party has emerged from the strong protest movement of Winter 2012/13. In Greece, a coalition of leftist parties has become the strongest political opposition but is divided regarding the question of the Eurozone membership. In several countries, technocratic governments headed by representatives of the financial sector, such as Lucas Papademos and Mario Monti, emerged and were supported by the core countries of the European Union. Similar to the case of Latin American crises (O'Donnell 1996), repressive and authoritarian reactions are emerging also in the EU, particularly in the periphery.

Conclusions and scenarios

It was already clear in the 1970s that global accumulation had clear-cut limits with regard to distribution, the provision of basic needs, and the destruction of nature (Cocoyoc Declaration 1974; Meadows 1972). Authors and activists in the tradition of the Latin American dependency approach pointed out that dependencies had to be overcome: moreover, it would be better to achieve this with collective self-reliance, in the sense of a common strategy of regions and countries in the periphery, than via national projects working in isolation to each other. The historical reality, however, saw a further radicalization of an already polarized and unsustainable system, with Latin America facing stagnation, further de-industrialization and a 'lost decade' in the 1980s. The repeated attempt to (re-)establish financialized models of accumulation in the Cono Sur (Southern Cone) states led to three decades that were characterized by extreme macroeconomic instability and exploding social inequality (Saludjian 2006: 115). As we have seen, de-industrialization has also taken place in the European periphery, and the economic growth provided by financialization was at best a flash in the pan. What we described as a financialized system bears the characteristics of severe distortions of the accumulation model. The 'neoliberal' answer to Keynesian economic models has been debt-driven since Reagan's 'military Keynesianism' of the early 1980s, and thus the 'growth' model in the era of financialization is dependent on debt. Channels of financialization do stimulate growth but hardly development. Above all, without a development strategy of (export) industrialization, asset price inflation is followed by austerity. Furthermore, and as we have seen, once Southern Europe became a less reliable export market after 2008, Germany's export strategy simply switched to BRIC countries (Brazil, Russia, India and China).

However, growing differences in productivity cannot easily be overcome in open market systems that link core and periphery. Currency devaluations (if still possible) make imports of technology and capital goods that are necessary for industrialization expensive, and a national stimulation of demand will increase imports of more advanced and/or cheaper products. In addition, region-wide industrial policies which might be effective in the long-term may well encounter legal difficulties regarding 'distortion of competition'. All of these processes favour countries which are already more economically and industrially advanced. Even France had to accept this in the early 1980s (facing Germany), and it will be a challenge today for any anti-crisis policy inspired by Keynes or Roosevelt that seeks to counter dependencies. A social democratic or Euro-Keynesian project (Patomäki 2013) or a 'Green Deal' (Brand 2012; Lipietz 2013), which aims at an expansionary policy in the core countries and include an active industrial policy in the periphery supported by substantial transfer payments, has the potential to be cohesive (see also Flassbeck and Lapavitsas Chapter 8, Grahl Chapter 10 and Niechoj Chapter 9 in this volume). Such policies, however, need a certain level of cross-country solidarity which would go against the grain of the economic governance in recent years.

Therefore, the continuation of a radicalized neoliberal EU integration project seems to be a realistic prospect. Such a project would be based on a further expansion of authoritarian elements of rules-based economic governance, a scenario which is already in place in the European periphery owing to the consequences of the last years of EU crisis management. Further increasing tensions within the EU, between the Eurozone member countries and those which are not in the Eurozone and between the core and the periphery, are to be expected. In the end, this is likely to be expressed in a deepened technocratic authoritarian integration of the European core countries and a possible disintegration of parts of the periphery.

In addition, social mobilization has turned out to be quite uneven in Europe. Europe-wide co-ordination of trade unions and leftist movements is at best very weak, and a Europe-wide solidarity of the working class is often missing. Instead, nationalist discourses have been strengthened in the core as well as in the periphery since the beginning of the crisis. Despite the rhetoric about broader 'civil society' approaches at the European level, there is a lack of social forces powerful enough to oppose the project of authoritarian radicalization in a serious way (Becker 2012; Becker and Hofmann 2014: 4; see also Clua-Losada and Horn, Chapter 12, in this volume). Compared to the 1980s and the social democratic project around Jacques Delors, the prospects of a progressive project seem to be much diminished today. The position of the working class relative to capital has been weakened further since the crisis started. Therefore, implementation of a social-democratic and ecologically sensitive European project seems to be very unlikely in the short and medium-term.

Based on the insights of dependency theory and the prevailing political trends, we conclude that national (or regional) attempts to regain autonomy as a precondition for national, and in part more self-reliant, developments are more likely. So far, attempts to regain autonomy can take a rather national-conservative (or national-liberal) or left-wing colouring. The nationalist policies in Hungary, the attempts to achieve independence in Catalonia, and David Cameron's announcement to hold a referendum on British EU membership are the first signs of such developments. The growing strength of the Left in Greek elections, and to a lesser extent in Spain, show that on a national level potentially progressive developments may also take place and which could be based on a rather self-reliant model of development as well. The idea of regaining autonomy seems to be of crucial importance for the field of monetary policy as well as for the regulation of the banking and financial sector.

Southern European economists building on dependency theory such as Romão (1983: 206) were already demanding a strengthening of self-reliant processes of accumulation in the periphery three decades ago. In today's world, self-reliance appears radically democratic and as a participatory concept that addresses not only distributive and socio-economic but also environmental concerns (cf. Galtung 1983). Of course, such a strategy was already hard to achieve back then. Therefore several authors in this tradition pleaded for solidarity and common policies among countries of the periphery (Galtung 1983: 28), a 'collective self-reliance' (Oteiza 1983) that is still difficult to achieve. Today and within the EU, such a concept faces strong political obstacles. Still, an exit from the Eurozone, as discussed in the case of Greece and other peripheral countries, seems to be a viable or even necessary option (see Flassbeck and Lapavitsas, Chapter 9 in this volume). At times, even prominent figures of the establishment, such as João Ferreira do Amaral, an advisor to the Portuguese president from 1991 to 2000, have come out in favour of exiting the Eurozone.

However, the progressive proposals for an exit differ widely with regard to the broader set of economic policies. Whereas Lapavitsas et al. (2012: 69) argue for the exit option as part of a broader radical project which includes debtor-led debt default, capital controls, a significant socialization of the banking sector and industrial policies, Ferreira do Amaral (2013: 117) defends a developmentalist strategy which focuses on re-industrialization. Despite some differences with Argentina, which dissolved the US dollar-based quasi-currency board and for some years forced a moratorium on its debts, this approach is also discussed as a role model for other Southern European countries (see Musacchio 2012). Similar to Argentina in 2001 and 2002, the exit from the Eurozone by Greece or other countries necessarily has to be supported by the implementation of controls on cross-border capital movements. For most of the EU countries that are not members of the Eurozone, it is obvious that they want to keep their own currency and relative autonomy in the field of monetary policy. Overall, centrifugal forces are being strengthened by the crisis and its management. It is becoming more likely that the EU as we know it today may fall apart. In any case, a further transformation of the EU is to be expected.

Note

1 We gratefully acknowledge that research for this chapter was supported by funds from the Oesterreichische Nationalbank (Anniversary Fund, project number: 15471).

References

Álvarez Peralta, I., Luengo Escalonilla, F. and Uxó González, J. (2013) *Fracturas y crisis en Europa*. Buenos Aires: Eudeba/Madrid: Clave intellectual.

Anderson, P. (2012) After the Event. *New Left Review* 73, pp. 49–61.

Amin, S. (1970) *L'accumulation à l'échelle mondiale*. Vol. II. Paris: Anthropos.

Arrighi, G. (1994) *The Long Twentieth Century. Money, Power, and the Origins of Our Times*. London/New York: Verso.

Becker, J. (2007) Dollarisation in Latin America and Euroisation in Eastern Europe: Parallels and Differences. In Becker, J. and Weissenbacher, R. (eds) *Dollarization, Euroization and Financial Instability. Central and Eastern European Countries between Stagnation and Financial Crisis?* Marburg: Metropolis, pp. 223–278.

Becker, J. (2008) Der kapitalistische Staat in der Peripherie: polit-ökonomische Perspektiven. *Journal für Entwicklungspolitik* 24(2), pp. 10–32.

Becker, J. (2011) Wachstumsmodelle und Krisenmuster in Osteuropa. *WSI-Mitteilungen* 64(6), pp. 270–277.

Becker, J. (2012) Blindstellen: ungleiche Entwicklung und ungleiche Mobilisierung in der EU. *Prokla* 42(3), pp. 467–476.

Becker, J. (2014) Finanzialisierung und globale Peripherie. In Heires, M. and Nölke, A. (eds) *Politische Ökonomie der Finanzialisierung*. Wiesbaden: VS, pp. 181–196.

Becker, J., Ćetković, P. and Weissenbacher, R. (forthcoming) Financialisation, Dependent Export Industrialisation and De-industrialisation in Eastern Europe. In Cozzi, G. Newman, S. and J. Toporowski (eds) *Finance and Industrial Policy: Beyond Finanancial Regulation in Europe*. Oxford: Oxford University Press.

Becker, J. and Hofmann, J. (2014) Editorial. *Kurswechsel* (1), pp. 3–10.

Becker, J. and Jäger, J. (2012) Integration in Crisis: A Regulationist Perspective on the Interaction of European Varieties of Capitalism. *Competition and Change* 16(3), pp. 169–187.

Becker, J., Jäger, J., Leubolt, B. and Weissenbacher, R. (2010) Peripheral Financialization and Vulnerability to Crisis: A Regulationist Perspective. *Competition and Change* 14(3–4), pp. 225–247.

Becker, J. and Weissenbacher, R. (2014) Berlin Consensus and Disintegration: Monetary Regime and Uneven Development in the EU. In Dymarski, W., Frangakis, M. and Leaman, J. (eds) *The Deepening Crisis of the European Union: The Case for Radical Change. Analysis and Proposals from EuroMemo Group*. Poznań: Poznań University of Economics Press, pp. 5–32.

Blanchard, O. and Leigh, D. (2013) Growth Forecast Errors and Fiscal Multipliers. *IMF Working Paper* WP/13/1, Washington, DC.

Brand, U. (2012) Green Economy and Green Capitalism. Some Theoretical Considerations. *Journal für Entwicklungspolitik* 28(3), pp. 118–137.

Bresser-Pereira, L. (2007) *Macroeconomia da estagnação. Críticia da ortodoxia convencional no Brasil pós-1994*. São Paulo: Editora 34.

Busch, K. (1991) *Umbruch in Europa. Die ökonomischen, ökologischen und sozialen Perspektiven des einheitlichen Binnenmarktes*. Köln: Bund-Verlag.

Cardoso, F.H. and Faletto, E. (1976) *Abhängigkeit und Entwicklung in Lateinamerika*. Frankfurt/Main: Suhrkamp.

Castellani, A. and Schorr, M. (2004) Argentina: convertibilidad, crisis de acumulación y disputas en el interior del bloque de poder económico. *Cuadernos del Cendes* 21 (57) Tercera época, pp. 55–81.

Cocoyoc Declaration, The (1974) Adopted by the participants in the United Nations Environmental Program (UNEP) and United Nations Conference on Trade and Development (UNCTAD) Symposium on 'Patterns of Resource Use, Environment and Development Strategies'. 8–12 October. Cocoyoc, Mexico. [Online] TRANSCEND (ed.) Available from www.transcendnordic.org/doc/08Cocoyoc Declaration/TheCocoyocDeclaration-English.pdf [Accessed 2 February 2014].

Dos Santos, T. (1969) El nuevo carácter de la dependencia. In Matos Mar, J. (ed.) *La crisis del desarrollismo y la nueva dependencia*. Buenos Aires: Amorroto, pp.11–113.

Drahokoupil, J. (2009) *Globalization and the State in Central and Eastern Europe. The Politics of Foreign Direct Investment*. London and New York: Routledge.

Dymarski, W. (2014) Impact of the Global Crisis on the Economic Performance of Central and East European Economies. In Dymarski, W., Frangakis, M. and Leaman, J. (eds) *The Deepening Crisis of the European Union: The Case for Radical Change. Analyses and Proposals from the EuroMemo Group*. Poznań: Poznań University of Economics Press, pp. 90–111.

Etxezarreta, M. *et al.* (2014) Boom and (Deep) Crisis of the Spanish Economy: The Role of the EU in its Evolution. In Dymarski, W., Frangakis, M. and Leaman, J. (eds) *The Deepening Crisis of the European Union: The Case for Radical Change. Analyses and Proposals from the EuroMemo Group*. Poznań: Poznań University of Economics Press, pp. 58–89.

EuroMemo Gruppe (2014) EuroMemo 2014. Europa spaltet sich. Die Notwendigkeit für radikale Alternativen zur gegenwärtigen EU-Politik. *Supplement der Zeitschrift Sozialismus* 3/2014.

Faria, L.A.E. (2007) Crisis financiera, estabilización y estancamiento en Brasil. In Becker, J. (ed.) *El golpe del capital. Las crisis financieras en el Cono Sur y sus salidas*. Montevideo: Coscoroba, pp. 89–107.

Ferreira do Amaral, J. (2013) *Porque devemos sair do euro. O divórcio necessário para tirar Portugal da crise*. Alfragide: Lua de Papel.

Fiori, J.L. (1999) Estados, moedas e desenvolvimento. In Fiori, J.L. (ed.) *Estados e moedas no desenvolvimento das nações.* Petrópolis: Vozes, pp. 49–85.

Frangakis, M. (2009) Europe's Financial Systems under Pressure. In Grahl, J. (ed.) *Global Finance and Social Europe.* Cheltenham: Edward Elgar, pp. 53–90.

Frank, A.G. (1979) *Lumpenburguesía: lumpendesarrollo. Dependencia, clase y política en Latinoamérica.* Barcelona: Laia.

Gallas, A., Nowak, J. and Wilde, F. (eds) (2012) *Politische Streiks im Europa der Krise.* Hamburg: VSA.

Galtung, J. (1983) *Self-Reliance: Beiträge zu einer alternativen Entwicklungsstrategie.* (Edited by M. Ferdowski) München: Minerva.

Heinrich, M. (2012) Zwischen Bankenrettung und autoritärem Wettbewerbsregime. Zur Dynamik des europäischen Krisenmanagements. *Prokla* 42(3), pp. 395–412.

Heymann, D. and Kosacoff, B. (2000) Introducción: comentarios generales sobre el comportamiento de la economía y temas abiertas al finalizar los noventa. In Heymann, D. and Kosacoff, B. (eds) *La Argentina de los Noventa. Desempeño económico en un contexto de reformas.* Buenos Aires: Eudeba, pp. 9–36.

Kay, C. (1989) *Latin American Theories of Development and Underdevelopment.* London and New York: Routledge.

Kentikelenis, A., Karanikolos, M., Reeves, A., McKee, M. and Stuckler, D. (2014) Greece's Health Crisis: From Austerity to Denialism. *The Lancet* 383(9918), pp. 748–753.

Krašovec, P. (2013) Slovenska revolucija traži svoju boju. *Le Monde diplomatique* (Hrvatsko izdanje). January 2013, pp. 5–6.

Kulikova, N.V. (2011) Krizis v Central'noj i Vostočnoj Evrope. In Kulikova, N.V. (ed.) *Central'naja i Vostočnaja Evropa. Uroki mirovogo krizisa.* Sankt-Petersburg: Altheia, pp. 10–42.

Lapavitsas, C. *et al.* (2012) *Crisis in the Euro Zone.* London: Verso.

Lehndorff, S. (2012) German Capitalism and the European Crisis: Part of the Solution or Part of the Problem. In Lehndorff, S. (ed.) *A Triumph of Failed Ideas. European Models of Capitalism in the Crisis.* Bruxelles: ETUI, pp. 79–102.

Lipietz, A. (2013) Fears and Hopes: The Crisis of the Liberal-productivist Model and its Green Alternative. *Capital & Class* 37(1), pp. 127–141.

López, I. and Rodríguez, E. (2010) *Fin de ciclo. Financiarización, território y sociedad propietarios en la onda larga del capitalismo hispano (1959–2010).* Madrid: Traficantes de sueños.

Marsh, D. (2011) *The Euro. The Battle for the New Global Currency.* New Edition. New Haven, NC and London: Yale University Press.

Meadows, D. *et al.* (1972) *The Limits to Growth: A Report for the Club of Rome's Project on the Predicament of Mankind.* New York, NY: Universe Books.

Mota, J., Lopes, A. and Antunes, M. (2014) A encruzilhada da economia portuguesa: da economia global ao memorando de entendimento. In Mota, J., Lopes, L. and Antunes, M. (eds) *Perspectivas para uma outra Zona Euro.* Coimbra: Coimbra Editora, pp. 211–250.

Musacchio, A. (2012) Umstrukturierung der Verschuldung und Wachstumsbedingungen: Griechenland und Argentinien im Vergleich. *Prokla* 42(3), pp. 433–453.

Myant, M. and Drahokoupil, J. (2011) *Transition Economies: Political Economy in Russia, Eastern Europe and Central Asia.* Hoboken: John Wiley & Sons.

O'Donnell, G. (1996) *El estado burocrático autoritario. Triunfos, derrotas y crisis.* 2nd edition. Buenos Aires: Editorial de Belgrano.

Oteiza, E. (1983) Collective Self-Reliance: Some Old and New Issues. In Villamil, J. (ed.) *Transnational Capitalism and National Development. New Perspectives on Dependence*. Brighton: Harvester, pp. 289–305.

Overbeek, H. (2012) Global Capitalist Crisis and the Future of the European Project. In Nousios, P., Overbeek, H. and Tsolakis, A. (eds) *Globalisation and European Integration. Critical Approaches to Regional Orders and International Relations*. London: Routledge, pp. 218–240.

Oberndorfer, L. (2012) Die Renaissance des autoritären Liberalismus? Carl Schmitt und der deutsche Neoliberalismus vor dem Hintergrund des Eintritts der 'Massen' in die europäische Politik. *Prokla* 42(3), pp. 413–431.

Panitch, L. and Gindin, S. (2012) *The Making of Global Capitalism. The Political Economy of American Empire*. London and New York: Verso.

Patomäki, H. (2013) *The Great Eurozone Disaster. From Crisis to Global New Deal*. London: Zed Books.

Romão, A. (1983) *Portugal face à C.E.E.* Lisbon: Livros Horizonte.

Saad-Filho, A. (2005) The Rise and Decline of Latin American Structuralism and Dependency Theory. In Jomo, K.S. and Reinert, E.S. (eds) *The Origins of Development Economics. How Schools of Thought Have Addressed Development*. London: Zed Publications, pp. 128–145.

Saludjian, A. (2006) *Pour une autre intégration sud-américaine. Critiques du Mercosur néo-liberal*. Paris: L'Harmattan.

Simonazzi, A., Ginzburg, A. and Nocella, G. (2013) Economic Relations between Germany and Southern Europe. *Cambridge Journal of Economics* 37(6), pp. 653–675.

Steinhilber, J. (2000) *Die 'Grande Nation' und das 'Haus Europa'. Frankreichs widersprüchlicher Entwicklungsweg*. Hamburg: VSA.

Tavares, M. da Conceição (1983) *Da substitução de importações ao capitalismo financeiro. Ensaios sobre economia brasileira*. Rio de Janeiro: Zahar Editores, 11th edition.

UNCTAD (2013) *World Investment Report 2013*. New York and Geneva: UNCTAD.

Wehr, A. (2010) *Griechenland, die Krise und der Euro*. Köln: Papy Rossa.

Weissenbacher, R. (2007) Historical Considerations of Uneven Development in East Central Europe. In Becker, J. and Weissenbacher, R. (eds) *Dollarization, Euroization and Financial Instability. Central and Eastern European Countries between Stagnation and Financial Crisis?* Marburg: Metropolis, pp. 35–83.

Ziltener, P. (2000) Die Veränderung der Staatlichkeit in Europa – regulations- und staatstheoretische Überlegungen. In Bieling, H.-J. and Steinhilber, J. (eds) *Die Konfigurationen Europas. Dimensionen einer kritischen Integrationstheorie*. Münster: Westfälisches Dampfboot, pp. 73–101.

6 Uneven development and 'European crisis constitutionalism', or the reasons for and conditions of a 'passive revolution in trouble'

Hans-Jürgen Bieling[1]

The academic debate on European integration was structured by the specific, often much too narrow focus of involved disciplines: economists were mainly concerned about the welfare effects of ever closer market integration; lawyers studied the stepwise gaining of independence of European law; sociologists developed some interest in transnational social stratification patterns and cross-border communication, that is, in the forms of an emerging European civil society and public sphere; and political scientists were busy analysing the making of national and supranational institutional settings and their impact on political decision-making. Occasionally, the narrow confines of disciplinary investigation and reasoning have been transcended. Nevertheless, it would be much too soon to speak of a vivid and productive interdisciplinary debate on the dynamics of European integration. On the contrary, precisely in times of severe crisis the participating academic disciplines have tended to relapse into old patterns of narrow-minded analysis, as they are particularly receptive to methodological conceptualizations along the national-supranational continuum. In consequence, this means that important dimensions of transnational capitalist accumulation and power relations, above all the complex processes of transnationally mediated uneven development, are ignored.

The aim of this chapter is to bring these processes into the debate by drawing on critical approaches which systematically transcend disciplinary boundaries in order to develop a political economy based, power and authority sensitive, framework of analysis. In this context, neo-Gramscian International Political Economy (IPE) is instructive in various regards. It explicitly investigates the particular articulation of economic, socio-cultural, and discursive processes; and it has developed useful theoretical concepts to analyse and interpret more recent European crisis dynamics, including the political initiatives of (non-)hegemonic European crisis management and regulation. Within the scope of this paper two concepts are particularly promising: first, the concept of 'European crisis constitutionalism', which specifies the older concept of 'new constitutionalism' (Gill 2003: 132) by highlighting the crisis and emergency driven, and somewhat ambiguous European adjustment measures; and second, the concept of 'passive revolution', which generally refers to the incremental, but in the context of the ongoing crisis contradictory, troublesome, and therefore precarious authority-stabilizing transformation of European financial capitalism from above.

The precarious nature of recent, crisis-induced adjustments of European modes of economic and financial regulation basically results from the still-lingering contradictions and unresolved crisis processes of European financial capitalism. The following section therefore outlines how this particular transnational type of capitalist development has come about and inasmuch it is characterized by particular features of 'uneven' and 'combined' development (Trotsky 1977: 26–27)[2] which in turn have generated or at least facilitated diverging and rival discursive constructions of the European crisis. While the first phase of the crisis was marked by a stepwise adoption of Keynesian-inspired views, the transition towards the so-called 'sovereign debt crisis' marked a shift towards the establishment of a European austerity agenda. Both phases, and that is the main argument of the second section, show specific features of a 'passive revolution', primarily promoted and organized by transnational capital and wealthier social classes, for example, owners of monetary and financial assets, mainly based in current account surplus and therefore creditor economies. The passive revolution strategy was implemented in the form of manifold – contradictory and complementary – measures of a 'European crisis constitutionalism' which, irrespective of their far-reaching societal impact, are still insufficient to politically balance and smoothly regulate the European economy and society. Moreover, the third section highlights that the political sociology of European integration is characterized by new socioeconomic and socio-cultural conflicts and tendencies of societal disintegration. The chapter concludes by outlining the changed patterns of cooperation and conflict between capitalist elites, capital and labour, and also the role of right-wing populist movements; or in short, the changing patterns of domestic and transnational power relations.

Conceptualizing the socioeconomic and political contradictions of European financial market capitalism

The recent reform dynamics and changed power relations within the European Union represent important and constitutive dimensions of a structurally transformed development of European capitalism. For quite some time now, academic observers have been identifying a transition towards the formation of financial market capitalism which has clear transatlantic and European features (Bieling 2013). Next to these features of cross-border interdependency, financial market capitalism is basically marked by the following characteristics: a privatization of public infrastructure and social security provision, above all pensions; a shareholder value oriented reorganization of management strategies and corporate governance systems; and a stronger role for equity markets and its main players such as institutional investors, investment banks, rating agencies or accounting firms. These and other transformations are structurally facilitated by an increasing amount of private property, above all real estate and financial assets (McKinsey Global Institute 2011), which, in a way, is an indicator of both capitalist over-accumulation, i.e. building-up of over-capacities in the area of investment goods, and a growing indebtedness of private, public and sometimes also corporate households.

The increasing size of the financial sector as well as the corresponding economic and political power of financial market players represents general but also domestically differing developments. The overall trends can be politically attributed to the dynamics of 'competitive deregulation', i.e. the processes of mutually lowering of regulatory standards (Rixen 2013; see also Wigger, Chapter 7 in this volume), which have been unleashed by the transition to the Dollar Wall Street Regime (DWSR) and the promotion of cross-border capital mobility since the 1980s (Gowan 1999). At the same time, domestic financial sectors still differ due to diverging modes of operation and interplay with other segments of economy and society. The latter aspect refers to specific domestic patterns of financialization, that is, the finance-led interpenetration and reorganization of the non-financial world depending on the domestically enabled access of finance towards fields such as pensions, public infrastructure, energy, housing and the like (Nölke, Heires and Bieling 2013).

The politics of the European Union have been functioning as a kind of intermediator between global and domestic developments. This applies to both dimensions, the production of an integrated financial market and the related, but domestically diverse, processes of financialization. Above all, in terms of financial market integration, European initiatives played an important role. Given the discursive presence and material weight of capital market based investment and modernization strategies, national governments, large parts of the financial services industries, increasingly also transnational non-financial corporations and the respective associations of these capital fractions pushed for ever more initiatives of financial liberalization and integration (Bieling 2003; Mügge 2006). The first steps have been a few liberalization directives on capital mobility, banking, insurance and securities markets in the context of the single market programme. In the course of the 1990s, the European Commission and venture capitalists initiated the set-up of a European risk capital market modelled on the American NASDAQ. Then, the implementation of Economic and Monetary Union (EMU) worked as a kind of catalyst for cross-border transparency of financial investments and for increased capital mobility. Furthermore, the Financial Services Action Plan (FSAP), launched in 1999 and strongly inspired by the booming 'new economy' in the USA, initiated additional Anglo-Saxon style changes in the mode of operation of finance (Cafruny and Ryner 2007; Grahl 2011). On top of this, the 'Lisbon Strategy' from 2000 made clear that the aforementioned integration efforts should be accompanied and stimulated by a range of reforms – in the areas of labour markets, pension systems or public infrastructure – all aiming to promote European capital markets.

In the official rhetoric of the European Commission the listed political initiatives should primarily serve two objectives (Bieling 2003: 210): first, to make the European economy more competitive by intensifying regulatory adjustment pressures and by facilitating the cross-border provision of cheap capital; and second, to create a level playing field in the financial markets for all competitors by abolishing the inherited regulatory shelters and privileges for selected financial players. The outcome was, however, not only more financial market competition but also the emergence of a transnational capitalist formation which, under the guidance of financial capital and in view of the still nationally organized redistributive systems of taxation and welfare regulation, produced new challenges for combating increasing social insecurity and inequality and politically balancing the aggravated processes of unequal development (Bellofiore, Garibaldo and Halevi 2010; Becker and Jäger 2012). The latter aspect particularly applies to the Eurozone where the abolition of the exchange rate mechanism in combination with the single interest rate policy prolonged stagnation in some countries but generated overheating tendencies in others. For instance, while the neo-mercantilist stimulation of the German economy through policies of wage restraint, labour market deregulation, and social cutbacks only materialized with a certain time lag, in the case of Ireland, Spain or Greece the comparatively low interest rates stimulated a finance-led investment and housing boom which, due to above-average inflation rates, deteriorated the relative competitive position.

What this implied became evident after the outbreak of the global financial crisis. This crisis could be seen as an extraordinary by-product of an inherently crisis-prone regime of finance-led or finance-dominated capitalist accumulation, strongly determined by the mode of operation of an US-centred global monetary and capital circuit (Cafruny and Ryner 2007: 24). The bursting of the so-called subprime bubble, therefore, immediately affected those economies with strong economic links with the US economy. Crisis contagion took place via two channels: first, via financial markets, since important European banks had extensively invested in subprime credits or mortgage-backed securities so that their impending collapse severely impaired their respective countries of origin; and second, via export markets which were strongly depressed as a consequence of the deep economic recession, first in the USA, but then also within the EU. While the relevancy of these two channels explains the immediate outbreak and progression of the crisis in individual European economies in 2008 and 2009, the prolongation, deepening and lasting impact of the crisis needs to be explained by the overall design of EMU (Aglietta 2012). Particularly significant here is the uniform monetary policy, but there is also the absence of a lender of last resort competencies, the insufficient cross-border fiscal, social, and macroeconomic cooperation, and the subsequent patterns of unequal – spatial and temporal – development.

Making sense of European crisis management

In the course of the unfolding of the crisis within the European Union some of the listed problems have been partially addressed. The concrete strategic position of involved political actors was determined by the interplay of socioeconomic interests, crisis impairment and ideological convictions. Yet, irrespective of country-specific views and proposals, it was soon evident that European crisis management was a matter which remained, by and large, orchestrated by political networks composed of national and supranational elites. While in the national arena, governments worked hand in hand with the financial industries, business associations and selectively involved trade unions in 'crisis corporatist' arrangements (Urban 2012; Bieling and Lux 2014), European crisis management was even more restricted to the political executive – national governments, the European Commission, the European Central Bank (ECB) – in close collaboration with market 'experts' and representatives of financial and non-financial (trans-)national capital. The European Parliament played no active role and was only involved in some issues of regulatory reform; and other social forces in civil society such as protest movements and trade unions only mattered if their initiatives fitted into the overall drive to stabilize European financial market capitalism. In this vein, the predominant discourse was primarily concerned to avoid a failure of the European project and the capitalist formation it is based upon.

So far, at least, European crisis management can be interpreted as an emergency-driven effort to stabilise, modernize, and adjust the transnational capitalist formation without fundamentally changing given power relations. Therefore, it quite well conforms to what Antonio Gramsci (1971: 104) once had labelled a 'passive revolution'. In some respects, the concept of 'passive revolution' is rather vague. Gramsci himself applied it to diverse phenomena and developments ranging from the rise of Christianity within the Roman Empire to the French Revolution after 1815, the success of Italian fascism in the 1920s and finally to the emergence of Fordism. Nevertheless, the concept is focused to the extent that it refers to processes of societal transformation which take place without a sudden, comprehensive, and radical change. Instead, passive revolutions are marked by three features: first, as revolutions 'from above' or from outside they show no signs of revolutionary explosion and take place without active involvement of the masses; second, they remain restricted to piecemeal economic or political reforms which aim to stabilize or restore inherited power relations; and third, irrespective of such intentions, eventually the reforms tend to change the composition of forces so that subaltern social classes or groups become increasingly marginalized. According to Gramsci, 'passive revolutions' show a lack of hegemonic capacities, which may be either caused by deficient productive forces so that they remain confined to incremental adjustments in state and civil society or by productive transformations without corresponding reforms of state-civil society complexes (Buci-Glucksmann 1981: 60). In both cases, the only molecular and partial changes show that no social force or no alliance of social forces is able to strategically organize societal transformations in a deliberate and hegemonic manner.

The process of an executive-dominated European crisis management precisely refers to such a constellation of 'passive revolution'. Over the past years national governments and state-like supranational institutions have been very active in attempting to stabilize European financial market capitalism by a series of ad hoc rescue measures and with an incremental adjustment of domestic and European regulation. In some ways, the rescue measures and procedures of initiating and negotiating reforms of the European system of financial, monetary and economic governance were chaotic. It is therefore difficult to discover any European master plan. What is possible, however, is to identify strategic priorities and ideological convictions of the involved actors as well as the most important stabilization initiatives. Overall, the different crisis management measures can be subdivided into two phases (Bieling 2012). In the first phase from Summer 2007 to Winter 2009/10, national governments were primarily concerned with mitigating the negative impact of the global financial crisis. Above all, they tried to rescue troubled banks and set up national rescue funds to stabilize the financial system; and next to their lender of last resort function, from Autumn 2008 onwards most governments launched economic stimulus programmes in order to cushion the deep recession. In both contexts, the European dimension was, more or less, confined to closely coordinating the domestic stabilization initiatives. Beyond that, however, the ECB started to play a more active role (Lapavitsas *et al.* 2012: 51). It counteracted the drying up of interbank credit markets through additional liquidity provision, and then it supported the counter-cyclical governmental programmes through a more expansive monetary policy.

Therefore, the first phase of European crisis management was characterized by a move into the direction of an emergency-driven Keynesian state interventionism. This move was further backed by increasing public criticism of unfettered financial markets in line with the Anglo-American model of capitalism, and there were many proposals for financial re-regulation in order to correct the undesirable developments of the past. Subsequently, most re-regulation proposals have been watered down (Rixen 2013) while discourses within the EU turned towards another focus. Against the background of the high public costs of bank rescues and economic stimulus packages, particularly the governments of current account surplus countries, the European Commission and fractions of globally oriented capital were less concerned about the still depressive economic situation, but increasingly with skyrocketing public debt (Jessop 2010). In this way, the second phase of crisis management was marked by the transition from the global financial crisis towards the so-called 'sovereign debt crisis' and 'euro crisis'.

To cope with these two crises the formerly hegemonic, but in the meantime still dominant, social and political forces negotiated new common instruments which can be seen as an embodiment of an underwhelming and widely criticized asymmetrical compromise (Bieling 2013). On the one hand, governments of highly indebted countries with a structural current account deficit pressed for the mobilization of public resources to further stabilize European financial capitalism. As they received the support of financial firms, associations, experts and think-tanks, they were able to push through the establishment of new interventionist instruments such as the European Financial Stability Facility (EFSF) and the European Stability Mechanism (ESM). In combination with an active ECB which announced, for instance, an Outright Monetary Transaction Programme (OMTP) to bring down interest rates on government bonds for highly indebted governments, these funds can be interpreted as the creation of limited common lender of last resort competencies. At least temporarily, such steps in the direction of a community with shared liabilities have stabilized EMU. At the same time, they had their price and were made conditional on the establishment of a range of austerity-oriented reform initiatives.

On the other hand, therefore, it was above all the governments of current account surplus countries which, backed by a transnational creditor community holding various kinds of financial and monetary assets and in cooperation with supranational actors, aimed to strengthen and generalize the political agenda of public budget consolidation (Bieling 2012). This was particularly evident in the case of the institutionalization of a so-called Troika – composed of the European Commission, ECB, and International Monetary Fund – authorized to negotiate and supervise the implementation of structural reforms and comprehensive austerity measures in countries receiving money from the EFSF and ESM. Beside, even apart from the conditionality of exceptional credit provision, the competitiveness and austerity oriented thrust has been strengthened by repeated reforms of the European system of financial and economic governance (Konecny 2012). Most important in this context were the introduction of a 'European Semester', the passing of a legislative 'Six-Pack' and 'Two-Pack', the agreement on a so-called 'Euro-Plus Pact', and, of course, the 'Fiscal Compact' whose ratification was defined as a basis for future financial support by the ESM.[3]

European crisis constitutionalism and the multifaceted dynamics of disintegration

All of these measures can be interpreted as components of a more recent process of 'European crisis constitutionalism' (Bieling 2013). In a way, this type of constitutional policy-making is in line with what, some years ago, Stephen Gill called 'new constitutionalism' (see also Oberndorfer, Chapter 11 in this volume). That is, the promotion of international treaties and supranational arrangements which:

> imply or mandate the insulation of key aspects of the economy from the influence of politicians or the mass of citizens by imposing, internally and externally, 'binding constraints' on the conduct of fiscal, monetary and trade and investment policies … In effect, new constitutionalism confers privileged rights of citizenship and representation to corporate capital, whilst constraining the democratization process that has involved

> struggles for representation for hundreds of years. Central, therefore, to new constitutionalism is the imposition of discipline on public institutions, partly to prevent national interference with the property rights and entry and exit options of holders of mobile capital with regard to particular political jurisdictions.
>
> (Gill 2003: 132)

In the past, within the European Union these aspects have been strengthened through the constitutionalization of major projects of integration such as the single market, EMU, financial market integration or eastward enlargement. It was fairly obvious that new constitutionalism as the politico-legal dimension of 'disciplinary neoliberalism' was not exclusively but most actively promoted by transnational productive and financial capital. Besides, small and medium-sized companies, small investors, owners of financial assets, large parts of established, in some ways privileged labour, and not to forget most governments and governing parties, have also been supportive of new constitutionalist propositions; and basically, it is still this transnational alliance of social forces which backs the crisis constitutionalist reforms now. However, despite such continuities 'European crisis constitutionalism' also differs from the former 'new constitutionalism' of the pre-crisis period. A few hints may illustrate this:

- First, recent 'European crisis constitutionalism' represents less a by-product of the formerly dynamic processes of market-liberal globalization but rather a response to the contradictions and crisis tendencies of European financial capitalism. Consequently, its legal and institutional reforms are much more contested and politicized.
- Second, crisis constitutionalist reforms are far less restricted to the promotion of capital mobility and competition, but also generate some forms of supranational statehood which have the purpose of politically intervening and steering economic processes. As outlined above, the intervention and steering capacities served above all to stabilize the European formation of transnational financial capitalism. At the same time, however, the implied manifold distributional effects are controversially seen by different social classes and national governments.
- Third, in view of these conflicts and the coercive nature of imposed reform conditionality, European crisis constitutionalism represents a decreasingly hegemonic mode of governance. This assessment is reinforced if one looks more precisely at its social basis, which now is predominantly based in current account surplus and therefore creditor economies, while being weakened in the European periphery, that is, in the current account deficit countries.

All of these characteristics and the socioeconomic consequences show that European crisis constitutionalism embodies the politico-legal dimension of a 'passive revolution in trouble'. Far from ushering in a new European formation of smooth capitalist development, the crisis constitutionalist dynamics remain marked by ambiguous, if not paradoxical developments. On the one hand, European crisis constitutionalism points towards further deepening of European integration by generating common institutions, competencies, and instruments, while on the other hand, it simultaneously contributes to undermining and putting into question the societal conditions and inherited rules of the integration process. Next to constitutionalist deepening there are obvious tendencies of socioeconomic and socio-cultural disintegration, too (Eppler and Scheller 2013). In a general sense, it is possible to identify at least three areas or fields of development which support this view.

The first development is immediately related to the socioeconomic consequences of European crisis management. Generally, but above all in the European periphery, the austerity agenda has obstructed economic recuperation and generated a vicious circle of public cutbacks, prolonged economic stagnation or even recession, shrinking fiscal revenues and increasing public debt (Busch et al. 2013: Table 6.1). An obvious effect of this constellation is an accelerated dismantling of the European social model and the erosion of social cohesion (Degryse, Jepson and Pochet 2013). This applies particularly to countries hit hard by the financial and economic crisis and compelled to overcome their presumed twin-crisis of sky-rocketing public debt and lack of competitiveness through a strategy of 'internal devaluation'; that is, a significant reduction of wages, social benefits and public services to unburden companies and the state (Schulten and Müller 2013). Consequently, it is above all some workers, the precariously employed, the young generation and unemployed, and recipients of social benefits who have to bear the costs of the crisis and crisis management. In view of the further weakening of collective bargaining, labour rights and a new wave of privatizing parts of the public sector and social security systems such as pensions, European societies suffer from a further increase in social inequality and insecurity. Against the background of rising unemployment, particularly among youths who are often rather well-trained people, and the manifold mortifications, frustrations and fears for the future, it is no exaggeration to assume that most European societies are confronted with a deep and increasingly solid 'social crisis'.

Disintegration is, however, far from confined to social crisis phenomena, but has also aggravated the crisis of democracy. Already before the outbreak of the global financial and the euro crisis there was an intensive debate on the scope and severity of the processes indicating the transition towards a so-called 'post democracy' (Crouch 2004); that is, towards a societal constellation in which democratic procedures are formally still intact, but in which large parts of the population retreat from active engagement with political issues. Indicators of this trend, such as shrinking voter participation, increase of floating voters and membership losses of mass organizations such as political parties or trade unions, were found in almost all EU member states (Mair 2006). Eventually, however, European crisis constitutionalism has significantly aggravated and partially politicized these tendencies.

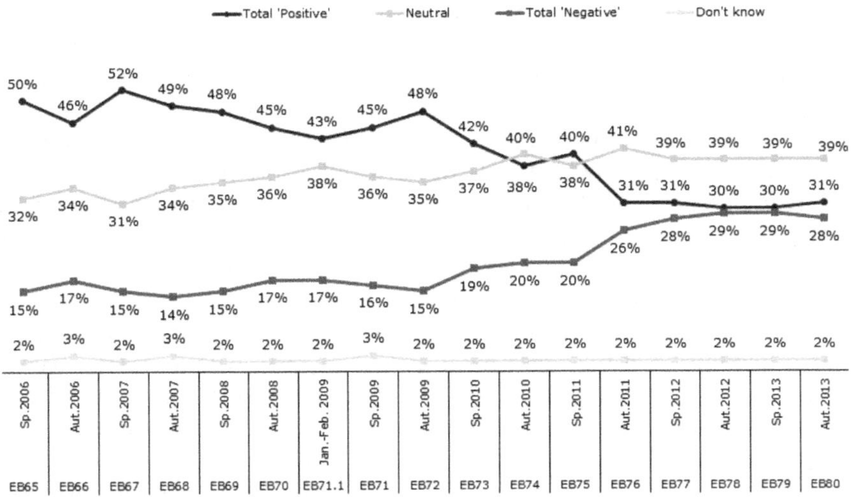

Figure 6.1 Public image of the EU
European Commission (2013: 6)

The aggravation resulted from the interplay of two components. One component was the further strengthening of the executive-dominated mode of integration. Above all this refers to national governments which have been guided by the German and the French ones as expressed in the neologism 'Merkozy' that defined the European reform agenda in cooperation with the European Commission, regulatory committees or – sometimes informal – expert groups. The immediate impact of this European 'executive federalism' (Habermas 2011: 8) was that not only the European Parliament but also domestic parliaments were increasingly sidelined and disempowered. Such anti-democratic developments were further reinforced by a second component, namely the predominant role of transnational finance and its leading representatives. Although seriously weakened after the outbreak of the financial crisis they have been able to mobilize public money by emphasizing their 'systemic' economic nature; and having been financially stabilized and strengthened again, they exerted strong economic and political pressure on European and national crisis management. The renewed transnational financial capitalist control was structural and discursive, but in some cases – one might remember the forced demission of Papandreou after considering a Greek referendum on the imposed austerity package, or the political inauguration of persons with very close ties to Goldman Sachs such as Papademos, Monti or Draghi – also of immediate personal political relevancy.

The socioeconomic and democratic crisis processes have had an impact on the further course of European integration. For a long while, the vast majority of the people have been in favour of the integration process since it was seen as generally supportive for economic growth, employment, social security, and not to forget peace. Due to the increased politicization of the EU, this so-called 'permissive consensus' eroded somewhat in the early 1990s, but was not substantially called into question. With the transition from the financial to the euro crisis and the crisis constitutionalist reforms, however, this situation seems to have changed (see Figure 6.1). Since Winter 2009/10, a much larger group of people is ready to withdraw political support for European integration. In this context, however, increasing de-legitimation has different, in some ways opposite causes: on the one hand, people within the current account surplus and creditor countries are less and less willing to financially stand up for rising public debt in the European periphery. Therefore, they tend to be more critical of a so-called 'transfer union' or union of shared liabilities. On the other hand, rising criticism within current account deficit and debtor countries feeds on opposite experiences, as the implementation of European reforms is often seen as an externally imposed austerity mandate which exceeds the available capacities of these countries to adjust to it without serious consequences. In view of these contradictory perceptions and interests, it is no surprise that populist sentiments have advanced into public debates and have also nourished international tensions and conflicts within the everyday business of the EU, especially as the politicians involved have difficulties in defining and negotiating compromises which are viable and take other European considerations into account.

The changing configuration of power in the Europe to come

Whether the outlined crisis phenomena will further deepen and cause even more trouble for the passive revolution of the European capitalist formation is difficult to foresee. It might be possible that economic recovery in North America and Asia will help mitigate the depressive situation. Whether such mitigation will suffice to restore public support for European integration and to re-balance the legal-institutional and socio-political changes within the European configuration of power is, however, unlikely. After all, the initiatives of European crisis constitutionalism all aimed to transform the mode of operation of the EU and the Eurozone in a mid- to long-term perspective; and in this way they have at least perpetuated and accentuated the relation of forces within the European capitalist formation. In that context, three tendencies seem to stand out:

The first tendency is that, within the transnational European power bloc which underpins transnational financial market capitalism, conflicts between the different fractions – Huw Macartney (2009) identified an 'Atlantic', 'Gallic' and 'Rhenish' fraction – have become more intense; and that in the struggle between these fractions about the future European economic order the German-led 'Rhenish' fraction and the current account surplus countries have gained the upper hand (see also Cafruny, Chapter 4 in this volume). Already before the crisis and as a consequence of competition-oriented wage restraint, which in turn was buttressed by cost-cutting labour market and social policy reforms in the 2000s, the German economy further transnationalized. The share of exports in relation to GDP moved from 25.7% (1991) up to 51.5% (2012), while stocks of German owned foreign direct investments almost increased tenfold in the same period. Moreover, within the EU, German transnational corporations adopted core positions within the transnationalized networks of interlocking directorates (van der Pijl, Holman and Raviv 2011); and given the extensive credit provision to foreign banks, corporations, and public households German banks and German state apparatuses took a leading role in European crisis management. Although from an economic and social perspective the crisis constitutionalist approach is very questionable, it was pushed through by German authorities in line with ordoliberal thinking in order to strengthen a rules-based, competition-oriented and non-interventionist mode of European economic governance (Dullien and Guérot 2012). The more self-assertive German reform strategy is, however, not confined to changing relations of forces between leading capital fractions. It also implies a clear accentuation of core-periphery relations within the EU as German readiness to make material concessions declined in the course of the crisis.

A second tendency is the weakening of organized labour. This tendency, which started to unfold as early as the late 1970s and early 1980s, is due to various transformations such as globalization, the transnationalization of production, rising unemployment, the deregulation of labour markets and social security systems, the privatization of public services, the increase of the service sector, and the individualization and erosion of working-class communities. Next to these and other developments, however, the transition towards financial market capitalism – that is, the rise of transnational finance and the stepwise financialization of production – welfare and social relations – mattered a lot as these processes corresponded with redistributive effects that were detrimental to labour (Peters 2011). From the 1980s onwards, in more or less all OECD countries, profit rates of productive and financial investments increased, while trade unions were not able anymore to realize collective bargaining results which represented a neutral distribution of inflation and productivity increases between capital and labour. This trend continued in the crisis apart from individual years such as 2009 or in specific country cases marked by a striking decrease in labour productivity (Schulten 2012), as both the recent crisis constitutionalist reforms and the European Troika (Schulten and Müller 2013) urged wage restraint and labour market deregulation. The latter were especially significant for the public sector, which in many countries in the European periphery plays a pivotal role in terms of collective bargaining. In some cases, these pressures led to strike waves and public protests, but without shifting the balance of forces in favour of labour.

Although most protests against European austerity have a solidaristic component, they have not been able to establish a strong progressive movement for European reform (see Clua-Losada and Horn, Chapter 12 in this volume). On the contrary, a third tendency is the upswing of right-wing populist parties. Like the former trends, this development is not completely new. Some right-wing populist parties have been established for years: in Austria the *Freiheitliche Partei Österreichs* (FPÖ), in Belgium the *Vlaams Belang*, in the Netherlands the *Partij voor di Vriheid*, in Denmark the *Danske Folkeparti*, in Italy the *Lega Nord*, in Hungary *Fidesz*, or in France the *Front National* (for an overview see Grabow and Hartleb 2014). What is new, however, is that in most cases right-wing nationalist movements prospered under conditions of crisis. On the one hand, there are also a couple more recently flourishing parties of this type: for instance, in Sweden the *Sverigedemokraterna*, in Finland the *Perussuomalaise* (True Finns), or in Germany the *Alternative für Deutschland* (AfD). And on the other hand, the longer established right-wing parties also had electoral success, consolidating and gaining more political weight within the respective national parliaments. Moreover, although for most of these parties transnational cooperation within the European context is still difficult due to ideological reasons, they started to form transnational European networks in the run-up to the European Parliament elections in May 2014 (Plehwe 2014).

All of these incremental shifts within international and societal power relations have been accentuated over the course of the past years. They can be seen as an important effect or by-product of the ongoing 'passive revolution'; that is, of the molecular adjustment within the political-institutional and discursive setting of European multi-level governance. At the same time, the incremental, but in some way uncontrolled power shifts indicate that the 'passive revolution' is far from leading towards an economically, socially and politically consolidated mode of development. On the contrary, it is generating or at least promoting the accumulation of social discontent and political troubles. At some points these troubles as the public expression of societal indignation come to the fore – in some cases with a socially progressive and solidaristic flavour, in others in nationalist guise – but without forming a strong transnational counter-hegemonic alternative towards the increasingly authoritarian management of the European economic order. Certainly, there is more than one reason for the still-limited forms of transnational cooperation on the part of subaltern social forces. One important factor is, however, that the severity of the crisis and the experiences of the European people differ significantly. These differences, in turn, can be attributed to the uneven capitalist development within the EU and the Eurozone (Becker 2012; Bieling and Lux 2014). This uneven development is not restricted to economic dynamics but also includes socio-cultural and political processes; yet eventually, it is precisely the contingency of these latter dimensions which still provides sufficient ground for alternative courses of political action.

Notes

1 I would like to thank Magnus Ryner for giving the inspiration for this title. When I talked with him about a special issue of the journal *Das Argument* on 'Neugründung Europas als passive Revolution' he asked back: 'but one in trouble, or'?

2 The notion of 'uneven and combined development' indirectly dates back to Marx's (1962[1867]) theoretical reflections on the concentration and centralization of capital, but was most prominently theorized in Trotsky's (1997 [1932]) *History of the Russian Revolution*. More recently, this topic has been brought up again in critical analysis due to the manifold and complex dynamics of crisis-mediated uneven transnational development, which include social structures, political institutions and regulations, discursive practices, cultural identities, etc. (see, for instance Morton 2010; Hobson 2011).

3 The last reform package of the European banking union has a slightly different focus. It aimed to limit the public costs of the stabilization and control of the highly vulnerable and interconnected banking system by establishing a system of centralized supervision of transnational banks, a common deposit insurance system, and European mechanisms for dealing with banks in default through direct financial support via the ESM or common winding-up rules.

References

Aglietta, M. (2012) The European Vortex. *New Left Review* 75. Second Series, pp. 15–36.

Becker, J. (2012) Blindstellen: ungleiche Entwicklung und ungleiche Mobilisierung in der EU. *Prokla* 42(2), pp. 467–476.

Becker, J. and Jäger, J. (2012) Integration in Crisis: A Regulationist Perspective on the Interaction of European Varieties of Capitalism. *Competition & Change* 16(3), pp. 169–187.

Bellofiore, R., Garibaldo, F. and Halevi, J. (2010) The Great Recession and the Contradictions of European Neomercantilism. In Panitch, L., Albo, G. and Chibber, V. (eds) *Socialist Register 2011. The Crisis This Time.* London: Merlin Press, pp. 120–146.

Bieling, H.-J. (2003) Social Forces in the Making of the New European Economy: the Case of Financial Market Integration. *New Political Economy* 8(2), pp. 203–224.

Bieling, H.-J. (2012) EU Facing the Crisis: Social and Employment Policies in Times of Tight Budgets. *Transfer: European Review of Labour and Research* 18(3), pp. 255–271.

Bieling, H.-J. (2013) European Financial Capitalism and the Politics of (De-)financialization. *Competition & Change* 17(3), pp. 283–298.

Bieling, H.-J. and Lux, J. (2014) Crisis-induced Social Conflicts in the European Union – Trade Union Perspectives: the Emergence of 'Crisis Corporatism' or the Failure of Corporatist Arrangements? *Global Labour Journal* 5(2), pp. 153–175

Buci-Glucksmann, C. (1981) *Gramsci und der Staat. Für eine materialistische Theorie der Philosophie.* Köln: Pahl-Rugenstein.

Busch, K. *et al.* (2013) *Euro Crisis, Austerity Policy and the European Social Model. How Crisis Policies in Southern Europe Threaten the EU's Social Dimension*. International Policy Analysis. February 2013. Berlin: Friedrich-Ebert-Stiftung.

Cafruny, A.W. and Ryner, M. (2007) *Europe at Bay. In the Shadow of US Hegemony.* Boulder, CO: Lynne Rienner.

Crouch, C. (2004) *Post-Democracy.* Cambridge: Polity Press.

Degryse, C., Jepsen, M. and Pochet, P. (2013) The Euro Crisis and its Impact on National and European Social Policies. *Working Paper* 2013.05. Brussels: ETUI.

Dullien, S. and Guérot, U. (2012) The Long Shadow of Ordoliberalism: Germany's Approach to the Euro Crisis, Policy Brief: European Council on Foreign Relations. [Online] Available from http://www.ecfr.eu/article/commentary_the_long_shadow_of_ordoliberalism [Accessed 10 September 2013].

Eppler, A. and Scheller, H. (eds) (2013) *Zur Konzeptionalisierung europäischer Desintegration. Zug- und Gegenkräfte im europäischen Integrationsprozess.* Baden-Baden: Nomos.

European Commission (2010) European Economic Forecast. *European Economy No. 7/10*. Autumn 2010 2010. Luxembourg: European Commission.

European Commission (2013) Public Opinion in the European Union: First Results, *Standard Eurobarometer 80*. Autumn 2013 2013. Luxembourg: European Commission.

European Commission (2014) European Economic Forecast. *European Economy No. 2/14*. Winter 2014 2014. Luxembourg: European Commission.

Gill, S. (2003) *Power and Resistance in the New World Order.* New York: Palgrave.

Gowan, P. (1999) *The Global Gamble. Washington's Faustian Bid for World Dominance.* London and New York: Verso.

Grabow, K. and Hartleb, F. (2014) *Europe – No, Thanks? Study on the Rise of Right-Wing and National Populist Parties in Europe.* Konrad Adenauer Stiftung and Centre for European Studies. Paderborn: Bonifatius GmbH.

Grahl, J. (2011) The Subordination of European Finance. *Competition and Change* 15 (1), pp. 31–47.

Gramsci, A. (1971) *Selections from the Prison Notebooks of Antonio Gramsci.* New York: International Publishers.

Habermas, J. (2011) *Zur Verfassung Europas. Ein Essay.* Frankfurt am Main: Suhrkamp.

Hobson, J.M. (2011) What's at Stake in the Neo-Trotskyist Debate? Towards a Non-Eurocentric Historical Sociology of Uneven and Combined Development. *Millennium: Journal of International Studies* 40(1), pp. 147–166.

Jessop, B. (2010) Cultural Political Economy and Critical Policy Studies. *Critical Policy Studies* 3(3–4), pp. 336–356.

Konecny, M. (2012) Die Herausbildung einer neuen Economic Governance als Strategie zur autoritären Krisenbearbeitung in Europa – gesellschaftliche Akteure und ihre Strategien. *Prokla* 42(3), pp. 377–394.

Lapavitsas, C. et al. (2012) *Crisis in the Eurozone.* London: Verso.

Macartney, H. (2009) Variegated Neoliberalism: Transnationally Oriented Fractions of Capital in EU Financial Market Regulation. *Review of International Studies* 35(2), pp. 451–480.

Mair, P. (2006) Ruling the Void? The Hollowing of Western Democracy. *New Left Review.* Second Series, No. 42, pp. 25–51.

Marx, K. (1962) [1867] *Das Kapital. Kritik der politischen Ökonomie.* Band I. MEW 23. Berlin: Dietz.

McKinsey Global Institute (2011) *Mapping Global Capital Markets.* August. [Online] Available from www.mckinsey.com/insights/global_capital_markets/mapping_global_capital_markets_2011 [Accessed 22 June 2014].

Morton, A.D. (2010) The Continuum of Passive Revolution. *Capital & Class* 34(3), pp. 315–342.

Mügge, D. (2006) Reordering the Marketplace: Competition Politics in European Finance. *Journal of Common Market Studies* 44(5), pp. 991–1022.

Nölke, A., Heires, M. and Bieling, H.-J. (2013) Editorial: The Politics of Financialization. *Competition & Change* 17(3), pp. 209–218.

Peters, J. (2011) The Rise of Finance and the Decline of Organised Labour in the Advanced Capitalist Countries. *New Political Economy* 16(1), pp. 73–99.

Plehwe, D. (2014) Durchmarsch der nationalen Neoliberalen? Die AfD und die neue europäische Rechte. *Blätter für deutsche und internationale Politik* 59(3), pp. 63–72.

Rixen, T. (2013) Why Reregulation after the Crisis is Feeble: Shadow Banking, Offshore Financial Centers, and Jurisdictional Competition. *Regulation & Governance* 7(4), pp. 435–459.

Schulten, T. (2012) Europäischer Tarifbericht des WSI – 2011/2012. *WSI Mitteilungen* 65(6), pp. 447–456.

Schulten, T. and Müller, T. (2013) A New European Interventionism? The Impact of the New European Economic Governance on Wages and Collective Bargaining. In Natali, D. and Vanhercke, B. (eds) *Social Developments in the European Union 2012*. Brussels: ETUI, pp. 181–213.

Trotsky, L. (1977) [1932] *The History of the Russian Revolution*. London: Pluto Press.

Urban, H.-J. (2012) Crisis Corporatism and Trade Union Revitalisation in Europe. In Lehndorff, S. (ed.) *A Triumph of Failed Ideas. European Models of Capitalism in Crisis*. Brussels: ETUI, pp. 219–241.

van der Pijl, K., Holman, O. and Raviv, O. (2011) The Resurgence of German Capital in Europe: EU Integration and the Restructuring of Atlantic Networks of Interlocking Directorates after 1991. *Review of International Political Economy* 18(3), pp. 384–408.

7 Enhancing 'competitiveness' in response to the European crisis

A wrong and dangerous obsession

Angela Wigger

Almost seven years after the eruption of the global economic crisis, the structural problems of the European Monetary Union and the widening centre-periphery divide seem far from resolved. The Southern Eurozone members are confronted with severe economic contractions and the disruptive impact of the crisis continues to aggravate, signalling that the crisis has not yet reached its zenith. Unemployment and underemployment are lingering, and poverty and social exclusion increasing. Precarious work is on the rise, while real wages continue to decline. The European Union (EU) responded to the crisis spasmodically in stages, subverting democratic decision-making at all levels. The EU responses comprise an imbroglio of Eurozone-specific and more general EU-28 regulatory emergency rules, new policy programmes and secondary law, a new economic governance framework, as well as intergovernmental treaties concluded outside the confines of the EU treaty framework. In addition to launching plans for a Banking Union, several budgetary and non-budgetary surveillance mechanisms were adopted with the goal to tighten fiscal discipline, such as the European Semester of 2010, the Euro Plus Pact and the Six Pack of 2011, the Treaty for Stability, Coordination and Governance, leading to the Fiscal Compact of 2012, or the Two Pack of 2013.

Whereas some of the above-mentioned regulatory and treaty-based packages already entailed a complementary macroeconomic agenda as a basis for national reform programmes, enhancing competitiveness has now become the mainstay of the EU's crisis management. The call for a 'Competitiveness Pact' by German Chancellor Merkel at the World Economic Forum in Davos in January 2013 gave the impetus for a European Commission proposal for a 'Convergence and Competitiveness Instrument' only a month later (European Commission 2013). The pace has been set: not only crisis-stricken member states but also the entire Eurozone has to step up reform efforts, such as negotiating 'Partnerships for Growth, Employment and Competitiveness', which consist of legally enforceable contractual reform arrangements between the Commission and individual member states in fields such as labour markets, markets for goods and services, the public sector and vocational education.

Already back in the early 1990s, economist Paul Krugman (1994: 44) criticized the EU's obsession with competitiveness as 'wrong and dangerous' as it draws on a misguided analogy according to which entire economies are competing on the global marketplace similar to corporations. Whereas in the 1990s the high-technology sector of the USA had been perceived as a mounting competitive threat, the EU now seeks to compete with China and other emerging economies. Boosting competitiveness may sound genuinely appealing and politically motivating, particularly against the backdrop of rising popular fatigue with further fiscal austerity and the concomitant rhetoric of an overall belt tightening. The impression that fostering competitiveness would branch out to a wide range of industrial policy strategies that aim at generating long-term socially and ecologically sustainable employment is however elusive. Competitiveness, in EU-speak, mainly concerns 'price and cost' competitiveness, building either implicitly or explicitly on the notion that not too much but too little competition is the root cause of the current crisis. Suggested reform measures are essentially premised on internal devaluation realized through enhanced inter-company competition, which is expected to lead to lower prices, an overall lowering of corporate taxes, and labour market reforms depreciating real wages. Intensifying inter-company competition as a way to reduce prices and internal devaluation through the labour market are intimately related: both essentially devalue labour.

The EU's crisis management hitherto has been characterized as 'muddling through' (Overbeek 2012) and lacking a clear vision (EuroMemorandum 2013). The vision of EU decision-makers is however very clear: the landslide 'Troika for all' seeks to recalibrate neoliberal structural adjustment programmes and extend competitive logics far beyond the corporate realm. This chapter seeks to demystify the power of the competitiveness agenda. Drawing on a critical political economy perspective, it argues that capitalist competition can be seen as one of the root causes of this crisis, and that pro-competition measures as a remedy to restore competitiveness only exacerbate structural imbalances and economic disintegration in Europe. Section one sketches EU crisis management and the reinvigorated emphasis on competitiveness as a two-tier strategy of price and wage reduction. Section two discusses the competition–competitiveness nexus, debunking the myth that competition serves to enhance consumer welfare and demonstrating that capitalist competition can be ruinous for labour and capital alike. Section three outlines theoretically and empirically the role of capitalist competition as part of the structural problem of overaccumulation, which underpins the crisis-ridden nature of capitalism. Section four investigates the labour–competitiveness nexus, while section five reveals the political configuration of driving and contesting forces. The conclusions ponder on how the competitiveness agenda narrows the gamut for a more progressive and democratically justified EU crisis management.

Structural adjustment through internal devaluation

When the crisis became manifest in Europe in 2007/8 in the form of a heightened liquidity shortage (credit crunch) and the threat of insolvency of major financial institutions with large US subprime exposure, joint action at the EU level was initially slow and uncoordinated. Recapitalizing the financial sector was considered key to preventing the collapse of the financial system and contagion to the real economy. EU governments acted resolutely and infused public funds (taxpayers' money) into domestic financial institutions considered of systemic importance (too big to fail), either in the form of massive loans or liquidity guarantees, or government sponsored mergers via corporate tax exemptions for bank takeovers, a (partial) nationalization of banks by the procurement of 'toxic' assets and state acquisitions of preferential shares, as well as government guarantees for deposits. The European Commission – the supranational competition authority in charge of supervising state aid *ex ante* – approved the vast majority of state aid cases on the basis of emergency rules, thereby acting as a *de facto* EU crisis-management authority. Financial aid between 2008 and 2010 amounted to €4.5 trillion, equivalent to 37 per cent of the EU's GDP and almost double the German annual GDP (European Commission 2011a). In conjunction with a steep decline in tax revenues, the bailout of the financial sector, and hence the transformation of private debt to public debt, exhausted national budgets. The credit crisis mutated into a European sovereign debt crisis, hitting particularly hard in the Southern Eurozone countries with growing current account imbalances and rapidly accumulating public debts and thus revealing the macroeconomic division between the 'core' and 'peripheral' member states that had been gradually built up since the advent of the euro in 1999.

The accusation that the states in crisis had lived beyond their means came to prevail in media outlets and among political decision-makers, and eventually served as a political legitimization for the imposition of painful austerity programmes by the Troika, limiting the capacity of Eurozone governments to run budget deficits and to adopt costly social and economic policies. Regaining the trust of financial markets and their rating agencies received all of the emphasis. In addition to a strict EU monitoring of national budgets and economic policy, EU efforts focused on fixing the institutional design of the European Economic and Monetary Union and the European Stability and Growth Pact through a range of regulatory and treaty-based measures. Once deficits and debt ratios stayed high and economic contraction and depression were aggravated, the Commission announced in its Quarterly Report on the Euro Area:

> While fiscal imbalances are at the forefront of the current policy debate, they are by no means the only area where policy action is needed. Recent developments have highlighted the urgent need for some euro-area Member States to restore their external balances and to improve their competitiveness.
>
> (European Commission 2011b: 21–22)

The rationale of fostering competitiveness is not new. Already the preambles of the Treaty of Rome of 1957 declared 'a high degree of competitiveness' a Community goal (Article 2, European Union 2014). In the post-war social order of embedded liberalism, stretching from the 1950s to the late 1970s, economic policies exemplified strong neo-mercantilist and protectionist traits. In the presence of the 'American Challenge' (Servan-Schreiber 1968) – the competitive threat posed by the much larger and technologically more advanced US companies, and later also Japanese companies – EU competition and industrial policy sought to facilitate national and later European champions (see Buch-Hansen and Wigger 2011). From the late 1980s onwards, competitiveness rankings, macroeconomic performance indexes, benchmarking best practices and scoreboards have formed the apex of the neoliberal organization of capitalism in Europe. Countless policies and programmes have reiterated the need for European economies to become more competitive ever since. The ill-fated Lisbon Agenda of 2000 of the European Council declared outcompeting the rest of the world an official EU policy. The Commission's successor strategy Europe 2020, promising smart, sustainable and inclusive growth, in many ways constitutes a revamped clone of the former Lisbon Agenda.

Now that EU economies are in a deep crisis, restoring competitiveness has become once more a top priority. Merkel's 'Competitiveness Pact' centres on the idea that the Commission proposes recommendations to Eurozone governments, leading to country-specific reform programmes in areas of lacking competitiveness. These recommendations would then be subject to confirmation by the Economic and Financial Affairs Council, after which individual member governments sign annually binding agreements on the implementation of reforms with the Commission. Without national parliaments or the European Parliament having a say on the substantive content, these bilateral reform contracts would then be an indispensable prerequisite for getting access to EU budgets under the so-called 'solidarity mechanism'. The macroeconomic adjustment programmes previously dictated by the Troika to some Eurozone countries would become constitutionalized regimes for all (see also Oberndorfer, Chapter 11 in this volume).

On the surface, the competitiveness agenda may appear as a perspicacious structural policy supporting knowledge-intensive industrial sectors and high-wage jobs in Europe. This impression is reinforced by the Commission's recent communication, entitled 'For a European Industrial Renaissance' (2014), where it is argued that 'a strong industrial base will be of key importance for Europe's economic recovery and competitiveness'. The adoption of flanking programmes such as the 'Regulatory Fitness and Performance Programme' (REFIT) and 'Competitiveness Proofing' may likewise appear as a revitalization of active industrial policy seeking to reverse the trend of deindustrialization – notably the transfer of manufacturing capacity to China and other emerging markets, which has accelerated not only in labour-intensive sectors but increasingly also in electronics and other high-tech industries. The

EU's reform agenda is indeed geared towards achieving external competitiveness and keeping pace with emerging world economies; however, not by going beyond the previous asymmetrical adjustment measures, such as adopting job creation programmes similar to the US crisis strategy. Instead, the epitome of the competitiveness strategy builds on the pursuit of export-led growth, notably through improving trade balances through selling more and importing less.

As nominal exchange rate devaluation is not an option, enhancing 'external competitiveness' effectively boils down to internal devaluation as a way of achieving a real depreciation. As the Commission explained (2011b: 22), 'alternative policies of "internal devaluation" can mimic the expenditure-switching effects of "external" exchange rate devaluation'. More concretely, European economies should become more resilient first, through more intense competition alongside a further deregulation of product markets and privatization, which is believed to reduce domestic production costs and prices; second, through a 'revenue-neutral' shift from taxes on labour to taxes on consumption, as well as reduced tax burdens on exports; and third, through 'wage moderation' (see European Commission 2011b). The burden of adjustment will be highest in so-called non-competitive Southern deficit countries, and rests on labour rather than capital. Internal devaluation is likely to worsen uneven economic development in the Eurozone. The next section outlines the competition dimension in greater detail.

The competition–competitiveness nexus

The overall theme of the competitiveness agenda is that Eurozone economies can compete themselves out of the crisis through 'pro-competition' reforms. Competitiveness is rather narrowly understood in terms of a removal of market barriers and exposure to more intense capitalist competition in the hope that domestic goods and services will become cheaper than foreign goods and services. European Competition Commissioner Joaquin Almunia (2014) is rather straightforward when arguing that intensified capitalist competition constitutes a main lever for re-establishing a competitive business climate and economic growth, and hence a first step towards stronger fiscal capacity and the realization of a 'Genuine Monetary and Economic Union'. The removal of barriers to competition in the service sector, public utilities such as energy, and network industries is considered particularly urgent. According to Almunia, competition enhances 'competitiveness and innovation, creates jobs and drives economic expansion' (ibid.). Competition, so the logic goes, creates incentives for companies to become more efficient, allowing them to stay ahead of rivals and increase productivity, which on an aggregate scale is expected to boost economic growth with a trickledown effect on employment across Europe. If we are to believe the Commission's Directorate General for Competition (European Commission 2014), the benefits of capitalist competition is inherently positive sum: 'consumers, taxpayers, workers and businesses – everyone is better off overall when competition exists in our markets'.

The Commission's unfathomable faith in capitalist competition, bolstered inter alia by strict competition regulation as a motor for economic growth, echoes countless textbooks in the tradition of neoclassical economics (broadly defined). It builds on the axiom that positive feedback loops in the form of higher competitiveness and better performance of entire economies can be expected if a plethora of discrete companies strive to innovate their products and realize efficiency gains, while at the same adjusting the supply of goods and services to consumer demand at ever lower prices. Although it is widely agreed that the stylized and imaginary world of 'perfect competition' – referring to some sort of harmonious equilibrium situation – is utopian, it nonetheless serves as an anchor point for policy recommendations. Neoclassical economics and its policy proponents acknowledge that seemingly atomistic competitors are not genuinely striving for price reductions but rather seek to secure and widen their profit margins through abusing dominant market positions, collude in cartels or adopt other types of restrictive business practices, which is why state-enforced competition rules guaranteeing free competition and free market access are considered indispensable. According to this view, a strict enforcement of competition rules forms part and parcel of a social redistributive policy, lifting society to ever-higher standards of economic wealth: through competition, prices are expected to converge towards marginal production costs, reducing the portion of realized surplus value for capitalists, which is to the benefit of consumers. Competition Commissioner Almunia (2012a, 2012b) praises a strict enforcement of EU competition regulation as 'the cheapest and most effective structural reform' that is 'at no extra cost for the taxpayer'.

EU competition regulation has formed part of the emerging supranational state apparatus since the Treaty of Rome 1957, which committed the founding member states to institute 'a system ensuring that competition in the internal market is not distorted' (see Article 3f). From the outset, the Commission, as a supranational competition authority, has been entrusted with far-reaching discretionary legislative and enforcement powers. However, EU competition regulation only acquired heightened agenda status with the acceleration of the common market project, enacted by the Single European Act in 1987, and the creation of the EU in the early 1990s (Wigger 2008). When free market ideologues took office at the Commission's DG Competition a more stringent enforcement of competition rules was adopted – together with a whole string of regulatory devices pandering to the creation of a bigger integrated market. The neoliberal turn was also reflected in the consolidated text of the Treaty of the European Union, where the notion of 'fair' competition was replaced by 'free' competition. Harsh competition was expected to form the backbone of economic growth. The whole *raison d'être* of EU competition regulation came to be subordinated to the maximization of the consumer welfare paradigm. Notions such as 'consumer surplus' became paramount for justifying the use of price theories and price modelling as a central reference point for determining anticompetitive conduct.

That capitalist competition serves the interest of consumers – and thus the vast majority of citizens – and that anticompetitive conduct harms consumers in the form of overcharges seems to strike a chord among a great variety of political persuasions, particularly during times of economic slump and recession when lower prices and economic growth through more consumption appear much-needed. Moreover, intensifying capitalist competition might seem less painful than the tight austerity packages that seek to curb sovereign debts through onslaughts on social rights and welfare state retrenchment. The freedom to compete is also often associated with broader notions of political freedom and individual self-determination. Neoclassical economics and its policy proponents, including the Commission, however create false impressions of prosperity and freedom (see also Wigger and Buch-Hansen 2013). How consumer welfare is distributed within society is of no concern as long as there is a net gain 'somewhere in the system' (Crouch 2011: 55–56). In addition, consumers – taken as a proxy for entire societies – frequently have no real voice apart from not consuming. As Marx wrote in the *Grundrisse* (1973[1939]: 650): '[i]t is not individuals that are set free by free competition; it is, rather, capital which is set free'. Competition 'is nothing more than the way in which many capitals force the inherent determinants of capital upon one another and upon themselves' (ibid.: 651).

Capitalists cannot escape competition, as this would lead to perishing. The coercive laws of competition compel capitalists to reinvest accumulated surplus capital to create even more surplus. In a context of competitive capital accumulation, capitalists that accumulate more quickly tend to drive out of business those that accumulate at a slower rate (Harvey 2006: 39). The elimination of competitors inevitably strengthens the winners and reinforces their advantages. Thus, those able to set the (price) standards of competition for others are the actual beneficiaries. Rather than market justice through some sort of a Darwinian natural selection process sorting out the rightful winners (the efficient and innovative) and losers (the inefficient and unprofitable), capitalist competition erects hierarchies in wealth and power. The perfectly competitive equilibrium of neoclassical economics is a chimera: as capitalism cannot be stationary and not everyone who plays can win, 'a situation in which all capitalist-employers make exploitation gains' is impossible (Schumpeter 1976[1943]: 28, 31). Thus, rather than being an expression of the ultimate individual freedom and the realization of self-interest, capitalist competition is zero-sum in nature.

Capitalist competition needs to be understood as a social relation that is essentially antagonizing: it pits not only capital against capital, but also capital against labour, and in the presence of a reserve army of unemployed, labour against labour. The competitive battle can intensify to the extent that the prices of competitors can only be undercut by reducing variable production costs through a further exploitation of labour and nature (Wigger and Buch-Hansen 2013). As Marx (1965 [1887]: 626) noted, '[t]he battle of competition is fought by cheapening of commodities. The cheapness of commodities depends, all other circumstances remaining the same, on the productivity of labour.' In other words, to cheapen commodities and remain profitable, capitalists have to constantly seek ways to enhance labour productivity and cheapening labour. Capitalist competition thus essentially deflates labour.

The Commission's dogmatic commitment to price competition, which quintessentially gives precedence to a microeconomic perspective and to short-termism, limits the focus to single company behaviour in relation to consumers only, while disregarding important 'labour' questions, such as working conditions and adequate wages. Lower wages and increased labour productivity are instead considered key to attract investment, leading to higher net exports and enhancing competitiveness.

The competition–crisis nexus and the structural problem of overaccumulation

The rationale of EU crisis management is that a decrease in prices improves competitiveness and ultimately net exports, which again is expected to stimulate further investments and to culminate in economic growth. Stiff capitalist competition also increases economic uncertainty, however, which can temper profit expectations and the propensity to invest and contribute to the structural problem of overaccumulation, and in a wider sense capitalist crises (Wigger and Buch-Hansen 2012, 2013). Overaccumulation refers to a surplus of capital relative to outlets that allow for a profitable reinvestment of that capital in the real production economy. In moments of overaccumulation, capitalists may temporarily hold on to their surplus capital and/or deleverage their debts. Capitalists do not adjust production to reduced demand but rather seek to widen capitalist production through expanding into geographically new markets, or to deepen capitalist production through the commodification of ever-new domains of social interaction. Alternatively, new opportunities for profitable capital investments may be found outside the realm of production, such as through speculation and investments in financial markets, or through mergers and acquisitions. As Marx (1975 [1847]: 134–135) observed, there 'are even phases in the life of modern nations when everybody is seized with a sort of craze for making profit without producing. This speculation craze which recurs periodically, lays bare the true character of competition'. In contrast to capital invested in real economic production, fictitious capital is almost limitless, which can precipitate financialization processes, referring to a broad-based transformation of the pattern of accumulation according to which profits accrue predominantly through financial channels rather than through trade and commodity production (Krippner 2011: 27–28). As the financial sector not only extracts and accumulates surplus created in the real economy but also attains value through the mere circulation of capital, particularly through leveraging and speculation, financial bubbles can arise. Such bubbles inflate until it becomes evident – through defaults or bankruptcies – that the debtors can no longer repay creditors. Once the accumulation of capital and the accumulation of debt get too much out of sync, a crisis erupts (Harvey 2006).

The current crisis is rooted in overaccumulation (see also Overbeek 2012). At the same time, capitalist competition has become truly global and all pervasive. Technological change and the removal of barriers to trade and investment on a global scale facilitated and enhanced processes of transnationalization in the realm of production, which drastically expanded the scale of competition. At EU level, the accelerated pace of the common market project since the late 1980s has been constitutive for corporations to grow in size, to mobilize capital more easily, and henceforth to invest in new spheres of production. The subsequent privatization of state-run industries, and processes of deregulation, as well as re-regulation at the supranational level, offered new prospects for transnational corporations to adapt to the challenges posed by global competition. The introduction of the euro eliminated exchange rate fluctuations and significantly reduced transaction costs for cross-border business deals of all sorts, which created further prerequisites for companies to expand. In the 1990s and the early twenty-first century, cross-border business transactions such as mergers and acquisitions, strategic alliances, and other forms of commercial intercompany agreements increased considerably. In the late 1990s, for the first time in history, the principal 'consuming' companies of mergers and acquisitions originated from the EU (UNCTAD 2000: 16).

Mergers and acquisitions particularly provided a welcome outlet for re-investing surplus capital. Prior to the outbreak of the current global economic crisis, the sheer number and volume of mergers and acquisitions set historically unprecedented records, culminating in a massive concentration. In 2006, eight of the ten worldwide largest mergers ever were concluded if measured in terms of the aggregated volume of the companies involved, while the sheer number of mergers reached an all-time high (see Wigger 2012). Boosted by processes of financialization and the emergence of (new) financial players, the acquisition and selling of companies had been strongly speculative in nature. Private equity companies, hedge funds and other institutional investors attracted huge amounts of liquidity to finance mergers and corporate buyouts and sought to exploit speculative arbitrages. In 2007 private equity houses were estimated to be responsible for more than 20 per cent of all global merger activity (see Wigger 2012). EU merger regulation has facilitated this process of economic concentration and the role played by financial capital. Ever since the adoption of EU merger control in 1989, the Commission cleared more than 4,600 transactions and blocked only 22 (Almunia 2012a). Economic concentration in fewer and larger capitals is however not the antidote to competition. Notably in a situation of overaccumulation and a general slowing down of the economy, as well as the growth of social inequality, the competitive race to offset products to affluent consumers remains fierce.

As part of financialization processes, capital accumulation in financial markets grew faster than the accumulation of industrial capital. Since the early 1970s, private and public investment in the economically advanced world has been characterized by a long-term downward trend. In the EU 'core' countries, private sector investment in the real economy, measured as gross fixed capital formation as a percentage of GDP, declined steadily (Barbiero and Darvas 2014). Prospects remain gloomy. As Collignon (2014: 24) argues, excessive austerity 'has killed the appetite for investment'. While corporate retained earnings have improved in Europe, investment ratios have come down further. Instead of investing in economic production, higher liquidity reserves are used to repay corporate liabilities or invest in financial markets (Collignon 2014: 21).

The growing geographical disproportionalities in the Eurozone are inherently linked to decreased levels of investment. In Germany, investments in domestic production facilities have slowed down due to sluggish local demands, while two-thirds of retained earnings have been lent to Europe's South. Hence, surplus countries (capital exporters) such as Germany or the Netherlands have been lending to deficit countries (capital importers). Countries such as Greece, Ireland, Spain and Portugal displayed a gradual increase in gross fixed capital formation from 1995 up to 2008/2009; however, when the crisis erupted, such investments collapsed from 25 per cent of GDP in 2007 to below 15 per cent in 2013 (Collignon 2014). Thus, once credit expansion based on capital inflows from current account surplus countries came to a halt, the debt-induced growth model of the Southern countries entered a crisis (Stockhammer and Onaran 2012: 13–14). The volume of investments in the EU-28 has shrunk further since the crisis erupted: from 21.3 in 2007 to 17.9 per cent of GDP in 2012 (Eurostat 2014). Thus, the Eurozone suffers primarily from insufficient investment and less from rigid labour markets. As the next section demonstrates, EU crisis managers, obsessed with bolstering the competitiveness of European economies, nonetheless seek internal devaluation through reducing unit labour costs.

The labour–competitiveness nexus in EU crisis management

According to the Commission, one of the key solutions to the structural imbalances in the Eurozone lies in an internal devaluation through the labour market. As part of the conditionalities for financial support, the Troika had already dictated public-sector wage cuts on some member states, expecting that private wages would follow suit. With currently twelve Eurozone countries falling under the excessive deficit procedure, the Commission demands similar reforms in other member states, thereby entering a policy domain that used to be the national preserve. The EU compares competitiveness of European economies on the basis of differentials in unit labour costs, building on the relation between wages and productivity. A member state economy increases its competitiveness if wages or statutory non-wage labour costs such as employers' social security contributions are reduced, or else labour productivity is increased. Moreover, EU decision-makers advocate further labour market flexibilization as wages for temporary and flexible labour tend to be lower, while experience-rated pay and entitlements to benefits can generally be avoided. Overall, the idea is to reorient labour markets and employment policies towards the supply-side and improve the profitability of domestic vis-à-vis foreign capital, which is expected to have positive signalling effects to investors.

Since the ascendancy of neoliberalism, wage shares relative to GDP have steadily declined in Europe. Pressures to cut unit labour costs are unequivocally linked to the relocation of production to low-cost labour areas through outsourcing and offshoring. Furthermore, economic concentration through mergers and acquisition has engendered restructuring measures and the closure of duplicate divisions, which impacted negatively on overall levels of employment. In addition, the appropriation of ever-larger shares of surplus capital from the real economy by financial institutions intensified neoliberal wage-compression, corporate restructuring and rationalization processes. Processes of deindustrialization, in conjunction with the growth of the tertiary service sector and technological change, have also depressed demand for labour. As Shutt (2010: 55) has argued, global job creation is not keeping pace with the supply of workers, and in Southern Eurozone countries such as Spain and Portugal, where industrial output has declined drastically in the absence of sufficiently high domestic and international demand, this has become manifest in high unemployment and underemployment. By comparing unit labour costs, Southern Eurozone countries have become less competitive vis-à-vis Germany and its successful export-led growth strategy (see also Flassbeck and Lapavitsas, Chapter 8 in this volume), which builds on vast labour market reforms and cuts in welfare expenditure throughout the first decade of the twenty-first century, leading to wage restraint, low social standards and low corporate taxes (Stockhammer and Onaran 2012: 15). Reforms that devalue labour in one member state, and hence improve so-called competitiveness, inevitably lead to the deterioration of labour conditions in another member state. Taking Germany as a benchmark, the suggestion of European decision-makers is to Europeanize 'Model Germany'. Emulating 'Germany' is however problematic. As Sablowski (2012) explains, lowering wages in Greece cannot solve the problem as Germany and Greece are not competing in the car industry, because there is simply no Greek car industry.

A range of EU member states have already adopted labour market reforms in the wake of the current crisis, varying from 'piecemeal although significant deregulatory measures' to 'far-reaching overhauls of the whole labour code' (Clauwaert and Schoenmann 2012). Reforms include easing employee dismissals and fostering temporary employment, reducing minimum wages, increasing working time for less remuneration, or introducing new conditionalities and time limits for unemployment benefits, as well as a further decentralization or weakening of collective bargaining and the use of individualized contracts more generally. Portugal, Spain and Greece eased job protection and abolished key worker's rights (ETUC 2014). Half of Spanish workers have temporary contracts and find themselves in a precarious and unprotected situation, in Portugal the minimum wage has been frozen, while Greece reduced the minimum wage by 22 per cent and an additional 10 per cent for the young, while abolishing national and sectoral collective bargaining (OECD 2014; ETUC 2014). As part-time and temporary work in many Eurozone countries does not qualify for social security benefits, a growing share of 'working poor' is confronted with cumulative precariousness, hitting particularly hard on women who are more generally overrepresented in short-time and part-time work (Euromemorandum 2013: 39).

The logic of internal devaluation through the labour market is based on the presence of strong external demand. As part of the global economic crisis, global demand is however weak, and austerity measures combined with lower wages also supress intra-EU consumption (see Stockhammer and Kohler, Chapter 2 in this volume). Competing on 'labour' is not a route to salvation but rather worsens the crisis and the persisting asymmetries within Europe. Moreover, as Stockhammer and Onaran (2012: 12) have suggested: 'High wages may also force capitalists to rationalize and thus speed up technological progress', while 'higher real wage growth can lead to higher productivity growth'. Lowering unit labour costs, either through intensified competition or outright wage repression, reduced employee protection and the dissolution of collective wage bargaining may be a comparative advantage and improve returns on capital, but it also engenders a dangerous race to the bottom. The shift in power is serious: the freedom of capital to exploit labour is maximized, and employment costs and risks minimized, whereas oppositional forces, including organized labour, find themselves marginalized as the next section demonstrates.

Driving and contesting forces of the competitiveness obsession

EU crisis management blatantly reflects the demands of organized transnational capital and its unrestricted access to political decision-makers. At a meeting in Berlin in March 2013, bringing together German Chancellor Merkel, French President Hollande and Commission President Barroso, as well as fifteen members of the European Roundtable of Industrialists (ERT), it was agreed that industrial competitiveness should be at the centre of EU policy making (ERT 2013a). More concretely, the Captains of Industry assembled in the ERT demanded more business-friendly regulations, such as tax reductions, less labour protection, more labour market flexibilization, lower severance payments to employees, as well as downward pressures on wages, the facilitation of mergers and acquisitions or what the ERT calls 'market-driven consolidation', and privatizations. Competition regulation should moreover 'enhance EU companies' ability to be competitive internationally' (ERT 2013b). Already back in the early 1990s, transnational factions of industrial capital deplored the lagging competitiveness with Japan and the USA. Similar to today, the ERT attacked what it saw as high tax levels and high social and energy costs, considering contracts between social partners and environmental legislation 'exorbitant' (*The Financial Times* 1994: 2).

The ERT subsequently established the Competitiveness Working Group and suggested a Commissioner for Competitiveness, entrusted with the task of scrutinizing EU legislation for its aptness to industrial interests, and preventing all kinds of directives that might harm the interests of large corporations attempting to compete on a global scale. Although such a Commissioner never took office, the persistent demand for reforms seems to bear fruit. The OECD (2014) also corroborates the ERT when recommending that all EU member states, including those less hard-hit by the crisis, should push forward reforms that enhance competitive pressures in both labour and product markets, lower the tax burden on corporate income and capital gains, lower unit labour costs through a significant reduction in nominal wages, and reduce 'the dualism between temporary and permanent jobs' – OECD-speak for greater labour market flexibility and wage fixing (OECD 2014).

On the contesting side, the EU crisis management has fuelled considerable social unrest and political protests in many parts of Europe, but most notably in Europe's South. Despite increased concerted actions of contesting forces seeking new pan-European left-wing alliances and a series of transnational campaigns, manifestos and petitions, as well as joint strike days and weeks of action against EU austerity policies (see Wigger and Horn 2014), the political Left, ideologically fragmented as it is, seems unable to chart an alternative future for European integration that wins the support of a vast constituency. In contrast, neo-populist Eurosceptic and increasingly radical right and even neo-fascist parties successfully harness feelings of discontent and insecurity. Many groups of the political centre-left have not discredited and delegitimized the neoliberal representation of competition as a remedy to rising poverty and social exclusion in full vigour and seem entangled by the enthralling competitiveness rhetoric. Suggested alternatives are at best defensive or reformist, demanding Keynesian crisis management or half-hearted piecemeal measures of social compensation and a deepening democratization of European integration. For example, competition is frequently poorly understood. Exemplary is the Group of the Progressive Alliance of Socialists and Democrats in the European Parliament (2008, 2010), which associates EU competition control with positively connoted terms such as 'freedom and equality', 'sustainability', 'economic and social solidarity', 'social and territorial cohesion', 'quality of life and an efficient and dynamic economy'. Competition policy is moreover considered 'a vital instrument for economic and social integration', 'guaranteeing consumer welfare and encouraging the optimum allocation of resources and in granting economic agents the appropriate incentives to pursue productive efficiency, quality and innovation but also low prices and employment' (ibid.).

Although the European Trade Union Confederation (ETUC) has started to increasingly challenge the far-reaching dismantling of social protection systems and unemployment benefit systems (see ETUC 2012a, 2012b), the uneven and combined nature of capitalist expansion in Europe has resulted in labour movements finding themselves in rather different positions and frequently with contradictory interests, rendering transnational labour solidarity a critical case (Bieler 2012). Moreover, when the crisis hit Europe, left-wing social forces including trade unions were effectively marginalized. None of the austerity or the hasty bailout packages has been implemented in cooperation with trade unions, whereas rescuing the financial sector has reinstalled the pre-crisis social configuration in which financial capital, notably banks from northern Europe, have been the most dominant social faction (Wigger and Buch-Hansen 2013). The lack of respect for social dialogue at the EU level is striking. As the ETUC (2014: 4) writes:

> trade unions could voice demands and critique in formal meetings with the Troika, being granted ten minutes to present their views, while Troika representatives reacted with a 'set response', replying with 'generalities' or in an elusive way. The exclusion of contesting forces from EU decision-making has been incremental since the ascendency of neoliberalism. As regards the field of EU competition regulation, due to confidentiality reasons, labour unions have not had access to pending competition cases, which structurally places labour at a disadvantage in getting heard. Similarly, whereas the Commission has installed a permanent dialogue with consumers in the form of an Annual European Competition and Consumers Day and the establishment of the European Consumer Consultative Group at Commission level, there has been no equivalent access installed for organised labour.

The EU crisis management goes paired with the incorporation of a range of 'authoritarian neoliberal' elements in the institutional outlook of its governing agencies, particularly by insulating key decision-making fora from any democratic control and strengthening the executive powers of non-elected bodies such as the European Commission and the judiciary at the EU level, all at the expense of legislative forces (see Oberndorfer 2012 and in Chapter 11 in this volume; Bruff 2014; Sandbeck and Schneider 2013). Decisions take place behind closed doors involving financial and transnational industrial capital, thereby constraining the room for manoeuvre for subaltern forces. This raises doubts about how far contestation can indeed be translated into a platform for opposition to the authoritarian neoliberal restructuring.

In conclusion

The perception that the effects of free competition are inherently positive sum is a political fiction. Unleashing competitive logics as an alleged panacea for the current crisis neither substitutes nor halts the draconian cuts in public spending, nor provides an avenue to economic growth. In fact, to the contrary: intense capitalist competitive pressures can be intimately connected to overaccumulation, and be one of the root causes for capitalist crises. EU-level crisis responses now rather straightforwardly target labour markets as a way of adjustment. Through bilateral contracts with the Commission, member states are expected to follow 'beggar thy neighbour' strategies with respect to labour market policies, such as increasing flexibilization, reducing severance pay, and allowing firms to set wage levels independent of collective bargaining agreements. The competitive undercutting of labour costs and enhancing labour profitability is believed to lead to more investment in Europe, and enhance Europe's competitiveness. However, intense capitalist competition, together with imposing perma-austerity and wage repression will only exacerbate the crisis further by redistributing wealth from wage earners to the owners of capital. Moreover, capitalist competition disunites more than it unites, which puts not only domestic but also pan-European worker solidarity and a coherent left-wing response under stress. Neoliberal remedies have not generated any economic success, but are only getting further recalibrated in their most authoritarian guise, which is further weakening oppositional forces considerably. At the same time, internal devaluation through price and cost competition stands in marked contrast to indolent and mild reforms in the financial sector. The obsession with competitiveness is not only wrong, but also dangerous.

References

Almunia, J. (2012a) The Role of Competition Policy in Times of Crisis. *Speech* 12/917. 6 December. Brussels. [Online] Available from http://europa.eu/rapid/press-release_SPEECH-12-917_en.htm [Accessed 25 June 2014].

Almunia, J. (2012b) Competition Policy for Innovation and Growth: Keeping Markets Open and Efficient. *Speech* 12/172. 8 March. Copenhagen. [Online] Available from http://europa.eu/rapid/press-release_SPEECH-12-172_en.htm?locale=en [Accessed 25 June 2014].

Almunia, J. (2014) Fighting for the Single Market. *Speech* 14/119. 11 February. Brussels. [Online] Available from http://europa.eu/rapid/press-release_SPEECH-14-119_nl.htm [Accessed 25 June 2014].

Barbiero, F. and Darvas, Z. (2014) In Sickness and in Health. Protecting and Supporting Public Investment in Europe. *Bruegel Policy Contribution* 02 (February).

Bieler, A. (2012) Globalisation and European Integration. The Internal and External Dimensions of Neoliberal Restructuring. In Nousios, P., Overbeek, H. and Tsokalis, A. (eds) *Globalisation and European Integration. Critical Approaches to Regional Order and International Relations.* New York: Routledge, pp. 197–217.

Bruff, I. (2014) The Rise of Authoritarian Neoliberalism. *Rethinking Marxism* 26(1), pp. 113–129.

Buch-Hansen, H. and Wigger, A. (2011) *The Politics of European Competition Regulation. A Critical Political Economy Perspective.* New York: Routledge.

Clauwaert, S. and Schoenmann, I. (2012) The Crisis and National Labour Law Reforms: A Mapping Exercise. *ETUI Working Paper* 04.

Collignon, S. (2014) Taking European Integration Seriously. Competitiveness, Imbalances, and Economic Stability in the Euro Area. In Collignon, S. and Esposito, P. (eds) *Competitiveness in the European Economy*. London: Routledge, pp. 13–45.

Crouch, C. (2011) *The Strange Non-Death of Neoliberalism*. Cambridge: Polity Press.

ERT (2013a) ERT Meets with Merkel, Hollande and Barroso on Europe's Competitiveness. Press Release European Roundtable of Industrialists. 18 March, [Online] Available from www.european-round-table.eu/node/565 [Accessed 18 March 2014].

ERT (2013b) Letter to Herman Rompuy. 4 June. [Online] Available from www.ert.eu/sites/default/files/2013%20June%20-%20ERT%20Letter%20to%20the%20EU%20Summit%20of%2027-28%20June%202013%20-%20Signed%20letters%20to%20all_0.pdf [Accessed 4 June 2014].

ETUC (2012a) Solidarity and Fairness are a Requisite for Saving the EU. Press Release, 25 June. [Online] Available from www.etuc.org/press/solidarity-and-fairness-are-requisite-saving-eu#.U6qSkxYWGf0 [Accessed 25 June 2014].

ETUC (2012b) *A Social Compact for Europe*. 5–6 December, Brussels. [Online] Available from www.etuc.org/documents/social-compact-europe#.U6qUBRYWGf0 [Accessed 25 June 2014].

ETUC (2014) *The Functioning of the Troika. A Report from the ETUC*. Brussels. [Online] Available from www.eesc.europa.eu/resources/docs/the_functioning_of_the_troika_etuc-report–2.pdf [Accessed 25 June 2014].

EuroMemorandum (2013) *The Deepening Crisis in the European Union. The Need for a Fundamental Change*. [Online] Available from www.euromemo.eu/other_publications/7347037.html [Accessed 25 June 2014].

European Commission (2011a) The Effects of Temporary State Aid Rules Adopted in the Context of the Financial and Economic Crisis. Commission Staff Working Paper, October, Brussels.

European Commission (2011b) *Quarterly Report on the Euro Area*. 10(3). Brussels. [Online] Available from http://ec.europa.eu/economy_finance/publications/qr_euro_area/2011/pdf/qrea3_en.pdf [Accessed 25 June 2014].

European Commission (2013) *Towards a Deep and Genuine Economic and Monetary Union. The Introduction of a Convergence and Competitiveness Instrument*. COM (2013) 165 final. 20 March. Brussels. [Online] Available from http://europa.eu/rapid/press-release_IP-13-248_en.htm [Accessed 25 June 2014].

European Commission (2014) How Competition Policy is Helping Economic Recovery. [Online] Available at http://ec.europa.eu/competition/recovery [Accessed 17 December 2014].

European Union (2014) *Treaty Establishing the European Community (Consolidated Version), Rome Treaty*, 25 March 1957, Brussels. [Online] Available from http://eur-lex.europa.eu/collection/eu-law/treaties.html [Accessed 25 June 2014].

Eurostat (2014) *The EU in the World 2013. A Statistical Portrait*. Brussels: European Commission.

Group of the Progressive Alliance of Socialists and Democrats in the European Parliament (2010) *European Competition Policy. For Social Cohesion, Quality of Life and an Efficient and Dynamic Economy*. Brussels. [Online] Available from www.socialistsanddemocrats.eu/sites/default/files/1009_Comeptition_policy_EN.pdf [Accessed 25 June 2014].

Group of the Progressive Alliance of Socialists and Democrats in the European Parliament (2008) *European Competition Policy and State Aid*. Brussels. [Online]

Available from www.yumpu.com/en/document/view/4549828/european-competition-policy-group-of-the-progressive-alliance-of- [Accessed 25 June 2014].

Harvey, D. (2006) *The Limits to Capital.* New York: Verso.

Krippner, G.R. (2011) *Capitalizing on Crisis. The Political Origins of the Rise of Finance.* Cambridge, MA: Harvard University Press.

Krugman, P. (1994) Competitiveness. A Dangerous Obsession. *Foreign Affairs* 73(2), pp. 28–44.

Marx, K. (1965[1887]) *Capital Volume 1.* Moscow: Progress Publishers.

Marx, K. (1973[1939]) *Grundrisse.* London: Penguin Classics.

Marx, K. (1975[1847]) *The Poverty of Philosophy.* Moscow: Progress Publishers.

Oberndorfer, L. (2012) Vom neuen zum autoritären Konstitutionalismus. *Kurswechsel* 2, pp. 62–67.

OECD (2014) *Economic Challenges and Policy Recommendations for the Euro Area.* Paris: OECD. www.oecd.org/about/publishing/Euro_Area_Brochure.pdf

Overbeek, H. (2012) Sovereign Debt Crisis in Euroland. Root Causes and Implications for European Integration. *The International Spectator: Italian Journal of International Affairs* 47(1), pp. 30–48.Sablowski, T. (2012) The Global Economic Crisis: Impoverishing Europe. *Global Research*, 16 May.

Sandbeck, S. and Schneider, E. (2013) The Sovereign Debt Crisis to Authoritarian Statism. Contradictions of the European State Project. *New Political Economy* 19 (6). [Online] Available from www.tandfonline.com/doi/abs/10.1080/13563467.2013.861411#.U6qhohYWGfl [Accessed 25 June 2014].

Schumpeter, J.A. (1976[1943]) *Capitalism, Socialism and Democracy.* New York: Routledge.

Servan-Schreiber, J.J. (1968) *The American Challenge.* London: Hamish Hamilton.

Shutt, H. (2010) *Beyond the Profit System. Possibilities for a Post-Capitalist Era.* New York: Zed Books.

Stockhammer, E. and Onaran, O. (2012) *Wage-led Growth: Theory, Evidence, Policy.* Political Economy Research Institute, Working Paper Series. 300. November.

The Financial Times (1994) EU Industry Concerned at Competition. Round Table seeks to stop drain of jobs to US, Asia. L. Barber, 25 November, Brussels, p. 2.

UNCTAD (2000) *World Investment Report. Cross-Border Mergers and Acquisition and Development.* New York: United Nations.

Wigger, A. (2008) *Competition for Competitiveness: The Politics of Transformation of the EU Competition Regime.* Dissertation, Department of Political Science, Vrije Universiteit Amsterdam.

Wigger, A. (2012) The Political Interface of Financialisation and the Regulation of Mergers and Acquisitions in the EU. *Journal of European Integration* 34(6), pp. 623–641.

Wigger, A. and Horn, L. (2014) Uneven Development and Political Resistance against EU Austerity Politics. In Pradella, L. and Marois, T. (eds) *Polarizing Development. Alternatives to Neoliberalism and the Crisis.* London: Pluto Press, pp. 90–102.

Wigger, A. and Buch-Hansen, H. (2012) The Unfolding Contradictions of Neoliberal Competition Regulation and the Global Economic Crisis. A Missed Opportunity for Change? In Overbeek, H. and Apeldoorn, B. Van (eds) *Neoliberalism in Crisis.* Basingstoke: Palgrave McMillan, pp. 23–44.

Wigger, A. and Buch-Hansen, H. (2013) Competition, the Global Crisis and Alternatives to Neoliberal Capitalism. A Critical Engagement with Anarchism. *New Political Science: A Journal of Politics and Culture* 35(4), pp. 604–626.

8 Confronting the failure of the European Monetary Union

Heiner Flassbeck and Costas Lapavitsas

The European Economic and Monetary Union (EMU) has been in turmoil since 2010 and its ability to survive remains in doubt. This chapter draws on Keynesian and Marxist perspectives to show that the fundamental reason for the turmoil is the divergence of labour costs among member states, leading to huge gaps in competitiveness. Above all, Germany has suppressed labour costs, gaining a competitive advantage over other EMU members that has allowed it to emerge as the main creditor and effective leader of the union. Austerity-based policies have not repaired the fundamental defect of the EMU, while plunging Europe into recession. For peripheral countries, but also countries of the core, including France, the EMU has become a trap.

At the root of the failure of the euro lie relations of capital and labour, particularly the retreat of labour in Germany since the end of the 1990s. The monetary union began with high hopes of cooperation and harmony in Europe, but the common currency has favoured capital against labour, increasing national frictions and facilitating German ascendancy. The main beneficiaries of the EMU have been exporters and large banks in Germany, while the losers have included working people and peripheral countries in general. Currently, peripheral countries are left with little option but to consider abandoning the EMU. It is important, therefore, to introduce orderly exit procedures that would minimize the cost of dismantling the failed monetary union, while opening fresh paths for social development and preventing friction among European nations. The interests of working people in core countries, furthermore, would be better served by a system of flexible but managed exchange rates. The longer the EMU perseveres in its current framework, the graver will be the danger of social and political catastrophe in Europe.

Was the euro primarily a 'political' project?

Contrary to what is frequently asserted, the euro was an economic, and not simply a political, project. Monetary cooperation in Europe started in the early 1970s after the collapse of the Bretton Woods system. The advantages of freely floating exchange rates, with putative monetary independence, were far from obvious, particularly for small open economies. As has been frequently shown, uncontrolled foreign exchange markets tend to over- or undershoot presumed equilibrium values (UNCTAD 2010). Even worse, market-determined exchange rates often move in the wrong direction for lengthy periods of time as a result of currency speculation. Countries with relatively high rates of inflation and thus relatively high interest rates tend to be swamped by inflows of short-term funds which drive up the domestic currency in real terms. In these circumstances, monetary authorities have to react to the vagaries of currency markets, and the formal freedom of a central bank from intervention has no meaning.

Countries that are not willing to leave the determination of the exchange rate to the whims of the markets are led to cooperate. Moreover, in the absence of cooperation, conflict is unavoidable as a change in one country's exchange rate always affects another. European monetary cooperation evolved in rather small steps for three decades before culminating in full monetary union in 1999. The move towards monetary union resulted from the experience of cooperation, and in particular from the requirement that the currency of one country should serve as anchor for the system as a whole.

The need for an anchor arises from the profound asymmetry between depreciation and appreciation. In a country trying to avoid (or stop) currency depreciation, the central bank must sell international reserves to increase demand for the domestic currency. Since reserves are always limited, small open economies are vulnerable to speculative currency attacks. In contrast, in a country facing appreciation the central bank could intervene by selling the domestic currency, which is potentially available in unlimited amounts. Hence an effective way to fend off speculation would be to have cooperation among countries with depreciating and appreciating currencies. The anchor of the system would be provided by one country with embedded current account surpluses and hence under pressure to appreciate. By the same token, the anchor country would tend to have lower inflation than the rest, thus avoiding depreciation pressures.

The obvious difficulty with such a system is that the monetary policy of the anchor country might not necessarily be the optimal policy for the group, even if it was ideal for the anchor country itself, and even if there was agreement on inflation targets across the group. This was the main problem of the Bretton Woods system in the 1950s and 1960s, when the US dollar served as the anchor currency. Decision-making by the US Federal Reserve System tended to take into account mostly the conditions of the US economy, rather than the requirements of the system as a whole.

The European Monetary System (EMS) was a system of adjustable exchange rates that preceded the EMU, and the country that would act as its anchor was obviously Germany. Consistently lower inflation in Germany meant that the Deutsche Mark never came under depreciation pressure, but rather tended to appreciate. By and large, Germany accepted its role as the de facto anchor of the EMS, but there is no evidence that German decision-making on monetary policy, including the setting of interest rates, actively considered the requirements of the system as a whole. Thus, as long as regional monetary cooperation remained the objective in Europe, it was logical that there would emerge a tendency to form a monetary union. In the 1990s, forming a monetary union seemed an equitable as well as economically sensible form of integration. If there was a genuinely multilateral union, all countries could participate on an equal basis to forming monetary policy, while taking into account the requirements of the group as a whole. The creation of the EMU had an economic logic and did not simply reflect a political wish to promote 'European unity'.

From a global perspective, the EMU offered its member states an enormous degree of freedom vis-à-vis the rest of the world as well as towards the international financial markets and the international multilateral organizations. For a lengthy period of time the EMU was able to prevent strong external shocks, and no single country had to take emergency measures to overcome problems of exchange rate misalignment or lack of international liquidity. However, the EMU also had profound social and economic implications for Europe that eventually resulted in a deep crisis.

The international and the domestic roles of the euro

Note first that the EMU is an unusual monetary union created as a Treaty-based alliance among sovereign states. On the one hand, the euro is an international form of money intended to be used by EMU enterprises and states in global transactions. Moreover, because of the weight of EMU countries in the world market, the euro naturally competes with the dollar as international reserve currency and means of payment deployed by third parties. On the other hand, the euro is the national domestic standard of all member states and thus, *de facto*, the national monetary standard of the entire EMU. There was no overriding need for the euro to have had both an international and a domestic role, and the combination of the two has resulted in extraordinary tensions.

Some clarity on this issue can be gained by deploying Marx's (1976 [1867]: 240–244) concept of 'world money'. The origins of this idea go back to the Mercantilists who, unlike the classical and neoclassical economists, never treated money as a mere 'veil' on real economic activity. Rather, money encapsulates the ability to pay as well as crystallizing wealth, and hence managing money becomes critical in a monetary crisis, a point that Keynes (1936: ch. 23) also came to appreciate. Liquidity preference and the handling of money by the state, both of which are key Keynesian ideas, have a Mercantilist flavour. For Marx, world money is the organizing element of the world market, where it acts as generally accepted international reserve of value but also as means of payment and value transfer among states and enterprises (Lapavitsas 2013). The world market lacks a homogeneous institutional and legal framework, and thus access to world money is vital to both enterprises and states participating in international transactions. In times of international crisis, possessing reserves of world money is critical to confronting contractions of economic activity.

The development of the world market during the last century can be seen as a process of transformation of world money. The traditional form of world money has been gold, and nations participating in the world market have had to keep gold reserves for payments and value transfers. The dominant countries of the world market since the early days of international capitalism have typically kept the most substantial hoards of gold. However, the twentieth century has been marked by the marginalization of gold, and a shift toward managed forms of world money.

The Bretton Woods system fixed the US dollar as the dominant form of world money in the post-war period. The US dollar is a form of domestic credit money – ultimately resting on government fiat – which acted as world money while being converted into gold at a fixed rate, even if only in inter-state transactions. Convertibility into gold allowed for fixed exchange rates, and thereby for imposing tough controls on interest rates, capital flows and the functional specialization of financial institutions across the world. The Bretton Woods system was the cornerstone of controlled finance in the post-war years, and supported US hegemony by allowing the dollar to function as world money. It collapsed in 1971–1973 essentially because the USA refused to operate its monetary policy in line with the requirements of the system as a whole, and eventually reneged on its promise to keep the dollar convertible into gold. Nonetheless, the USA still contrived to keep the dollar as world money, even if on a different basis.

Since the end of the Bretton Woods system the world market has entered a historically unprecedented period in which the dollar has continued to act as the main form of world money, but without being compulsorily convertible into anything containing value. The international functioning of the dollar as reserve currency and means of payment has been underpinned simply by the domestic fiat and the international power of the US government. In addition, the dollar has been supported by customary acceptance and practical attachment of other nations to its international functioning. Fixing exchange rates among the major trading currencies has consequently become much more difficult, while interest rate controls, capital controls and functional regulation over finance have been rendered more complex.

The functioning of world money has become contested terrain among the leading countries in the world market, since success in transforming a domestic currency into a form of world money offers considerable advantages. First, it loosens constraints on monetary policy; if the domestic currency could be used to pay abroad, the central bank would face no overwhelming external pressure to raise interest rates and to adjust monetary policy in case of a current account deficit. Second, it removes the need to hold substantial reserves of means of payment which typically earn very low returns. Third, it imposes on others the need to hold reserves of the currency, a task that in recent years has been relegated overwhelmingly to China, Japan and developing countries. Given that reserves pay very low returns, the issuing country effectively receives a tribute from those who use its money as reserve. This is an unprecedented development in the history of capitalism since the dominant countries in the world market have historically had to keep gold reserves, and thus to bear the costs of keeping money capital in idle form. Under current conditions, the costs of holding reserves have been shifted onto other countries, while the issuers of world money receive a return. Fourth, issuing world money affords enormous political power as it offers the means of intervention in inter-state affairs.

The euro is a peculiar competitor to the dollar since it has been created *ex nihilo* rather than being an already-existing domestic money that was transformed into world money. Indeed, the domestic role of the euro has been manufactured with considerable institutional difficulty, and has never managed to be fully compatible with its world role. The international functioning of the euro, moreover, has been influenced by the interests of large European exporting capital plus the large European banks that have deployed the euro to facilitate global expansion. There is no comparison between the euro and the dollar in these respects. The dollar is the incumbent form of world money, supported by the institutions and the customary practices of several international markets. In contrast, the euro has had to earn the trust and acceptability of participants in the world market. The task was made easier because the euro has inherited some of the international mantle of the Deutsche Mark. Nonetheless, securing the international role of the euro and making it compatible with its domestic functioning have been major problems for the EMU.

The institutional machinery to achieve these aims includes, above all, the European Central Bank (ECB) created to operate monetary policy independently of national governments (Lapavitsas *et al.* 2012: Parts I and II). The ECB presides over a homogeneous inter-bank market in which all member-state banks can obtain liquidity on formally equal terms. The explicit mandate of the ECB is to maintain price stability within the EMU, keeping inflation at slightly below 2%, and thus ensuring the acceptability of the euro globally and against the dollar. In addition, the institutional framework of the euro has included mechanisms to ensure fiscal discipline, thus further supporting the international acceptability of the euro. The main vehicle has been the Growth and Stability Pact, imposing on member states the arbitrary limits of 3% of GDP for budget deficits and 60% of GDP for the national debt. However, responsibility for hitting these targets was left to individual states, thus creating a source of friction for the EMU as a whole.

In short, on the one hand the institutional machinery of the EMU has focused heavily on monetary and fiscal issues aiming primarily to ensure the international acceptability of the euro. On the other hand, adjustment of labour costs – thus the management of competitiveness within the EMU as a whole – was left mostly to national institutions. In other words, the domestic function of the euro in the labour market was left largely to the discretion of each member state. This was a decisive flaw of EMU since capital–labour relations differ profoundly among member states, as do the historical, institutional and cultural characteristics of the labour market in each country. Not surprisingly, systematic divergences emerged among member states with regard to unit labour costs, and thus with regard to inflation and competitiveness. The result has been disruption of the international functioning of the euro.

One final point to mention is that command over world money is a measure of political power across the world which, in the case of the euro, means German international power (see also Cafruny, Chapter 4 in this volume). It ought to be stressed that the EMU was not originally a plan to promote German ascendancy, but rather a formal, treaty-based alliance establishing rights and obligations for member states, and relying strongly on the ideology of Europeanism (Carchedi 2001). Nonetheless, for reasons that are made clear in the following sections, the euro has rebounded strongly in favour of Germany, which has emerged as the country able to set economic and social policy across Europe. However, given that the clash between the international and the domestic functioning of the euro has not been resolved, Germany's preeminence remains extremely fragile.

The importance of controlling inflation and nominal unit labour costs

The main requirement for avoiding a clash between the international and the domestic functions of the euro is to achieve convergence of inflation rates. Systematic divergences of competitiveness within the EMU could then be avoided, and the international acceptability of the euro would have a clear and predictable foundation. The importance of inflation convergence did not escape the ECB, which set the target at slightly below 2%. However, for the ECB, the sole means of achieving the target was monetary policy, and this meant controlling the money supply and/or changing the rate of interest according to circumstances. The element that was consistently ignored was the high and stable correlation between growth of nominal unit labour costs (ULC) and the inflation rate.

The cost of labour is a vital component of the total cost of production for the economy as a whole, since in a vertically integrated production process not only final consumer goods but also intermediate and capital goods are produced by employing labour. In empirical terms, nominal unit labour costs are the best instrument for forecasting and controlling inflation, as Figure 8.1 shows.

It is a practical rule of thumb in policy making that the difference of the actual (p^a) from the target (p^*) rate of inflation is equal to the difference between nominal wage growth (w) and the sum of national productivity growth (pr) plus the inflation target (p^*), i.e.,

$$pa - p^* = w - (pr + p^*) \qquad (1)$$

For the EMU to function sustainably, the rate of growth of wages in each member country should not exceed the rate of growth of productivity plus the inflation target (see also Niechoj, Chapter 9 in this volume). If this rule was

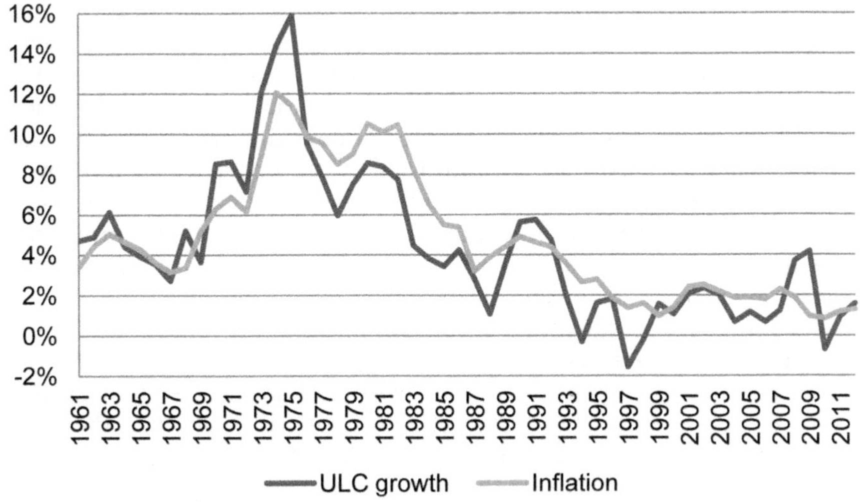

Figure 8.1 ULC[1] growth rates and inflation for EMU[2]
2 12 countries: Belgium, Germany, Finland, France, Greece, Ireland, Italy, Luxembourg, Netherlands, Austria, Portugal, Spain
AMECO database (as per November 2012); own calculations

applied systematically over the medium- and long-term, ULC growth and national inflation rates would converge towards the inflation target. Real wages would rise in line with national productivity and there would not be significant divergences in national competitiveness. The rule implies that, in real terms, each member country would avoid both 'living above its means' and 'living below its means'. This would provide a basis for the domestic and the international functioning of the euro to become compatible with each other.

Applying the rule would have the further merit of stabilizing domestic demand since real wage growth is the most important determinant of domestic consumption growth. If nominal wages were adjusted at a rate equivalent to national productivity growth plus the inflation target, domestic demand would expand sufficiently in each country (and in the union as a whole) to compensate for the possible negative impact of new technology on employment. Moreover, to counteract unexpected and unpredictable cyclical changes in productivity it would be preferable to adjust nominal wages to the trend growth of productivity for short periods of time. By taking into account the inflation target (rather than the actual rate of inflation) the growth of wages and demand would be stabilized, thus preventing short-term and one-off price shocks from having a lasting inflationary impact, as they would have if they were passed immediately into wage settlements.

If the rule was followed, it would be possible for national economies but also for the EMU as a whole to move along a stable growth path, led by the growth of private consumption based on positive income expectations of households (at least as long as productivity growth could be expected to remain positive). External trade could also be balanced because, if ULC moved in line with the inflation target in all countries irrespective of national productivity paths, real exchange rates and competitiveness would be stable. Finally, stabilizing real wage growth in line with productivity growth would imply rejecting the neoliberal insistence on flexible and readily adjustable wages. There would be no need to make real wages lag behind productivity growth presumably to cure unemployment, if there was stable growth of domestic income and competitiveness.

It is also worth stressing that differences in either the level of wealth or in real wages would not necessarily preclude formation of a monetary union between a poor and a rich country. In any country the claims of all groups of economic agents must obey a budget constraint with respect to the overall income produced: no country can consume more than it produces in the long-term, and hence the claims of different groups, including workers, must be balanced out against each other at a given level of total income. If the customary balancing of claims was disrupted, there would be severe conflict over income distribution and the result would probably be a bout (or even a spiral) of inflation. However, if the rule of nominal wage growth was applied, wages would be in accord with national productivity: low wages in the poorer countries would reflect low productivity, and high wages in richer countries would reflect high productivity. Unit labour costs would not diverge systematically between a poor and a rich country, if both avoided bouts of inflation arising out of distributional conflicts. Consequently, there would be no risk of sustained trade imbalances as long as the structure of trade and the structure of products available to both countries displayed a degree of overlapping.

The euro malfunctions domestically and internationally

The institutions of the EMU have, from its inception, focused on maintaining fiscal discipline, aiming to keep public sector deficits at or below 3% and the national debt at or below 60% of GDP; at the same time, they have paid no attention to the link between nominal unit labour costs and inflation. No direct relationship has ever been demonstrated between fiscal discipline and an inflation target, and all postulated indirect links have been very weak. Above all, there is no evidence that either the current budget deficit or the size of the public debt has a significant impact on the inflationary performance of an economy (see Sill 2005). Thus, by ignoring the path of nominal unit labour costs, or rather by entrusting it to relations among capital, labour and the state in each member state, the EMU has sown the seeds of its structural crisis.

The main cause of the malfunctioning of the EMU has been the domestic wage policy of Germany. As the monetary union began to take shape, the German government started to put pressure on labour unions to restrict the growth of nominal and real wages, presumably to confront unemployment. In the tripartite agreement of 1999 labour union leaders agreed to abandon the formula hitherto deployed to determine wage growth by guaranteeing a share of productivity gains for workers. Instead, complying with neoliberal logic, the unions agreed to 'reserve productivity growth for employment' (Flassbeck 1997; Flassbeck and Spiecker 2005). This agreement meant a fundamental break with the tradition of German economic policy to target a low and stable inflation rate. Historically, Germany had been characterized by moderate wage settlements aiming to keep increases in real wages (nominal wages adjusted for inflation) in line with increases in productivity (GDP divided by the number of hours worked). The implications of abandoning this practice attracted very little attention in the triumphant neoliberal atmosphere of the late 1990s.

The new German approach to the labour market meant that nominal unit labour costs remained flat throughout 1999–2008, and thus Germany systematically undershot the ECB inflation target. In peripheral Europe, in contrast, growth in nominal wages exceeded the sum of national productivity growth and the EMU inflation target by a small and rather stable margin. The result was the gradual emergence of huge divergences in unit labour costs among EMU countries. France was the only country to have generated a path of nominal wage growth in line with national productivity performance and the inflation target. This is shown in Figure 8.2, which traces the path of ULC from the inception of the euro, and establishing the systematic undershooting of the inflation target by Germany.

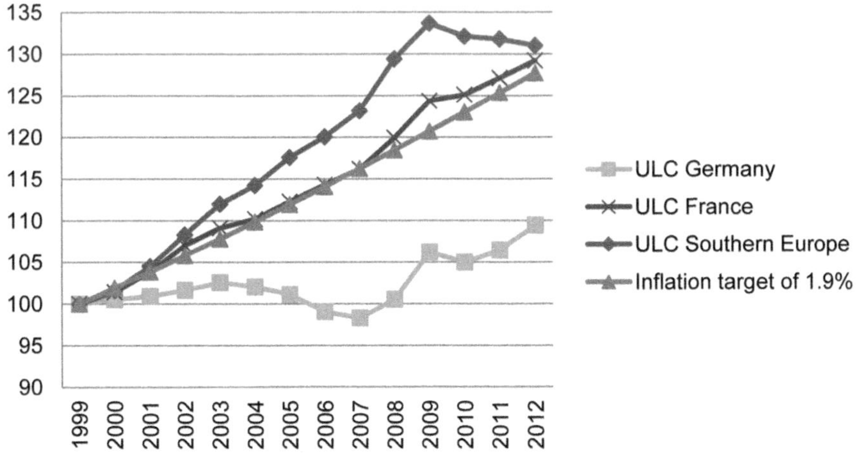

Figure 8.2 ULC[1] in Germany, France and Peripheral Europe[2] (1999 = 100)
2 Spain, Italy, Greece and Portugal
AMECO database (as per November 2012); own calculations

The cumulative effect of ULC divergences has been dramatic and equivalent to a substantial depreciation of the implicit real exchange rate of Germany. A huge gap in competitiveness has emerged to give Germany an absolute advantage in international trade, and allowing it to undersell competitors within the EMU without loss of profit margin for German producers. If peripheral Europe has been 'living above its means' during this period, Germany has also been 'living below its means'. The impact on international transactions within the EMU has been enormous: German current account surpluses grew persistently, while peripheral Europe registered large deficits; France has also been registering widening current account deficits, as is shown in Figure 8.3. These imbalances are a new phenomenon in Europe, since trade relations were broadly balanced at the beginning of the currency union and for many years before. Even after the devastating shock of the global crisis of 2007–2009, the trend towards large German surpluses has persevered.

A persistent absolute advantage of one country (or a group of countries) against a similar country (or group of countries) is clearly unsustainable other than in the short-term. The reason is that persistent current account deficits imply the accumulation of external debts, which must inevitably be financed by the surplus country. The origin of the debt problem of peripheral Europe can thus be seen in Figures 8.2 and 8.3.

For a deficit country it is vital to eliminate both the gap in competitiveness and the resulting imbalances on current account, if lenders are to be convinced that it will repay its debts in the future. The final repayment of any

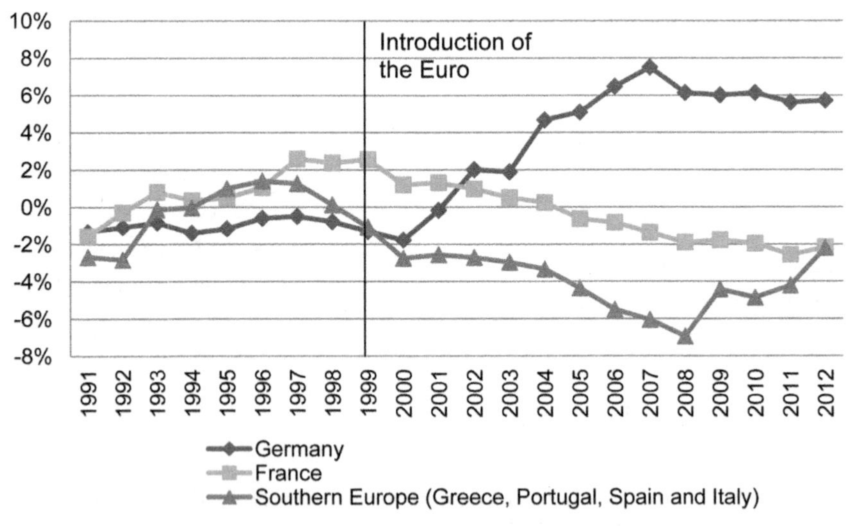

Figure 8.3 EMU current account balances as percentage of GDP
Note: Negative values represent a current account deficit
AMECO database (as per November 2012); own calculations

international debt is, of course, payment in kind; thus, it is necessary for the debtor country eventually to run a current account surplus, while the creditor country must run a deficit (Keynes 1929). It follows that the European periphery would be able to service and repay its debts only if it produced current account surpluses by restoring its competitiveness, either through wage adjustments or through changes in exchange rates.

The imperative of adjustment at the core

The approach chosen by the EU to deal with the crisis – discussed in further detail in sections VII and XII – essentially amounts to improving international competitiveness in the periphery by cutting, or moderating, wages. This policy, sometimes erroneously called ‘internal devaluation’, and amounting to downward adjustment of inflation, is worse than pointless. Domestic demand in these countries is normally more important than external demand, and wage cuts have backfired badly by reducing domestic demand. Furthermore, the strategy of emulating Germany means that peripheral countries would have to go through an extended period of catching-up in competitiveness. Yet, there would still be no prospect of achieving large current account surpluses over an extended period of time, or of significantly raising export share in GDP. The reason is that to reap these benefits peripheral countries would have to develop a lasting absolute advantage compared to Germany. As Figure 8.4 shows, they would have to drop below the German ULC for a sustained period of time if they are to reverse the impact of the current

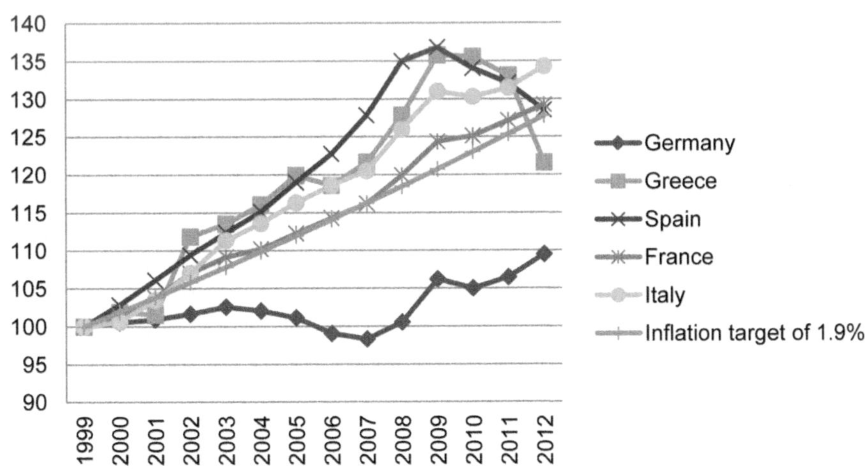

Figure 8.4 ULC[1] from 1999 to 2012 for selected EMU countries (1999 = 100)
Note: 1 ULC defined as gross income per capita in ECU/Euro of dependent employees divided by real GDP per total employed persons
AMECO database (as per November 2012); own calculations

account deficits registered in the first ten years of EMU. Democratic countries can hardly sustain five to ten years of falling living standards and rising unemployment. In practice, the EMU has become a trap for peripheral countries.

This is why the adjustment process has to be symmetric at the very least. This means that the country whose exchange rate is implicitly undervalued has to undertake an upward adjustment, i.e. have faster wage increases, as deficit countries undertake a downward adjustment. The most reliable yardstick for the success of the adjustment efforts on both sides is the inflation target. To restore the international competitiveness of deficit countries, it would be necessary to have a rise of ULC and inflation in the surplus country up to the point where external balance would be achieved on both sides over the entire life of the monetary union (the first ten years included). This would necessarily be a slow and highly unstable process.

Austerity and the tough choices ahead

In 2010, after the crisis had emerged fully, the so-called Troika of the EU, the ECB and the International Monetary Fund (IMF) formulated adjustment programmes based on austerity and comprising two main elements: fiscal adjustment and 'structural reforms'. The programmes reflected the German belief that 'austerity is the only solution'[1] and were to be imposed on all countries requesting financial support when access to international capital markets ceased, or was blocked *de facto* by very high interest rates. The Troika has been obsessed with the apparent fiscal problems of the periphery of the Eurozone, and thus insisted countries receiving financial support should consolidate public budgets at any cost and as quickly as possible.

The programmes have produced complex and on the whole negative results. The Troika focus on fiscal adjustment has implied cuts in government spending and higher tax rates, which in an environment of already weak aggregate demand have worsened the economic outlook still further. The ensuing contraction of output has typically brought further difficulties in collecting tax revenues, while public expenditure has been pushed up by payments of social security and unemployment benefits. To be sure, by 2012 the financial markets had been partly stabilized thanks to the liquidity interventions of the ECB that brought interest rates down. Yet, the fire was merely placed under control rather than being extinguished, since the banking system of Europe continued to weaken and fragment, while uncertainty about the future of the Eurozone remained high (Lapavitsas and Lindo 2014)

In 2013 the rate of unemployment in the EU stood at about 11%, and in some southern European countries total unemployment exceeded 25%, while youth unemployment even approached 60% (European Commission 2013). More than anything else, these figures reflected the failure of austerity-based adjustment programmes, which deprived the debtor countries of the Eurozone of the means of fighting recession and indeed imposed pro-cyclical policies on a scale last seen in the 1930s. It is wishful thinking to expect the contraction induced by the fiscal stance to be offset by a positive reaction by the private sector, giving rise to so-called 'non-Keynesian' effects. Cuts in public expenditure at a time of high uncertainty among firms about demand and high uncertainty among households about income generally lead the private sector to reduce spending, and the result is to increase uncertainty even further. To assume that households have perfect foresight about both future income streams and tax burdens, and would thus raise consumption in the expectation of falls in future taxes, is merely to wish the problem away. In practice, heightened uncertainty in the private sector makes it necessary for the governments to spend *more*, or to *reduce* taxes, in order to change perceptions in the private sector and to encourage higher private consumption and investment.

'Structural reforms', on the other hand, effectively mean labour market reforms or, in plain language, wage cuts and a worsening of the conditions of labour. For the German policy establishment the way out of the crisis consisted in improving the competitiveness of all Eurozone countries, which implies copying the German attitude toward labour costs. This approach is bound to fail, while causing large social disruption across the Eurozone. Summarily put, lowering wage growth would restore competitiveness in the periphery very slowly as long as Germany continued to keep its own wage growth low. Even worse in the short run, a simultaneous lowering of wages across several countries would lead to a drop in domestic demand, which in all European countries is by far the largest component of total demand. Therefore, unemployment would probably rise further, while trade flows within the EMU would decline.

The Troika's policies of fiscal austerity and wage reductions, leading to falls in unit labour costs, have contributed to the deepening of the crisis after 2010, and the worst outcome, by far, has obtained in Greece. The country has brought down its unit labour costs more violently than any other Eurozone member, thus entering a depression leading to a cumulative reduction of its GDP of about 25% during 2008–2013 (El.Stat. 2014). Despite these 'achievements', Greek international competitiveness would still not have reached a level sufficient to allow the country to reap benefits in terms of sustained increases in exports, as was shown in Figure 8.4.

Finally, if France and Italy were to pursue an adjustment path similar to that of peripheral countries, the result would probably be a depression accompanied by deep and long-lasting deflation across the Eurozone. It is likely that social and political upheaval would follow, as well as a shift in public opinion against the monetary union and against the notion of European integration more generally. If France and Italy did not pursue adjustment along the lines of Troika programmes, they would continue to lose competitiveness, thus making it impossible to rebalance their external trade. The depth of the structural problems of the EMU and the absurdity of austerity-based adjustment programmes is vividly apparent in the impossible dilemma faced by these large countries.

Conclusion: Towards an orderly exit procedure

In view of the preceding analysis, it is apparent that a general solution for the Eurozone crisis could arise if there was an international cooperative effort including major adjustment in the surplus countries, especially Germany. Such an approach would allow for the international and the domestic role of the euro to become more easily compatible with each other. For that, however, the national hierarchies and relations of power within the Eurozone would need to be overcome or sidelined, and there is no evidence that this is a feasible prospect within the EU. Indeed, Germany is extremely unwilling to alter the fundamentals of its economic policy, which have ensured its dominance in export markets (see also Cafruny, Chapter 4 in this volume). Moreover, given the dysfunctional nature of the adjustment programmes imposed on peripheral economies, it is no surprise that the cost of remaining within the EMU has escalated rapidly, while the benefits of membership have shrunk relentlessly.

Some light on the difficult choice faced by peripheral countries was shed by the 'rescue' of Cyprus in March–April 2013. Cyprus was the first country to be detached from the generally agreed convertibility of money within the Eurozone, since the Cypriot authorities imposed restrictions on the movements of capital at the behest of the Troika. In effect, the currency union has ceased to exist as an integral entity since one of its constituent parts has not been able fully to honour its monetary obligations. Moreover, the adjustment programme delivered an overwhelming shock to Cyprus virtually overnight, destroying the service sector on which the economy has been based. Deep concerns have emerged regarding the future of Cyprus inside the Eurozone, and it became feasible openly to consider exiting the monetary union.

Furthermore, in the course of the negotiations the ECB forced the Cyprus government to accept the conditionality demanded by the EU, at the threat of withholding liquidity to the country's most vulnerable banks. This was a grave violation of the putative role of the ECB in the EMU, which is supposed to act as the central bank of all member states and which is certainly not meant to blackmail governments. The conditionality attached to adjustment programmes is a political issue dealt with through negotiations among (at least formally) sovereign states. In contrast, liquidity provision by the central bank is supposed to be an entirely economic matter. If bank regulators considered that the business model of an individual bank was no longer viable, the bank should be wound down in an orderly manner and depositors should be protected, as laid down in EU rules and regulations.

However, in the case of Cyprus, the business model of its major banks became the subject of government negotiations, and the ECB sided with the governments of core countries by putting unbearable liquidity pressure on the Cypriot government in order to force rapid restructuring. Even worse, the ECB was prepared to countenance losses for depositors in Cypriot banks, including those covered by law (Lindo 2014). Its intervention reflected the hierarchical nature of the EMU, creating a bad precedent that has damaged the confidence of depositors in the common currency. Equal treatment of all those who hold bank liabilities across the monetary union is a precondition for a functioning monetary order, and it has been badly violated. Cyprus and other countries for which the economic costs of membership are increasing while the benefits are shrinking have been forced to consider the exit option. There is, however, no easy way out of a currency union such as the EMU. To devalue a currency that is already in circulation and to break its fixed convertibility to another currency, as in Argentina in 2002, is straightforward compared to the logistical and political difficulties of introducing a new currency.

By far the biggest problem would be to prepare the population psychologically. It would be extremely difficult to keep such an important step secret, or to execute it overnight, even if some actions would have to take place quickly. The fear of losing part of or all savings would induce depositors to withdraw deposits from domestic banks, with the result of inducing a bank run that would threaten collapse of the banking system. Consequently, it would be necessary immediately to impose severe administrative controls on banks as well as controls on capital flows. In the case of Cyprus, however, the Troika has already imposed enormous losses on depositors as well as restricting banking transactions and capital flows. Much of the spadework of preparing for exit has already been accomplished (Cutillas, Lapavitsas and Munevar 2014).

In addition to banking problems, exiting the euro would also create difficulties for monetary circulation. Electronic money could be converted rapidly, depending on the law governing particular contracts, but banknotes would take time to print. It would probably be necessary for the state to print fiat money with local circulation – including small denomination bonds of various descriptions, often issued by local authorities, that would have a local circulation – to meet the needs of liquidity until the new currency would be firmly in place. For some time there would be monetary turbulence and parallel systems of pricing in operation.

The most complex technical problem of exit, however, would be finding a viable new foreign exchange regime. The new currency could be introduced at an administrative rate of 1:1 to the euro, but it would then obviously depreciate rapidly in the foreign exchange markets. For a small country with a high import share in GDP, the magnitude of the devaluation would be crucial. If the rate was left entirely to the market, there would be a significant risk of a fall that would go far beyond what would be warranted to restore the country's competitiveness. A very deep devaluation would profoundly disturb the ability to import, thus raising the spectre of having to call upon the IMF shortly after the Troika would have left the country. To preclude this outcome, it would be worth even considering a safety net provided by other EU countries.

It is important to stress that countries considering exit from the monetary union would think twice before also exiting the EU, since the common market guarantees important access to export markets (at least, once competitiveness is restored). Moreover, the EU could easily provide a safety net for countries considering exit, even by reviving aspects of the EMS that preceded the EMU, and which still exists formally. A new EMS could allow countries to peg their new currency at a reasonable rate to the euro, thus reducing the risk of becoming a punching ball in the international financial markets. Such an 'orderly exit' would avoid a falling out among European nations, without keeping countries in the straitjacket of EMU.

The fundamental point, nevertheless, is that Europe should acknowledge the failure of the currency union. The notion that there might be political unification that would in effect transform the euro into proper domestic money is not realistic, for the simple reason that a European 'demos' capable of providing legitimacy to domestic money simply does not exist. And nor is a system of fiscal transfers feasible, or even desirable, among independent and sovereign nations. Its implication would be that Germany would be transferring money to its neighbours to enable them to buy its products, and would thus be able to dictate the conditions of everyday life in Europe.

At the core of EMU failure lies German economic policy as well as the inability of other European countries to force Germany to follow an alternative path. It is imperative to stress that a currency union is not a necessary part of the institutional arrangements that would allow the nations of Europe to coexist without friction and social destruction. Given the experience of the EMU, national currencies would allow countries to use devaluation as an instrument of economic policy, thus fending off attempts by one country economically to dominate the others. Historically, devaluation has been the most frequently used mechanism to respond to an aggressive trading partner without engaging in outright protectionism. A system of orderly management of exchange rates would be the best option for Europe to avoid a general economic disaster that would lead to renewed national friction. Ridding the continent of the straitjacket of the EMU might also open new possibilities for social progress in both the periphery and the core.

Note

1 As Wolfgang Schäuble, the German Finance Minister, declared to the *Financial Times* on 5 September 2011.

References

Carchedi, G. (2001) *For Another Europe: A Class Analysis of European Economic Integration*. London and New York: Verso.

Cutillas, S., Lapavitsas, C. and Munevar, D. (2014) *Capital Controls: A Practical Guide*. RMF Occasional Policy Paper 8. [Online] Available from www.researchonmoneyandfinance.org/imagjunees/occasional_policy_papers/RMF-OPP-8-Cutillas-Lapavitsas-Munevar.pdf [Accessed 27 June 2014].

El.Stat. (2013) *Quarterly National Accounts.* Q4m. [Online] Available from www.statistics.gr/portal/page/portal/ESYE/BUCKET/A0704/PressReleases/A0704_SEL84_DT_QQ_04_2013_01_P_GR.pdf [Accessed 27 June 2014].

European Commission (2013) *Draft Joint Employment Report.* COM(2013) 801 final. [Online] Available from http://ec.europa.eu/europe2020/pdf/2014/jer2014_en.pdf [Accessed 27 June 2014].

Flassbeck, H. (1997) Und die Spielregeln für die Lohnpolitik in einer Währungsunion? *Frankfurter Rundschau*, 31 Oktober 1997, p. 12.

Flassbeck, H. and Spiecker, F. (2005) Die deutsche Lohnpolitik sprengt die Europäische Währungsunion. *WSI-Mitteilungen* 58(12), pp. 707–713.

Keynes, J.M. (1929) The German Transfer Problem. *Economic Journal* 39, pp. 1–7.

Keynes, J.M. (1936) The General Theory of Employment, Interest and Money. In *The Collected Writings of John Maynard Keynes, Volume VII.* London and Basingstoke: Macmillan.

Lapavitsas, C. (2013) The Eurozone Crisis through the Prism of World Money. In Wolfson, M. and Epstein, J. (eds) *The Handbook of the Political Economy of Financial Crises.* Oxford and New York: Oxford University Press, pp. 378–394.

Lapavitsas, C. *et al.* (2012) *Crisis in the Eurozone.* London: Verso.

Lapavitsas, C. and Lindo, D. (2014) *The 'Draghi Effect' on Eurozone Banks: Shrinkage and National Fragmentation.* RMF Occasional Policy Paper 6. [Online] Available from www.researchonmoneyandfinance.org/images/occasional_policy_papers/RMF-OPP-6-Lapavitsas-Lindo.pdf [Accessed 27 June 2014].

Lindo, D. (2014) *Banking in Cyprus: A Crisis Made in the Eurozone.* RMF Occasional Policy Paper 1. [Online] Available from www.researchonmoneyandfinance.org/images/occasional_policy_papers/RMF-OPP-1-Lindo.pdf [Accessed 27 June 2014].

Marx, K. (1976 [1867]) *Capital.* Vol. I. London: Penguin/NLR.

Sill, K. (2005) Do Budget Deficits Cause Inflation? *Business Review.* [Online] Philadelphia Federal Reserve Bank. Q3, pp. 26–33. Available from https://philadelphiafed.org/research-and-data/publications/business-review/2005/q3/Q3_05_Sill.pdf [Accessed 27 June 2014].

UNCTAD (2010) *Trade and Development Report.* New York and Geneva: United Nations.

Part III

Possible futures

9 Which future for Europe?

A scenario analysis of European integration

Torsten Niechoj

Today, the idea of a 'United States of Europe' is no longer an attractive option for most European populations. As the European Commission's Eurobarometer of December 2013 shows, there has been a clear downward trend in the positive and a clear upward trend in the negative image of the European Union (EU) since 2010 (European Commission 2013: 6). Similarly, pessimism on the future of Europe rose significantly in 2010 and again in 2011 (European Commission 2013: 9). The impact of the financial market crisis and the following sovereign debt crisis have left their marks (see also Bieling, Chapter 6 in this volume).

The past was characterized by an increase in European integration, namely the single market, the monetary union and the Eastern enlargement. This evolution of the EU was not always a continuous and smooth process, but nevertheless one without major steps backwards concerning the degree of integration. This is no longer guaranteed. Currently, i.e. in the beginning of 2014, many issues within the euro are not settled which affect the whole European project of an economic and political union. Public debt is high in all member states, unemployment rates are enormous in some countries, gross domestic product (GDP) is still declining in several countries and the regulation of the financial sector is a rather slow progress. A country's exit from the euro area or a split-up of the area is still not out of question. Paradoxically, even mastering the current challenges of the euro area might lead to political tensions within the EU. The sovereign debt crisis has led to a two-speed Europe with an extension of integration within the euro area. It was pushed forward by pure necessity rather than being the outcome of well-prepared and acclaimed decision processes coordinated with the other member states of the EU. As a result, we see more integration, i.e. fiscal coordination, pacts and agreements and a strengthened role for the European Central Bank (ECB), within the euro area. But this does not hold for the rest of the EU, where the level of integration stays the same. So the flip-side of this is a widening institutional and maybe even mental gap between members and non-members of the monetary union. It seems that a division between core and periphery, i.e. between an increase in economic and political integration within the euro area and a lack of integration into the rest of the EU, is taking place.

Crucial for both, the sovereign debt crisis and the emergence of a two-speed Europe, was the introduction of the monetary union, initiated and prepared by the Maastricht Treaty. With the euro, an important adjustment mechanism for economic shocks has been eliminated. There are no longer national currencies that can depreciate or appreciate in order to restore price competitiveness. Moreover, a single interest rate is set by the ECB for all member states of the euro area. The same nominal interest rate has diverging effects on the member states of the euro area due to differences in the national inflation rates and different business cycles within the countries. The euro is also the currency in which all debt is denominated. The member states, however, no longer have full control over this currency. Responsibility for it is now shared by all members of the euro area, represented by the ECB. As a consequence, an individual country can no longer decide (on its own) to devaluate its debt by issuing more money or to reduce its debt via debt restructuring. Therefore, the euro area is bound together by the same currency on the one hand, and on the other hand it does not show the same economic development. Key indicators such as GDP growth rates, unemployment or productivity still point to large economic differences within this area (Niechoj 2012). If the institutional arrangements within the euro area are not able to balance or cushion these differences, tensions will emanate. And this is likely, because the euro area is no homogeneous group of countries demonstrating vital power and prosperity. On the contrary, several countries are in dire straits while others are currently performing relatively well. There are systemic reasons for this asymmetry, and again the monetary union contributed crucially to the aggravation and persistence of the imbalances in the euro area.

In this chapter, a scenario analysis is conducted to depict possible future developments for Europe in order to discuss the extent to which the specific institutional framework of the euro area and the still-present causes of the last crises will challenge the economic development in the euro area and the EU in the following years, maybe decades. These causes will be identified and the events following the introduction of the euro are analysed using a post-Keynesian framework. Then I will review the current institutional arrangements, developed as a response to the turmoil generated by the financial market crisis and the European sovereign debt crisis. Finally, three scenarios and their implications will be constructed, covering different degrees of European integration.

Scenario analysis as a policy tool

Forecasts are used to predict future economic activity in the short and medium term. International organizations offer forecasts for the EU and the euro area on a regular basis. For 2014 and 2015, the European Commission (2014) forecasts a slow recovery with low but positive growth rates for both the EU and the euro area, also for nearly all of the member states. Even for Greece a change to positive growth rates is projected for 2014, although the

Commission acknowledges a fall in GDP of 3.7 per cent for 2013. Inside the EU and within the euro area, large asymmetries in GDP growth rates persist due to differences in private consumption, investment and net exports. The Organisation for Economic Cooperation and Development (OECD 2013: 12) also provides a forecast for the euro area (and some of the member states) that shows a similar picture for the near future, with real GDP growth of 1.0 per cent in 2014 and of 1.6 per cent in 2015 for the euro area. Unemployment rates are projected to remain significantly higher than before 2008, especially in Spain and Greece (OECD 2013: 101–102, 147–148, 191–192). The forecast of the International Monetary Fund (2014: 53–57) further substantiates the view of an expected slow recovery. Domestic demand is still depressed against the background of both the austerity measures and private deleveraging, which is reflected in low inflation rates.

Common to all these projections is their focus on the next one or two years and the assumption of *given political and institutional conditions*. For the estimation of the future economic development the current setting is assumed to be constant; otherwise, no clear direction of development could be projected. In contrast to such forecasts, this chapter views the institutional setting as a variable. Based on different political frameworks, scenarios are depicted in order to show the impact of modifications of the institutional setting on the evolution of economic activity within the euro area and hence on the EU as a whole. Such a scenario analysis is a tool for strategic decision-making and policy advice depicting the consequences of differently changing settings (Ringland 1998). Due to the slowness of political reforms and their implementation and due to cumulating effects, a scenario analysis for the euro area has to focus on the medium- and not the short-term. Some determinants of future developments are relatively persistent and largely predetermined; hence, scenarios hinge on the uncertain or variable determinants. This can be spelt out in the context of future European scenarios as different combinations of monetary, fiscal and wage regulations for the euro area, which are subject to political decisions. The scenarios presented here are in no way innovative, and they focus on the dimension of integration. A basic scenario extrapolates the current policy framework and its advancement in small steps. This scenario is accompanied by two scenarios representing an increase and a reduction of integration in Europe.

Basically, this differentiation is present in other scenario analyses of the euro area as well. Buiter and Rahbari (2012) discuss the institutional framework of 2011 in comparison to a set of scenarios covering variants of deeper fiscal integration and a set of break-up scenarios, in which exits of strong and weak member states are gone through. In an in-between scenario, viewed as most likely, the solvency problems of states emanate and are solved by debt restructuring where the burden is for the most part borne by private creditors. In the same year, the Economist Intelligence Unit (2011) developed an outlook based on four scenarios. The first one extrapolates the situation in 2011 and offers a semi-pessimistic look into the future. The second scenario discusses an increase in fiscal integration by establishing some kind of euro bonds, i.e. jointly issued government bonds of all euro area member states implying a joint liability and collective guarantee for debt (cf. the seminal proposal on euro bonds by Delpla and von Weizsäcker 2010). Exits of peripheral or core countries characterize the next scenario. The last scenario resembles the first scenario. No institutional changes but, in comparison to the first scenario, recovery is achieved quickly because confidence is restored soon and austerity works. A recent scenario analysis, Scenario Team Eurozone 2020 (2013), which is based on preparatory work by Rodrigues (2012), also reviews four scenarios. The first is an extension of the current situation, the second and third discuss a complete break-up of the euro area and the exits of some countries. The last one again describes a change towards a fiscal union.

A similar structure for the scenarios is used here. In difference to these studies, however, this chapter will highlight the importance of the causal factors in the recent crises that will shape future development. Only if the destructive potential of the recent crises and their systematic causes are revealed, can the lasting consequences for the euro area be identified. Depending on the concrete elements of the future institutional setting in Europe, currently unresolved problems and existing challenges are addressed by policy measures and institutional amendments – or not. If not, this will dampen economic activity and might lead to ongoing turbulence in the future. The scenario analysis presented here is based on a post-Keynesian perspective emphasizing imbalances within the euro area due to the aggressive export-led growth models of some countries in combination with the incoherent institutional framework of the monetary union (Joebges, Lindner and Niechoj 2010; Niechoj *et al.* 2011; Niechoj 2012 and 2014; for a comparative overview of approaches including the view expressed here, see Priewe 2012).

Asymmetric economic development before the crisis (t_{-1})

The monetary union can be seen as a structural break for the EU. Before the union, depreciations and appreciations of currencies were the rule. As a consequence, the business environment was characterized by a high degree of uncertainty. Firms had to face high transaction costs and to procure significant amounts of money for hedging. In order to dampen the negative effects of volatile exchange rates a semi-fixed exchange rate regime, the European Monetary System, was established. Speculations against currencies, however, led to several re-alignments and the system eventually proved to be dysfunctional (Polster 2002). With the introduction of the common currency, the euro, currency crises no longer threaten the member states of the second-largest currency union in the world. Monetary policy is now concentrated in a single actor, the European Central Bank, which sets a unique nominal interest rate for all member countries in order to control inflation and to avoid deflation.

Within this revised institutional framework, differences in inflation rates have important consequences. First, a high inflation rate often indicates high wage increases. If so, and if it corresponds to real wage increases, then private consumption will be fostered in countries with higher inflation rates, whereas in other countries the development of private consumption will lag behind. If, on the contrary, inflation rates are below the ECB target, it indicates problems for firms seeking to raise prices and to make profits, which dampens future expectations of sales and thus production. Secondly, the national real interest rates, which are the common nominal interest rate minus the national inflation rates, differ as well. Although investment decisions are based on several factors, the real interest rate is an important element in firms' decisions to expand production and to invest in product and process innovations. Low real interest rates contribute to an increase in investment and thus GDP; moreover, they favour an increase in consumption credits and hence private consumption and again GDP.

Thirdly, diverging price developments of export goods and services translate in a common monetary union into an increase or fall in price competitiveness. When wages and profits in the sectors participating in the production of export goods and services increase faster in one country than in other member states, no exchange rate adjustment corrects for this. The price increase will result in lower sales if the product is not differentiated enough from other similar products. If one country manages to keep the price increases low compared to other countries, then it should be able to increase exports. Advantages in price competitiveness are, vis-à-vis countries outside the euro area, only temporary because exchange rate adjustments undermine these increases permanently. As there is no such mechanism within the euro area, the differences remain. Furthermore, an appreciation of the euro due to a rise in the export surplus for the rest of the world does not completely erode the price advantage of the country in question. The euro area and its exchange rate represent the whole area, exchange rates thus adapt to an average of all member states. For an export-oriented country this means that it can keep its price advantage longer, compared to the situation before the euro (see Lapavitsas and Flassbeck, Chapter 8 in this volume).

These three mechanisms help to explain the asymmetric economic development within the euro area after its establishment (cf. for a detailed discussion and presentation of empirical data, Niechoj and van Treeck 2011: 246–258; Niechoj 2012: 391–397; Niechoj 2014: 108–122). Countries such as Germany, Austria and the Netherlands followed an export-led growth model, based on wage restraint and aiming at increases in price competitiveness. The development in other countries was characterized by consumption-led growth, financed partly by foreign credits (see also Becker *et al.*, Chapter 5, and Stockhammer and Köhler, Chapter 2 in this volume). A third group of countries, including France and Italy, showed mixed elements of both groups mentioned above.[1] What happened was that the export-led countries moderated their wage increases, which dampened private consumption but fuelled exports. Then the revenues of these exports could be used to finance the imports of the countries in the second group, which prospered during the first years of the monetary union.

To be sure, exports, imports, credits and liabilities are no pure intra-euro area issue. However, due to the roughly balanced current account of the euro area with the rest of the world, it seems justifiable to consider the euro area as a closed economy in this respect. The outcome of this situation was a rise in the net international investment position of the export-led countries and a decline in the consumption-oriented countries. High GDP growth rates in, for example, Spain or Greece resulted from the low real interest rate and strong private consumption in these countries. A rise in domestic demand normally also leads to an increase in imports, which further deteriorates the trade balance. Normally, the trade balance is the dominant part of the current account. The different patterns in exports and imports thus gave rise to growing current account imbalances. From 1999 to 2007 the export-led countries showed increasing positive current accounts for most of the years, the consumption-led countries correspondingly negative current accounts (Table 9.1). During the following years the differences persisted but did not further accumulate. In 2012 and 2013 the impact of the austerity measures became visible in the current accounts: due to the fiscal retrenchment, imports dropped and (among others) Portugal and Spain showed a positive trade balance and positive current accounts in 2013.

Until 2007, this constellation was in favour of the consumption-led countries. The main indicators of economic performance, developed far better in these countries than in the export-led countries. Germany's real GDP growth, for example, performed far below the euro area average until 2007, while Spain showed increases well above the average. Unemployment rates also declined in consumption-led countries but increased in Germany and other export-led countries.

The financial market crisis changed this picture. What happened? (See also Horn et al. 2009; Joebges and Niechoj 2010; Niechoj and van Treeck 2011.) The collapse of the US housing market and the cascading negative impacts on the banking system resulted in a sharp fall in GDP in 2009. Both exports and investment confidence broke off. Private debt on a large scale was not repaid. Financial investors and banks became insolvent. For two main reasons, this problem for private actors turned out to be a problem for governments as well. Firstly, if such actors are in trouble and if spill-over effects exist because financial actors are cross-linked with each other and bankruptcies might lead to a collapse of the whole financial sector, the government has to step in and stabilize the banking system. Secondly, the economic downswing which accompanied the financial turmoil also required a fast and strong response by the governments. Many member states issued fiscal stabilization programmes, in other words financed investment programmes and consumption stimuli by debt in order to compensate partly for the loss in private consumption and investment. After 2007, public debt in the euro area rose by

Table 9.1 Current accounts in the euro area in billion euro

	Germany	*Netherlands*	*Austria*	*Belgium*	*Finland*	*France*	*Ireland*	*Italy*	*Spain*	*Greece*	*Portugal*
1999	-25.9	16.4	-2.9	11.8	8.6	35.0	0.1	11.5	-15.5	-6.5	-10.6
2000	-36.2	26.6	-1.5	10.6	10.0	17.2	-0.4	-2.3	-25.3	-16.4	-13.6
2001	-3.5	23.3	-1.6	11.2	11.7	19.6	-0.6	3.6	-29.5	-16.8	-14.3
2002	42.7	28.2	6.0	16.0	12.2	14.9	-0.5	-4.2	-27.4	-19.8	-12.0
2003	40.4	29.2	3.9	15.4	7.4	8.1	1.2	-10.5	-31.6	-21.2	-9.6
2004	102.5	42.2	5.2	13.2	9.6	3.9	-0.2	-4.9	-49.5	-19.4	-12.3
2005	113.4	38.4	5.3	9.7	5.5	-10.8	-4.9	-12.8	-67.8	-20.9	-15.9
2006	150.0	48.7	8.3	10.8	7.7	-14.8	-6.6	-22.3	-88.9	-28.7	-17.3
2007	182.5	48.1	10.9	13.2	7.6	-25.7	-10.4	-20.1	-105.2	-39.3	-17.2
2008	152.1	28.1	13.7	3.7	5.8	-36.6	-10.2	-44.9	-104.3	-41.9	-21.7
2009	145.1	18.2	7.4	2.4	3.4	-33.2	-3.8	-30.2	-50.0	-33.2	-18.2
2010	159.5	29.6	10.3	9.3	3.0	-36.1	1.8	-54.5	-45.7	-28.4	-17.9
2011	163.2	44.3	4.6	1.7	-2.7	-49.1	2.0	-48.3	-41.6	-24.5	-12.3
2012	187.9	45.9	5.5	-0.9	-2.7	-42.4	7.3	-8.4	-12.5	-10.3	-3.7
2013	192.1	55.7	9.0	0.2	-0.3	-39.9	11.6	13.6	11.3	-4.2	0.7

Source: Eurostat Ameco 2013

19 percentage points within three years. This, together with the confession of statistical irregularities in Greece after the introduction of the euro, brought the debt situation of the European states to the forefront for the first time.

During the early years of the monetary union, nominal interest rates for public debt did not diverge within the euro area. Since 2010, large spreads have emerged. For some countries it became increasingly difficult to borrow fresh money at reasonable interest rates. Debt servicing became a problem for those countries which did not focus on an export-led growth model in the past and which had already accumulated a negative net investment position. Their government bonds lost value, which aggravated the debt situation in the national banking sector again because national banks normally hold a significant amount of national government bonds. Before 2010, it had seemed as if there was no difference in holding Greek or German government bonds but then Greek government bonds became a burden and contributed to a further deterioration of the situation of the Greek banking sector. Again, the state had to stabilize the national banking system. Greece needed more money. Creditors were no longer willing to lend money – or only at high costs. Greece could not respond by issuing more money because it no longer had sole control over Greek euros. Financial investors in government bonds also started to rethink their exposure to other countries in similar situations, such as Portugal or Spain, and started to shift their assets towards countries with a better reputation, mainly export-led countries like Germany. The crisis spread.

Responses to the sovereign debt crisis (t_0)

The political systems at national and supranational levels responded with conditional rescue packages and major reforms of the European institutional setting (Niechoj and van Treeck 2011: 259–261). Financial assistance, first for Greece and later also for Ireland, Portugal, Spain and again Greece, was provided on bilateral basis or within a newly established supranational agency, the European Financial Stability Facility (EFSF), which was later transformed into the current and permanent European Stability Mechanism (ESM). The member states of the euro area have jointly guaranteed the bonds these agencies have issued since their establishment and have also paid a capital of €80 billion to the ESM. By doing so, access to further credits was guaranteed at low interest rates for the countries that otherwise could no longer borrow from the capital markets at reasonable costs. In order to reduce the debt-to-GDP ratio, these programmes included conditions to reduce public spending and to reform the national economies. They are monitored by the so-called Troika of European Commission, International Monetary Fund and ECB. In June 2012, the heads of the governments of the euro area also decided to give the ESM permission to directly lend to national banks. This allowed for support for Spain without the direct involvement of the Spanish government.

Reforms of the governance structure of the euro area covered a series of new or revised institutions. The Stability and Growth Pact (SGP) was modified and strengthened in the form of five regulations and one directive, which is the reason for these amendments of the pact being called the 'six pack'. The SGP now requires an adjustment path for indebted countries, which are required to reduce their debt-to-GDP ratio to 60% within 20 years. Moreover, a new, so-called Macroeconomic Imbalances Procedure was set up as part of the SGP. It consists of a warning system, based on a scoreboard of macroeconomic indicators, to identify imbalances between the countries. As the main tool for reducing these imbalances, labour market reforms are prescribed. Financial sanctions are possible, and the thresholds for taking action are often asymmetric: a current account deficit of up to 4 per cent of GDP but a surplus of up to 6 per cent is permitted. Moreover, the net international investment position has only a negative ceiling of 35 per cent, but no positive threshold. Increases in nominal unit labour costs, indicating the price competitiveness of a country, above 9 per cent can be punished, but there is no equivalent for low or negative values as in the case of German wage restraint. In other words, this structure offers leeway for and favours the export-led growth model.

Other institutional reforms go into the same direction. The Euro Plus Pact aims to increase price competitiveness by wage restraint in the public and private sectors. The Fiscal Compact deepens fiscal surveillance by prescribing the implementation of budgetary rules similar to the SGP at the national level, and even amending national constitutions in order to increase the rules' binding force. Furthermore, the European Court of Justice was assigned with the power to impose financial sanctions. The European Semester mainly streamlines the temporal procedure of all the existing pacts, reports and guidelines at European level. A further 'two pack' is currently under consideration, aiming only at member states of the euro area and further strengthening fiscal monitoring.

Besides the political level, the ECB, in charge of monetary policies within the euro area, reoriented its policies and responded to the fall in GDP in 2009. Since the end of 2008, the ECB has lowered the interest rate for main refinancing operations from 3.75 to 0.25 per cent in November 2013. Since July 2012, banks have zero interest rates for their deposits at the ECB, the rationale for this being the reduction of the cost of credits and hence the stimulation of private investment. In a situation of dampened expectations, and this still holds for the situation in the beginning of 2014, banks are, however, not willing to extend their lending activities. So this instrument is important but limited in effect. It also does not address the prohibitively high financing costs in Greece and Portugal and – for certain periods in time – for Ireland, Italy and Spain since 2010.

After hesitant behaviour in the beginning, the ECB has successfully reduced the spreads by purchasing government bonds on the secondary market, i.e. the central bank does not buy directly from the states but reduces the pressure on yields of already issued government bonds, which are a good indicator for the interest rates governments would offer if they issued new bonds. The crucial point was a speech by Mario Draghi, president of the ECB, in July 2012 when he promised to purchase as many bonds as necessary, or in his words: 'Within our mandate, the ECB is ready to do whatever it takes to preserve the euro. And believe me, it will be enough' (Draghi 2012). A few months later, in September, the ECB concretized the statement by announcing a procedure called Outright Monetary Transactions (OMT), which allows for an unlimited purchase of government bonds on the secondary market if the country in question has accepted reform conditions defined by the EFSF or the ESM. As the latest development, a banking union is currently in preparation. Its core is the so-called Single Supervisory Mechanism as a new mandate of the ECB (Council Regulation [EU] 2013, No 1024/2013), and it is expected that from Autumn 2014 the ECB will acquire powers to supervise the largest private banks in the EU. Further pillars of the banking union are under discussion, although nothing has been decided and institutionalized yet. A second pillar might be an insolvency procedure for banks, including a privately financed fund of €55 billion to cover the costs of liquidations, a third pillar of national deposit protection funds.

Three scenarios for European integration (t_{+1})

The following scenario analysis will differentiate between three scenarios covering different degrees of European integration. Scenario 1 extends the existing political and institutional trend. Major reforms and structural changes besides the amendments of the past are excluded from this scenario. As the overview of the section before has shown, the existing institutional framework has already addressed several challenges of the past but has still not resolved all important issues. Therefore, this scenario is called the *'muddling through'* scenario. Scenario 2 – *'unified in disintegration'* – assumes a major reform of the euro area, the disintegration of the euro area, which paradoxically leads to a reduction of political and institutional differences by eliminating the strong role of the euro area within the European Union. The last scenario, *'a union within a union'* is based on a further extension of European integration within the euro area. Thus, the three scenarios cover an extrapolation of the current status quo plus the two poles of integration and disintegration of the euro area (Figure 9.1).

What would happen, if the institutional framework stays constant? Would any loose ends lead to escalating troubles in the future? In this *muddling through* scenario, public spending behaviour is limited both by the rules of SGP and Fiscal Compact and the ongoing consolidation programmes. Therefore, no fiscal stimuli from public budgets will contribute to a sound upswing within the next years. On the contrary, the focus on balanced budgets will complicate stabilization policies and a strong recovery of the euro area in the future. Especially in times of a non-functioning monetary policy,

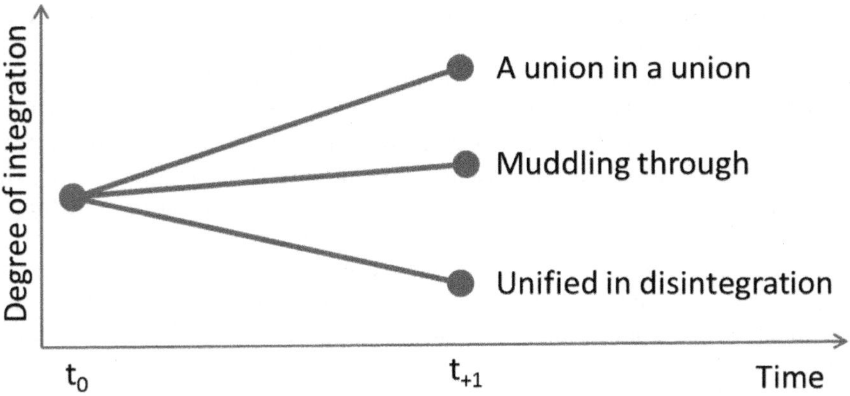

Figure 9.1 Three scenarios of European integration
Source: Own depiction

where low interest rates do not trigger investment, this limitation is noticeable. It is claimed that what should kickstart the economies are ongoing efforts to reduce employment protection and to increase the level of commodification of labour. The German example shows that this is a dangerous tool: it aggravated labour market segmentation and did not translate into rising real wages and high GDP growth rates (for a discussion cf. Herzog-Stein, Lindner and Zwiener 2013; Möller 2014; Niechoj 2014). So wage policy is the second policy area that cannot set growth-enhancing stimuli.

As mentioned before, monetary policy can also not initiate a self-supporting upswing in the current situation. Additionally, this policy mix endangers the economic cohesion of the euro area. If all countries followed the German example of wage restraint and if no fiscal policy could compensate, then there will be a race for price competitiveness nobody can win. Even if some countries succeed in gaining price competitiveness, other countries will have to accept import surpluses because not all countries can have an export surplus. By definition, some must have a deficit: therefore, the future will be characterized by current account imbalances, too. Without a fiscal union and transfers, drastic cuts in wages, like in Greece, can cushion the divergence – but only at extreme social costs. Surely, against the rest of the world, a surplus of the euro area and a beggar-thy-neighbour policy is possible. Nevertheless, here the exchange rate mechanisms still exist. Price advantages run dry, and price increases have to stay constantly below those of competitors outside the euro area in order to maintain the export surplus. Moreover, wage restraint common to all member states of the euro area would bring the threat of deflation to the forefront. In a deflationary environment, the real debt of firms increases because prices fall and revenues are not sufficient to pay back the nominally fixed debt. This would lead to higher levels of company insolvency and investment would decline further.

All in all, these prospects are not favourable for the euro area. Low GDP growth rates will be the rule, not the exception. The bright spot is that these low growth rates are not endangering public finances, although normally they would. The key indicator for public debt is the debt-to-GDP ratio. If GDP growth is low, even slight increases in debt might lead to a rising debt-to-GDP ratio. What keeps the area together in this scenario is, however, that governments can refinance their debt at relatively low interest rates as long as the ECB purchases bonds on the secondary market or if the ESM starts to buy government bonds. As long as this is guaranteed, governments can service their debt despite low growth rates. In other words, ECB and ESM have accepted, at least informally, the role of the lender of last resort for public debt.

It has to be noted that this outlook hinges crucially on the assumption that no second financial market crisis happens. Although the private sector has started to deleverage, financial institutions are still not able to prevent a further crisis. The supervision of the banking union is an improvement but not a sufficient one: for example, there is still no separation of commercial and investment banking functions. A negative impulse could shake the whole banking system again.

A second scenario promises to reduce the imbalances within the euro area and to restore price competitiveness through the re-introduction of exchange rates. In the scenario *unified in disintegration* countries re-establish their old own currencies. If countries leave the monetary union, the consequences will differ for countries with current account surpluses or deficits. If we assume that Germany, as the country with the largest current account surplus, leaves the monetary union this will reduce the pressure to increase price competitiveness in other member states. It would also lead to a depreciation of the euro and capital inflows to Germany as a new reserve currency for the world. It is likely that other countries such as the Netherlands or Austria would follow. Maybe a second currency area within the EU, consisting of these countries, would emerge.

From the point of view of countries with long-term current account deficits in the past, such a development would have a mixture of positive and negative effects in the short run. The euro's depreciation and the loss of a strong competitor in prices within the euro area would translate into an improvement of current accounts. Price competitiveness will rise and imports will become far more expensive. As a result, current accounts would improve but the reduction of imports might worsen the living conditions in these countries if this effect is not compensated for by strong exports. As the recent example of Greece shows, a country that has no broad export basis will not necessarily gain from a rise in price competitiveness. For Germany (and followers), the immediate appreciation would result in a significant loss in price competitiveness vis-à-vis the rest of the world. Current account surpluses would shrink. Calls for even sharper wage restraint within Germany could lead to a loss in domestic demand and hence reduce GDP growth rates even further.

A similar development is to be expected if not Germany but a country (or more than one) of the group of countries in dire straits were to exit. With their own currency, depreciation would be possible again. Price competitiveness could be restored, but at the cost of rising prices for imports. It is likely that capital would take flight towards the euro area, even with capital controls. In addition, the impact of a break-up of the EU and the euro area as a political project are expected to be disastrous. The momentum of change towards a higher degree of economic policy coordination, pushed by pure necessity during the last years, would be reversed. If the monetary union unravels, there will no longer be a strong case for fiscal coordination, not to speak of wage coordination. The member states will return to a situation *ex ante*, to the times of the European Monetary System that failed in the past.

The third scenario, *a union within a union*, completes economic integration in the fields of fiscal and wage policies and strengthens monetary surveillance and the role of the ECB. From a political point of view, the realization of this scenario is a highly demanding one. For example, there would still be institutionalized limits to debt but the balanced budget rules would be transformed into a golden rule: if a state borrows money for investment purposes, i.e. later generations will gain from it, this money does not count for the debt-to-GDP ratio and the deficit criterion of the SGP. Fiscal coordination is no longer restricted to surveillance but includes transfers between the countries, e.g. via an enlarged common budget of the European Commission, in order to target sectors and regions lagging behind with much more financial power than at the moment. Wage policies would be coordinated within countries and between countries. Therefore, large spreads of inflation rates could be avoided and domestic demand would be strengthened in countries such as Germany that had to face real wage stagnation in the past. The banking union would be extended: surveillance of all large banks, not only the largest ones, would be concentrated at supranational level. Commercial and investment activities of banks would be separated in order to avoid negative spill-overs of the speculative banking on financing firms' investments and other commercial activities.

Next, short-term speculation would be reduced by the introduction of a transaction tax. Moreover, the ECB would explicitly accept its role of a lender of last resort and not only step in until the ESM is ready to take over. The reason for this is that the ESM will always be limited in capacity because it is dependent on the capital markets to provide sufficient money. Furthermore, the ECB would introduce the tool of asset-backed reserve requirements in order to become able to dampen overheating economies and to stimulate growth in sluggish economies. Such a development would allow for growth-enhancing policies which would decrease the debt-to-GDP ratios in various countries. Fiscal policy would be stimulated when and where necessary, and wage policies would take care of the inflation differentials and foster domestic demand. Monetary policy would create a growth-friendly interest rate environment, well-tailored to all countries and based on inflation being kept under control by wage policies. Public debt would not continue to rise; states could borrow at reasonable interest rates. Nevertheless, if a country faces a deterioration of credit conditions, the ECB can act as a lender of last resort. In this scenario, and only in this scenario, intra-European imbalances can be actively reduced and the impact of a further financial market crisis on the real economy is significantly lower than in the other two scenarios. As has probably become obvious through this chapter, this will not be the future. The muddling-through scenario, with all of its drawbacks, seems much more likely.

Conclusions

This chapter has shed light on the cumulating tensions after the introduction of the euro that still challenge the whole project of European integration. Not only could the euro not reduce the differences in economic development within the euro area, it also paved the way for two growth models which both failed. The first is an export-led model, the second a debt-financed consumption model. There is a dependency between both growth models: the export-led growth model dampens domestic demand but generates current account surpluses, while the debt-financed consumption growth model absorbs these exports and finances the current account deficit with credits offered by export-led countries that are eager to lend money to countries with higher GDP growth rates. For two reasons – a sharp decline of real interest rates for some countries and an undervalued currency for other countries – the introduction of the euro fuelled this fragile dependency which, finally, ended in the sovereign debt crisis in Europe and especially the euro area. The trigger for this was the situation in Greece, the specific form of the crisis being a consequence of the financial market crisis that transformed private into public debt.

Against this background, three scenarios for the future development of the euro area were constructed. The first two scenarios cannot address the still-virulent causes of the current crisis. They do not depict stable situations, because the institutional capacities necessary for addressing the underlying tensions are not sufficiently developed. The last scenario lists such capacities, but their realization is unlikely.

All scenarios also impact on the EU. The muddling-through scenario describes a euro area with low GDP growth rates and continuing challenges. The political agenda of the EU will be dominated by attempts to address these challenges in the future. Moreover, economic stagnation in the euro area pulls down economic activity in the rest of the EU, too. The second scenario of an exit of one or more countries endangers even more the political and economic outlook. If countries leave, it proves that the political architecture was not ready for an economic union. Economically, at least for a transitionary phase, the (ex-)euro area will suffer from a split, and so will the rest of the EU. Surprisingly, the last scenario, which is the most promising for the euro area, might not be favourable for the EU. On the one hand, it increases the level of integration within the euro area and hopefully establishes a well-functioning framework. On the other hand, it raises the gap between the euro area and the rest of the EU. All countries which do not belong to the euro area are less integrated and partly excluded from supranational coordination and decisions. For the global level, though, the last scenario is preferable, because it promises to produce a stable euro and stabilized economic development with sound GDP growth rates and thus increased trade volumes.

Note

1 Note that Ireland is a special case. It belongs to the countries in dire straits due to its large financial sector that was hit hard by the crisis. Contrary to consumption-led countries, however, the Irish economy normally is characterized by a trade balance surplus. Although for most of the countries trade balance and current account develop in the same direction, because the trade balance is part of the current account and normally dominates it – in the Irish case large transfers of profits to other countries turned the current account into deficit several times despite a positive trade balance.

References

Buiter, W. and Rahbari, E. (2012) The ECB as Lender of Last Resort for Sovereigns in the Euro Area. *CEPR Discussion Paper* No. 8974, May. Centre for Economic Policy Research.

Council Regulation (EU) (2013) No 1024/2013: Council Regulation of 15 October 2013 conferring specific tasks on the European Central Bank concerning policies relating to the prudential supervision of credit institutions. *Official Journal of the European Union*. L 287. 29.10.2013, pp. 63–89.

Delpla, J. and Von Weizsäcker, J. (2010) *The Blue Bond Proposal*. Bruegel Policy Brief [Online]. Brussels. Available from www.bruegel.org/download/parent/403-the-blue-bond-proposal/file/885-the-blue-bond-proposal-english [Accessed 15 February 2014].

Draghi, M. (2012) Speech by Mario Draghi, President of the European Central Bank, at the Global Investment Conference in London, 26 July 2012 [Online]. Available from www.ecb.europa.eu/press/key/date/2012/html/sp120726.en.html [Accessed 17 February 2014].

Economist Intelligence Unit (2011) *State of the Union: Can the Euro Zone Survive its Debt Crisis?* EIU Special Report. [Online] Available at http://pages.eiu.com/rs/eiu2/images/EuroDebtPaperMarch2011.pdf?mkt_tok=3RkMMJWWfF9wsRow5%2FmYJoDpwmWGd5mht7VzDtPj1OY6hBkvILiJK1TtuMFUGpsqOOyXFFA%3D [Accessed 15 February 2015].

European Commission (2014) European Economic Forecast. Winter 2014. *European Economy* 2/2014 Brussels. [Online] Available from http://ec.europa.eu/economy_finance/publications/european_economy/2014/pdf/ee2_en.pdf [Accessed 30 April 2014].

European Commission (2013) *Standard Eurobarometer 80. Public Opinion in the European Union*. First Results. Autumn. Brussels [Online]. Available from http://ec.europa.eu/public_opinion/archives/eb/eb80/eb80_first_en.pdf [Accessed 12 February 2014].

Eurostat Ameco Database (2013) Update of 5 November 2013 [Online]. Available from http://ec.europa.eu/economy_finance/ameco/user/serie/SelectSerie.cfm [Accessed 17 February 2014].

Herzog-Stein, A., Lindner, F. and Zwiener, R. (2013) *Is the Supply Side all that Counts? How Germany's One-sided Economic Policy has Squandered Opportunities and is Damaging Europe.* IMK Report 87e. Düsseldorf [Online]. Available from hwww.boeckler.de/pdf/p_imk_report_87e_2013.pdf [Accessed 12 January 2014].

Horn, G. *et al.* (2009) *Von der Finanzkrise zur Weltwirtschaftskrise. Wie die Krise entstand und wie sie überwunden werden kann.* IMK Report 38. Düsseldorf [Online]. Available at www.boeckler.de/pdf/p_imk_report_38_2009.pdf [Accessed 11 February 2013].

International Monetary Fund (2014) *World Economic Outlook.* April 2014. Washington DC [Online]. Available from www.imf.org/external/Pubs/ft/weo/2014/01/pdf/text.pdf [Accessed 30 April 2014].

Joebges, H. and Niechoj, T. (2010) *Rettungsmaßnahmen im Euroraum – kurzfristig sinnvoll, aber nicht ausreichend.* IMK Report 52. Düsseldorf [Online]. Available from www.boeckler.de/pdf/p_imk_report_52_2010.pdf [Accessed 11 February 2013].

Joebges, H., Lindner, F. and Niechoj, T. (2010) *Mit dem Export aus der Krise? Deutschland im Euroraumvergleich.* IMK Report 53. Düsseldorf [Online]. Available from www.boeckler.de/pdf/p_imk_report_53_2010.pdf [Accessed 17 February 2014].

Möller, J. (2014) Hartz IV and the Consequences: Did the Labour Market Reforms Destroy the German Model? In Collignon, S. and Esposito, P. (eds) *Competitiveness in the European Economy.* London and New York: Routledge, pp. 129–142.

Niechoj, T. (2012) Germany – Best Practice for the Euro Area? The Janus-faced Character of Current Account Surpluses. In Herr, H. *et al.* (eds) *From Crisis to Growth? The Challenge of Debt and Imbalances.* Marburg: Metropolis, pp. 389–419.

Niechoj, T. (2014) How Promising is Wage Restraint for a Large Economy? The Example of Germany Before and During the Current Crises. In Collignon, S. and Esposito, P. (eds.) *Competitiveness in the European Economy.* London and New York: Routledge, pp. 107–128.

Niechoj, T. and van Treeck, T. (2011) Policy Responses to the Euro Debt Crisis: Can they Overcome the Imbalances that Caused the Crisis? *Intervention. European Journal of Economics and Economic Policies.* 8(2), pp. 245–266.

Niechoj, T. et al. (2011) *German Labour Costs: A Source of Instability in the Euro Area. Analysis of Eurostat Data for 2010.* IMK Report 68e. Düsseldorf [Online]. Available from www.boeckler.de/pdf/p_imk_report_68e_2011.pdf [Accessed 17 February 2014].

Organisation for Economic Cooperation and Development [OECD] (2013) *OECD Economic Outlook* 2. No. 94. OECD Publishing [Online]. Available from http://dx.doi.org/10.1787/eco_outlook-v2013-2-en [Accessed 15 February 2014].

Polster, W. (2002) *Europäische Währungsintegration. Von der Zahlungsunion zur Währungsunion.* Marburg: Metropolis.

Priewe, J. (2012) European Imbalances and the Crisis of the European Monetary Union. In Herr, H. *et al.* (eds) *From Crisis to Growth? The Challenge of Debt and Imbalances.* Marburg: Metropolis, pp. 331–360.

Ringland, G. (1998) *Scenario Planning. Managing for the Future.* Chichester: John Wiley & Sons.

Rodrigues, M.J. (2012) Mapping Future Scenarios for the Eurozone. Friedrich Ebert Stiftung. [Online] Available at http://library.fes.de/pdf-files/id/ipa/09194.pdf [Accessed 8 August 2013].

Scenario Team Eurozone 2020 (2013) Future Scenarios for the Eurozone: 15 Perspectives on the Euro Crisis. Friedrich Ebert Stiftung [Online]. Available at http://library.fes.de/pdf-files/id/ipa/09723.pdf [Accessed 8 August 2013].

10 Social Europe and the crisis of the European Union

John Grahl

Among citizens of the European Union, identification with the EU and support for its institutions have been reduced to low levels by the EU's dysfunctional response to the global financial crisis and its aftermath. The long-standing democratic deficit of the EU has certainly widened as austerity policies have intensified. In this chapter, it is accepted that it is economic policy rather than social policy which is the central factor in this malaise. However, social policy failures are certainly a contributory factor; and the two issues overlap in that it is above all the social consequences of economic failure, and in particular youth unemployment, which work to undermine confidence in the EU and the cohesion of its member countries. The introduction of more positive social policies and a much higher priority for social objectives could support a recovery of the EU in two respects. Firstly, social policies could provide an appropriate mechanism for the transnational transfers needed to underpin an effective monetary union. Secondly, the promotion of social objectives would work to narrow the gap between the goals pursued by EU leaders and the actual concerns and values of European citizens.

The slow death of social Europe

Although social partnership, social dialogue and the social dimension are constantly invoked in the EU, social policy is a realm of soft law, of declarations of principle, of 'policy communities', of the non-binding social charter and of the open method of co-ordination. If the topic changes to economics – to the single market, or to fiscal deficits – one is in a very different world of hard law and justiciable rights, of detailed supervision, of precise numerical constraints and of quasi-automatic sanctions for transgressors. It was not always thus. The story of social policy in the process of European construction begins with ambitious and effective commitments to protect those damaged by the integration process and continues with a drive to level social standards upwards. However, after the turn to market-led restructuring in the 1980s, the EU's social policies were narrowed, attenuated, marginalized and, in the current crisis, abandoned or indeed reversed. In the heroic age of integration, articles 49–50 of the Treaty of Paris, establishing the Economic Coal and Steel Community (ECSC), stated:

> The High Authority is empowered to procure the funds necessary to the accomplishment of its mission: by placing levies on the production of coal and steel; by borrowing …
>
> The levies are intended to cover: … the non-reimbursable assistance provided for in Article 56, concerning readaptation …

Article 56 then spelt out:

> If the introduction of technical processes or new equipment within the framework of the general programs of the High Authority, should lead to an exceptional reduction in labor requirements in the coal or steel industries, creating special difficulties in one or more areas for the re-employment of the workers released, the High Authority, on the request of the interested governments … may facilitate, in accordance with the methods provided for in Article 54, the financing of such programs as it may approve for the creation, either in the industries subject to its jurisdiction or, with the concurrence of the Council, in any other industry, of new and economically sound activities capable of assuring productive employment to the workers thus released … will grant non-reimbursable assistance to contribute to: the payment of indemnities to tide the workers over until they can obtain new employment; the granting of allowances to the workers for reinstallation expenses; the financing of technical retraining for workers who are led to change their employment.

Milward (2000) confirms that these promises were kept, the main beneficiaries being Wallonian coal miners. Today, however, the notion that the employers in an industry should, collectively, compensate the employees dismissed in function of restructuring could be characterised by the Orwellian term: *crimethink*.

The widening of the integration process with the Treaty of Rome saw an extension of social policy ambitions. Three aspects stand out: on French insistence, the rights of female workers were explicitly reinforced (women workers in Germany at that time received very inferior wages, and competition from them could have been disruptive). Article 119 stated:

> Each Member State shall during the first stage ensure and subsequently maintain the application of the principle that men and women should receive equal pay for equal work.

Secondly, German employers were enthusiastic to push up wages and enhance social provision in other member states. At that time they had no subsidiaries in other countries and had therefore a strong interest in avoiding 'social dumping.' According to article 118:

> the Commission shall have the task of promoting close co-operation between Member States in the social field, particularly in matters relating to:

- employment;
- labour law and working conditions;
- basic and advanced vocational training;
- social security;
- prevention of occupational accident, and diseases;
- occupational hygiene;
- the right of association, and collective bargaining between employers and workers.

Today, of course, German multinationals are ready to dump socially cheapened products on their employees in Germany itself (see also Cafruny, Chapter 4 in this volume). Thirdly, the Common Agricultural Policy, although increasingly dysfunctional in economic terms, can be seen as a highly successful social policy at least in its first decades. A huge ageing population of small farmers in both France and Germany benefited from this 'planned retreat', to use Schumpeter's expression, when they might otherwise have been crushed by the rise of modern agri-business.

These positive impulses, aligning member state governments and employers with the interests of workers and citizens persisted through the 1960s and 1970s. Wide-ranging social reforms were promulgated in what was then the European Economic Community (EEC) and these had the effect of levelling up standards of social provision. A key ruling by the Court of Justice was that an Italian worker in France was entitled to French child support payments for his children in Italy. Italy was, of the original six member states, clearly the one with the least developed social protection regime.

The assumption that economic and social progress would run in parallel within the integration project began to be challenged in the 1980s. The neoliberal turn in European construction, embodied in the single market programme of legislation, gave decisive priority to competition and market access over social policy. At the same time, the scope of economic integration was widened in ways which greatly increased the range of social problems that could arise. Integration up to the 1980s concerned above all merchandise trade. Now there was increasing pressure to establish a single market for services, including many public services, with direct implications for the social models of member states. Increasingly, also, investment and capital flows were liberalized within the EU, placing a new set of pressures on business enterprises and employment systems.

Commission head Jacques Delors (1997: 95), who presided over the single market programme, suggested at first that the priority given to market completion was tactical, that social advance would follow and indeed be carried by the development of the EU's internal market. Later, he himself was compelled to concede that the postponement was to be *sine die*. Repeated refusals by some of the larger member states to increase the EU budget prevented the gradual emergence of the federal social protection regime which many had previously expected. In fact, the division of competence could be roughly described by saying that the EU now had substantial control over economic policy while the member states retained substantial autonomy in social policy. With the single market programme and the reinforcement of the four freedoms (free movement of capital, labour, goods and services), economic interventions and structural industrial policies became very difficult for member states because they often conflicted with the EU's competition rules. Likewise, the use of public procurement to preserve domestic jobs or assist domestic companies increasingly ran foul of the single market regime. The majority of member states which entered the monetary union also lost macroeconomic instruments, not only monetary policy but increasingly budgetary policy as it was constrained by the rules of the Stability Pact.

Most social policy decisions on the other hand, remained at the member state level. This may be partly because the different welfare states had developed in different ways so that their integration would always be a formidable task. But member states tended to guard their control over social policy because social policy measures were the main instrument remaining to them to respond to the disturbances and disruptions arising from the European and global economies. It is notable that the Scandinavian countries, with the most developed social policy regimes, were reluctant to accept an integration of social provision which could have threatened the higher standards they had achieved.

Employment and labour market regulation, at the intersection of economic and social policy fields, was subject to a mixed regime, codified in the Social Chapter of the Maastricht Treaty. Divided competence was perhaps unavoidable here. On the one hand, to leave labour market policies completely to the member states might compromise the competition regime if labour market interventions were used to influence economic outcomes; on the other hand, a unified labour market regime across the EU as a whole would hardly be welcome to big corporations, which value their ability to regime shop and the regime competition which follows from such shopping (see Wigger, Chapter 7 in this volume). The relevant protocol established full EU competence (legislation by Qualified Majority Vote) over: health and safety of workers; working conditions; information and consultation; equality between men and women; integration of excluded persons. Outside these areas, legislation had to be based on unanimity among member states and certain topics were explicitly excluded from EU action and thus reserved to member states: wages; trade unions; strikes and lockouts. This partition of responsibilities largely survived until the global financial crisis of 2007–2008 when, without any amendment to the Treaties, it was simply abandoned.

Meanwhile, the EU maintained a certain activism in the narrow field of social policy left to it – essentially labour market regulation. On the very reasonable assertion that working hours was a health and safety issue, a working time directive was adopted in 2003. However, most EU labour market legislation following Maastricht concerned atypical employment contracts, such as temporary work or agency-supplied labour. The aim was to place certain restrictions on the way 'flexible' labour could be used and on the use of such labour simply to reduce wage costs. However, the meaning of the EU directives was ambivalent. In some member states, such as Britain or Ireland, the effect was to strengthen the position of flexible workers but in many member states the EU legislation could not have any effect because national regulation already imposed stronger constraints on employers. Thus, this legislation could also be seen as working to promote the labour flexibility agenda by suggesting that atypical contracts were under more effective social control than was in fact the case. In any case, this legislative agenda was largely exhausted by the new century and no new labour market reforms followed. One can also note a certain instrumentalization of social policy in the Lisbon agenda – the central strategic document of the EU in the first decade of the present century – as social policy was to contribute to the EU's growth and employment targets by making for better functioning labour markets.

From the turn of the century a number of policy initiatives tended to destabilize the previous division of competence between the EU and the member states, as the Commission and the Council sought to strengthen the single market in ways that must weaken national social models. A draft takeover directive prepared by the Commission would have completely deregulated takeovers and made most defences against takeovers by incumbent company managements illegal. The Internal Market and Services Directorate General saw deregulation as necessary for the full liberalization of the EU capital market, and the central strategy of the EU's Lisbon Agenda was introducing the 'knowledge-based' economy. This was a project which required Europe to become, in the notorious words of the European Commission's (2001: 17) report to the Stockholm Council, 'the cheapest and easiest place to do business in the world'. Had the draft directive been adopted it would have swept away any regulatory restrictions on takeovers designed to protect jobs. In fact it was rejected by the European Parliament in a dramatic tied vote, and the Commission was compelled to substitute a very diluted directive.

A second initiative threatening established social policy regimes came from the Commission's Directorate General for the Internal Market under the robust leadership of Frits Bolkestein. The draft directive on services in the internal market put forward a ready and easy path to service market integration. Companies providing services in any member state could continue to be regulated from the member state in which they were established. Since it was becoming possible for them to register in the member state of their choice, this in effect meant that all service providers would be able to opt for the lightest regulation available anywhere within the Union. Bolkestein thought the comprehensive deregulation to which this was bound to lead was very desirable, since he considered most if not all regulation of service provision to be 'bureaucratic protectionism'. There was a clear threat to employment regimes because the regulation of service provision overlaps with the regulation of service employment, for instance by specifying required qualifications. Quite apart from its implications for employees, the directive as drafted might have brought about juridical chaos since one would never have been able to predict which regulatory regime would apply to which service in which country. Because of this, and after a very determined campaign against it by the trade unions, the directive was seriously diluted in the European Parliament, although even the diluted version may imply substantial deregulation of the service sector.

Decisions in the Court of Justice seemed to confirm the increasing willingness of EU institutions to sacrifice established social advances to the drive for market-led integration. The rule in the EU is that workers from one country who take up employment in another are subject to the employment and social protection regimes of the latter. However, for 'posted' workers, who are only briefly in another member state a complete change of regime – for pensions or social insurance, for example – might be impractical. The posted workers directive was designed to close any possible loopholes by shielding national employment regimes from erosion by such workers. In a series of judgements the EU Court subverted the directive by declaring that trade union actions to uphold the principle of nationally determined working conditions for all workers within a given member state were illegal. Subsequent regulatory changes were quite inadequate at restoring the intended effects of the original directive (Ewing and Hendy 2009; Cremers 2011; Ewing 2011).

One can also detect a change of approach in areas of social policy where member states retained substantial competence. The drive for labour market flexibility, largely involving regulatory change at member state level, was strongly supported at EU level and, especially after the introduction of the euro, became one of the main types of 'structural reform' continually recommended by the Commission as the path to competitiveness. It became clear, however, that the flexibility drive had been, in social terms, all too successful. Many millions more EU workers found themselves on atypical contracts by the early years of the new century, and the adverse implications in terms of insecurity and inequality could not be disguised (for the links between flexibility and precarity, see Standing 1999). At this point the Commission started to promote enthusiastically the notion of 'flexicurity'. Rhetorically this seemed to promise the best of both worlds – rapid and effective labour market responses to changing economic circumstances together with improved working conditions and strong social protection. This impression was reinforced by invoking Denmark and the Netherlands, both with enviable social models, as key examples of how the two objectives could be reconciled.

The actual meaning of the flexicurity discourse was almost the opposite of this. The intention was to recognize the adverse consequences of atypical contracts by *weakening standard contracts.* Nor was it intended to promote a general upward convergence of social protection and employment systems towards the Danish or Dutch models. On the contrary, flexicurity was to take quite different forms across member states: in one country its primary meaning might be to make it easier to dismiss employees, in another to deregulate public services, in a third to privatize state-owned enterprises. The theme of flexicurity was given an ethical veneer by the suggestion that the 'insiders' – those on standard, indefinite, employment contracts – should make concessions in view of the losses already suffered by the 'outsiders' on temporary contracts or subject to otherwise precarious conditions. This suggestion was spurious since the dilution of standard protections was always likely to affect the most vulnerable employees concerned – the weakest 'insiders' – and thus to exacerbate the continuous widening of social and economic inequality.

Although the definition of employment contracts was a matter for the member states, the 'open co-ordination' practised by the Commission seems, on this occasion at least, to have found a response at member state level. France led the way as Nicolas Sarkozy and Dominique de Villepin, at that time allies under the presidency of Jacques Chirac, initiated a substantial reduction of the historic rights embodied in the *Code du Travail* (Filoche 2008). More recently scholars at the European Trade Union Institute (ETUI) have documented a flood of employment law 'reforms' across nearly all member states, and all are designed to reduce employment rights and limit social protection (Clauwaert and Schömann 2012).

This wheel only turns one way. The ambitious social objectives of the ECSC and early EEC are abandoned. With the single market programme a compromise leaves most social policy with the member states and only certain aspects of employment regulation are retained by the EU. That compromise is itself undermined as the EU turns from establishing minimum working conditions to encouraging deregulation at member state level, and as the absolute priority given to the competition rules and market-led integration leads to increasingly aggressive legislative and judicial constraints on social policies. What would follow, as a response to the crisis of the European Union, was a direct and comprehensive assault on the social policy regimes of the weakest states.

In the debtors' prison

In the wake of the global financial crisis, the Commission and the Council tolerated a brief widening of public sector deficits to brake the drastic decline in aggregate demand. As early as 2009, however, they were demanding rapid fiscal consolidation. Marco Buti, Commissioner for Economics and Finance, wrote in October of that year:

> Withdrawal of the fiscal stimulus, accompanied by structural fiscal consolidation measures, would improve the conditions for price stability and so allow for an appropriate macroeconomic policy mix. Ambitious reforms of labour, product and financial markets are essential and should be an integral part of a consolidated exit strategy.
>
> (European Commission 2009: 6)

Thus the usual 'supply-side' deregulation, privatization and liberalization measures were now to replace the maintenance of aggregate demand. There followed a general drive for austerity, implemented by a thorough reinforcement of the central surveillance of member state policies and, in the case of those actually or potentially constrained to borrow from EU institutions, a comprehensive loss of policy autonomy. The policies imposed on these debtor states by the EU amounted to the dismantling of their social models. The main elements of the 'surveillance union' introduced since the European crisis are the 'Euro-plus Pact', the 'six-pack', the 'two-pack', and the 'Fiscal Compact'. (See les Économistes Atterrés 2012 and, for the earlier measures, Dräger 2011 and also Stockhammer and Köhler, Chapter 2 in this volume.) The economic consequences of the regime established by these measures are discussed elsewhere in this book. From the point of view of social policy two points can be made.

The first concerns the division of competence between the EU and the member states: the so-called 'Merkel Method' completely subverts any established limits to central control by herding member state governments into agreements which 'voluntarily' commit them to centrally determined disciplines. Neither the European Parliament nor national parliaments have played an active part in the construction of the surveillance union which emerged. From the start, European integration has tended to reinforce the hypertrophy of executive power as against that of legislatures, both because of the central role of the Commission as its own executive arm and because the Council, although it also has legislative functions, represents national executives (see also Oberndorfer, Chapter 11 in this volume).

The thinking embodied in this set of agreements, treaties and laws directly threatens member state social models in two respects. In macroeconomic terms it reduces all policy issues to the lack of competitiveness in the weaker economies. Competitiveness is to be restored by downward pressure on wages and prices, reinforced by labour market 'reforms' designed to make such pressure harder to resist, and by budgetary consolidation which cannot avoid being at the expense of social provision and of redistribution. The 'structural reforms' supposed to contribute to competitiveness are the usual neo-liberal measures – privatization (including fire sales of state assets), liberalization of procurement, and deregulation – which can undermine the wages, working conditions and job security of public sector employees but have otherwise very dubious consequences and have no clear relationship to economic recovery. Indeed the whole approach is likely to fail in the medium-term, because it will tend to discourage the investment needed to reduce the gap in economic performance between the countries affected and the stronger ones. Already, for example, there are big outflows of more highly skilled and better qualified workers from the crisis-struck economies (Benton and Petrovic 2013: 9).

For those countries which have had to accept emergency finance from the 'Troika' (that is the Commission, the International Monetary Fund and the European Central Bank (ECB) acting as creditors) there are no limits at all to central intrusion into their social, political and economic life. The most extreme case is that of Greece, where major changes to employment relations and labour market functioning were imposed. Memoranda of understanding between the Troika and the Greek government short-circuited the democratic process. In the Memorandum of Understanding (MoU) of February 2012, tenured job security was abolished in a single sentence:

> Prior to the disbursement [that is, before the Greek government receives any money from the Troika, JG], clauses on tenure (contracts with definite duration defined as expiring upon age limit or retirement) contained in law or in labour contracts are abolished.
>
> (European Commission 2012: 148)

Minimum wages and negotiated pay scales were treated likewise:

> Prior to the disbursement, the following measures are adopted:

- The minimum wages established by the national general collective agreement (NGCA) will be reduced by 22 percent compared to the level of 1 January 2012; for youths (for ages below 25), the wages established by the national collective agreement will be reduced by 32 percent without restrictive conditions.
- Clauses in the law and in collective agreements which provide for automatic wage increases, including those based on seniority, are suspended.

(European Commission 2012: 147)

Explicit targets for rapid wage reductions were laid down:

> Given that the outcome of the social dialogue to promote employment and competitiveness fell short of expectations, the Government will take measures to foster a rapid adjustment of labour costs to fight unemployment and restore cost-competitiveness, ensure the effectiveness of recent labour market reforms, align labour conditions in former state-owned enterprises to those in the rest of the private sector and make working hours arrangements more flexible. This strategy should aim at reducing nominal unit labour costs in the business economy by 15 percent in 2012–14.
>
> (European Commission 2012: 147)

Thus, since the social partners had not agreed to a drastic wage deflation, it would simply be imposed. If such decisions were taken by the Commission acting as an EU institution, they would be completely *ultra vires*. The Maastricht Treaty explicitly excludes any EU competence in wages policy.[1] But acting as a creditor, and eliciting the compliance of debtor governments, the Commission can simply step over any such putative limits to its power.

There is insufficient space here to examine the details of the MoU, because that document itself spells out in remorseless detail the ways in which the

Greek social model is to be dismantled. Public sector employment plays an important social role in all advanced countries, by offering employment on somewhat better conditions than at the lower end of private sector labour markets and by adding to the total of relatively secure jobs. The MoU imposes, in order to 'modernize' the public administration, reductions in 'public employment by 150 thousand in end-2010 to end-2015' (European Commission 2012: 131). Mass privatizations are also imposed, to the tune of 15 billion euros by the end of 2015, although Greek citizens could hardly expect fair prices from purchasers – venture capital groups and the like – who are aware that the sales are forced. One feature of the 'reforms' imposed on Greece and other debtor states is an insistence on opening up public procurement to external suppliers. These measures, almost bound to increase imports and very likely to reduce profits and employment in domestic firms, could only further lower the level of activity in their economies. The Commission pushes these policies forward, not as a response to the crisis, but in order to promote its dogmatic and inflexible market integration agenda despite the fact that they intensify pressure on the debtors.

A full account of the impact of austerity on the Greek employment system is in Karamessini (2012). Only one other social policy measure, among very many in the MoU, will be mentioned. In order to reduce labour costs the Troika required a 5% cut in social security contributions. This was to be achieved in a 'budget-neutral' way, that is, by implementing corresponding reductions in the pensions and social protection expenditures which the contributions financed.

Of course, the Greek experience is in some respects exceptional. (For details of the social consequences of the policies adopted, see Laskos and Tsakalotos 2013: 91–112; the same source also gives full details of their complete economic failure.) However, what is not in the least exceptional is that drastic social regression has, on a very widespread basis, followed upon EU austerity. The Directorate-General for Employment and Social Affairs reports:

> Poverty among the working age population has increased significantly in two out of three EU Member States over the last four years [2008–2012, JG]. More than 50 million people aged 18–64 now live at risk of poverty in the EU; 28 million cannot afford the necessities for a decent life; and over 30 million live in a jobless household. Altogether, this covers nearly a quarter of the working age population.
>
> (European Commission 2014: 129)[2]

Consider, in contrast to Greece, the case of Ireland, star inmate of the debtors' prison and now due for early release. It is certainly the case that specific economic advantages, in particular the presence in Ireland of many export-oriented US and German multinationals, enabled the Irish to obtain a positive stimulus from increased exports rather than being compelled simply to compress imports by reductions in purchasing power. The social costs of austerity, however, are very marked. The 2013 National Reform Programme reports:

> Overall the under-25 age group had an unemployment rate of 30%. This compares to an unemployment rate of 13.5% for prime age workers. Of particular concern is the continued increase in the share of youth unemployed who are out of work for more than one year. They now account for two out of five of all youth unemployed. Despite the high rate of youth unemployment, the absolute number of young unemployed people has fallen somewhat. This reflects demographic developments arising from birth trends in the 1980s and 1990s, the tendency for some young people to stay longer in education rather than seeking work in a depressed market and the impact of emigration.
>
> (Ireland 2013: 14)

The Troika often inserts clauses into its memoranda of understanding and its adjustment programmes requiring the maintenance of a social safety net or the protection of the most vulnerable. How little these caveats mean is illustrated by the Irish Reform Programme's report on poverty:

> In 2011, a third of the Irish population (33.6%) was in combined poverty, i.e. consistent poverty, at-risk-of poverty or basic deprivation. This equates to 1.5 million people. This was an increase of 2.6 percentage points on the 2010 rate of 31%.
>
> (Ireland 2013: 32)

This deterioration takes place despite the Irish government's claim that it implements more effective anti-poverty redistribution than in other member states.

Apart from those inside the debtors' prison, there are member states inflicting every imaginable form of austerity on themselves in the hope of avoiding incarceration. Banyuls and Recio (2012: 209) analyse the case of Spain: after a brief period during which it had tried to prevent a drastic decline in the level of aggregate demand, 'the government performed a strategic u-turn in May 2010, fully accepting a programme of budget adjustment and structural reforms with a neoliberal bent'. The elements of this programme included all the usual austerity measures: cuts in public spending; cuts in public sector wages; freezing of pensions; 'reforms' of the labour market; privatizations. One aspect, much favoured by the German government and other defenders of the austerity drive, is that constitutional limits to state borrowing have been introduced in Spain in accordance with the Fiscal Compact.

Such constitutional or quasi-constitutional limits on either fiscal or monetary policy are dangerous both to the economy and to democracy. In the thinking behind them it is presumed that such constraints can be imposed because decentralized institutions and market forces will bring about any necessary adjustments at minimal cost and because discretionary policies determined by democratic processes are likely to be dysfunctional. Economic history offers many counter-examples to both beliefs (see EuroMemo Group 2013; Sapir 2002: 137).

The law of the strong

It was Walter Hallstein who first said that the European Community was a creature of law. For the sake of the irony one can cite the claim on the EU's website:

> The European Union is based on the rule of law. This means that every action taken by the EU is founded on treaties that have been approved voluntarily and democratically by all EU member countries. For example, if a policy area is not cited in a treaty, the Commission cannot propose a law in that area.[3]

In the austerity drive, however, democratic and voluntary treaties have become infinitely malleable. According to the political scientists, Shaw and Wiener (2000: 78–9):

> EU constitutionalism … is about transgressing but not ultimately transcending the established divide between domestic law in which constitutionalism is a comfortable discourse, and international law which swings between the formal legitimacy offered by the principle of *pacta sunt servanda* operating between formally equal and sovereign states which holds together the EU from an external perspective and a more base power politics involving realistically unequal relations of political and economic power.

With the 'Merkel method', that 'more base' power politics and the reality of unequal relations have recently multiplied the number of such transgressions.[4] Transcendence, however, remains a distant prospect unless one accepts as such the increasing willingness of commentators to announce that certain *pacta non sunt servanda*.[5]

The democratic deficit of the EU is an extreme case of a more general phenomenon. In general, the problems for democracy posed by globalization have become a central theme in contemporary political science. Only a few examples will be alluded to. Crouch, reflecting on his 2004 book *Post-democracy*, writes that firstly,

> the global class of major shareholders … had an ideology (neoliberalism) to express themselves and had the power to exercise major political influence. The second process was economic globalisation, which meant that power was increasingly being exercised by international business

> interests ranging at will over trans-national territories beyond the reach of nation states, the level at which democracy remained largely trapped.
>
> (Crouch 2013)

Streeck (2013) paints an even darker picture:

> If the capitalism of the fiscal consolidation state can no longer sustain the illusion of growth shared in a socially just way, the moment arrives when the paths of capitalism and democracy must part. Today the most probable outcome would be the completion of the Hayekian model of society in which the dictatorship of the market economy is protected from democratic correction. Its legitimacy depends on this, that those who once formed the people of the state, would have learnt to consider legal market functioning and social justice to be the same thing and to conceive themselves as a people united by market relationships. Its stability would require effective instruments by which the others, who do not wish to accept this, can be ideologically marginalised, politically disorganised and kept physically in check.
>
> (p. 235)

Rodrik (for example 2011) has explored these tensions. His 'trilemma' rules out a successful combination of nation-states, deep integration into the global economy and democratic politics. An escape would require either a globalization of 'democratic governance along with markets' or the rewriting of trade and investment agreements to permit greater autonomy at the level of the nation-states. Crum (2013) maps Rodrik's trilemma very convincingly onto the current political problems of the eurozone. In principle, the EU could act to shield its member states against many of the pressures which the global economy puts on their democracies. In practice, it intensifies these pressures because it subordinates all internal objectives to the pursuit of 'competitiveness' and because its absolute priority is always market access and competition rules.

Scharpf (2011), in a study of macroeconomic policy-making, finds threats to both 'output' and 'input' legitimacy. As regards the first:

> the 'rescue-cum-retrenchment' regime presently imposed on GIPS countries [Greece, Italy, Portugal, Spain, JG] can only be considered a disaster of output-oriented legitimacy. Two-digit and still rising rates of unemployment, massive real-wage cuts, and rising social inequality will surely not generate outcome satisfaction.
>
> (p. 193)

In spite of this, GIPS governments may for a while retain input legitimacy by blaming austerity policies on their predecessors:

> But they must still struggle with the perception that the 'undertakings' they had to sign in order to obtain the guarantees of the Financial Stability Fund read less like self-chosen programs than like the protocols of an unconditional surrender … To a lesser degree, the same problems arise in all EMU member states in consequence of the measures required and sanctioned by the Excessive Deficit or Imbalance Procedures … where the Commission's requirements would violate politically salient interests, preferences and values of national constituencies, compliance may once again undermine democratic legitimacy.
>
> (p. 194)

Scharpf's view would seem to be that the EU and the EMU as such are not seen as directly legitimate. They borrow their legitimacy from national political systems where credible claims can be made as to the value of participation in these institutions. If EU rules and decisions undermine the legitimacy of member state governments, that debt goes unpaid and the European institutions themselves are undermined. The core of the legitimacy problems of the EU (see also Bieling, Chapter 6 in this volume), now acknowledged even by the president of the Commission,[6] is economic: the imposition of an economic model which is dogmatically held to be the only one feasible. Since this claim is invalid the consequence is economic failure, and since it denies the citizens of EU countries the right to determine what forms of economic organization should be chosen and in what way conflicts should be resolved it undermines the democratic process.

However, social policies are an important aspect of the EU crisis (Grahl and Teague 2013). In the first place, the destabilization of member state social models, with no compensating policies at EU level, reflects the reversal of ends and means in the EU. Member states would still endorse the declared social objectives of the EU, for instance as these are expressed in Article 1 of the Maastricht Treaty:

> The Community and the Member States shall have as their objectives the promotion of employment, improved living and working conditions, proper social protection, dialogue between management and labour, the development of human resources with a view to lasting high employment and the combating of exclusion.

However, the next sentence adds: 'To this end the Community and the Member States shall implement measures which take account of … the need to maintain the competitiveness of the Community economy' (European Union 1992; see also Wigger, Chapter 7 in this volume).

This theme of external competitiveness, invariably used to justify the strategies and structures of the EU, is in reality highly questionable. Economic progress in low-income countries, surely a very desirable development, would be bound to raise their productivity relative to that of the EU and thus diminish the 'competitiveness' of the latter. On the other hand, the EU members have flexible exchange rates and thus can avoid the macroeconomic problems associated with rapid import penetration. It is clearly the German export sector which benefits most from the monetary union, although the weaker economies of the Eurozone are bearing most of the costs of its preservation (see Flassbeck and Lapavitsas, Chapter 8 in this volume). Thus, although the adoption of a more practical and effective economic model would be the key to resolving the EU crisis, one aspect of a more realistic approach to economic policy would be to recognize that social objectives are as important as economic ones and cannot be continuously sacrificed to the latter.

Secondly, EU-level social policies, with adequate funding, could be a practical and politically successful way of implementing an economic policy aimed at reducing unemployment and lowering the imbalances between member states. Stockhammer (2012) argues that 'a European welfare state would be economically viable in that it would address or prevent many of the imbalances that led to the present crisis'. He identifies three key components of a Keynesian policy package: a wage policy aimed at higher wages in the countries with trade surpluses, rather than wage cuts in the weaker ones; controls over financial flows; and 'a robust mechanism of redistribution across regions' which could take the form of a European social security system. Galbraith (2007: 6) has made a convergent argument on the value of a European Pension Union.

An initiative in the same direction has come from the European Commission's Directorate General for Employment Affairs, which has promoted a Youth Guarantee requiring intervention to assist the millions of young Europeans without work. It is politically astute to concentrate on the plight of young people – their neglect represents the neglect by the EU of its own future. However, many member states do not have the resources to operate a comprehensive programme for their young unemployed, and the resources of the EU's central budget are quite insufficient to finance the programme. The value of the initiative is therefore chiefly political – it reminds the strongest member states of their failure to respond to the most pressing needs of the Union.[7]

Conclusion

Perhaps the most alarming aspect of the EU's current economic strategy is not the dysfunctional austerity drive, nor the absolute priority given to the competition regime, nor the lack of democratic control over the ECB, nor the assault on national social protection regimes, nor the attempt to resolve imbalances almost entirely at the expense of the weakest member states. What is truly alarming is that these very dubious positions are being perpetuated by writing them into treaties, or by giving them constitutional or quasi-constitutional status. The distrust of democratic decision-making is so extreme that electorates have been virtually prevented from changing the priorities, the objectives or the instruments of the present strategy (see Oberndorfer, Chapter 11 in this volume).[8] The consequence must be that the structures of the European

Union will represent a major obstacle to any movement for the reassertion of democratic decision-taking, and that in consequence such movements will be unable to progress except by challenging the project of European integration.

In these circumstances it is logical to propose a radical redefinition of the European project, a 'refoundation' of the EU, as called for recently by some scholars attached to the Social-Democratic Party in Germany. Nida-Rümelin *et al.* (2013: 11) argue:

> The basic social rights, enshrined as directly applicable EU law, must be given precedence over competition rules. In the Treaty texts it must be clearly spelled out that the EU exists to promote not only economic growth, but also social progress.

Without such a fundamental change of direction by the EU, it is difficult to foresee how the European project can be rescued from the increasing disillusion and hostility of the peoples it exists to serve.

Notes

1 Maastricht Treaty, Social Protocol, article 2, paragraph 6: 'The provisions of this Article shall not apply to pay, the right of association, the right to strike or the right to impose lock-outs' (European Union 1992).
2 Note that Eurostat methods minimize the increase in poverty because the definition involves median incomes, which have fallen rapidly in many member states.
3 http://europa.eu/about-eu/basic-information/decision-making/treaties/index_en.htm
4 See EuroMemo Group (2013) 'Key elements of the "Merkel method" are: strengthening intergovernmental proceedings in negotiations during the crisis; an insistence that only the proposed strategy is feasible; and especially extracting political and economic concessions in exchange for monetary aid' (footnote 14).
5 For example, Bernier (2011) who urges, 'désobéissons à l'Union européenne'. See also Cassen (2012).
6 'Socially and politically, one policy that is only seen as austerity is, of course, not sustainable. We haven't done everything right … The policy has reached its limits because it has to have a minimum of political and social support.' José Manuel Barroso, cited in the *Guardian*, 22 April 2013.
7 The opening remarks of this chapter, which characterized the social policies of the EU as 'ceremonial', should in no way be taken as a criticism of the present activities of the Directorate General for Employment and Social Affairs. Indeed this DG has, since the appointment of a new Commission in 2009, challenged in an increasingly forthright way the *pensée unique* of the EU institutions as a whole. The Commissioner, Laszlo Andor, has repeatedly stressed the social costs of current EU economic policies and called for social policy initiatives corresponding to the EU's power and responsibilities. However, it remains the case that social policy in the EU is completely subordinated to competition rules and restrictions on budgetary policies.
8 'What is the point of voting for a Keynesian candidate if Keynesianism is ruled out by the constitution?' Oral remark of Engelbert Stockhammer, EuroMemo workshop, September 2013.

References

Banyuls, J. and Recio, A. (2012) Spain: The Nightmare of Mediterranean Neoliberalism. In Lehndorf, S. (ed.) *The Triumph of Failed Ideas: European Models of Capitalism in the Crisis.* Brussels: ETUI, pp. 199–218.

Benton, M. and Petrovic, M. (2013) *How Free is Free Movement? Dynamics and Drivers of Mobility within the European Union.* Brussels: Migration Policy Institute Europe. March.

Bernier, A. (2011) *Désobéissons à l'Union européenne.* Paris: Fayard/Mille et une nuits.

Cassen, B. (2012) Désobéissance civique pour une Europe de gauche. *Le Monde Diplomatique*, October, pp. 4–5.

Clauwaert, S. and Schömann, I. (2012) *The Crisis and National Labour Law Reforms: A Mapping Exercise.* ETUI Working Paper, April 2012.

Cremers, J. (2011) *In Search of Cheap Labour in Europe.* Brussels: CLR/EFBWW/International Books.

Crouch, C. (2013) The Possibility of Post-democracy. *Fabian Review* 125(4), pp. 22–24.

Crum, B. (2013) Saving the Euro at the Cost of Democracy. *Journal of Common Market Studies* 52(4), pp. 614–630.

Delors, J. (1997) 'Avons-nous trahi le projet économique et social?' *Entre mondialisation et nations, quelle Europe?* Semaines sociales de France. Paris : Bayard.

Dräger, K. (2011) *Sado-monetarism Rules Ok?! EU Economic Governance and its Consequences.* [Online] Available from www.euromemo.eu/show/4028166.html?searchshow=sado-monetarism [Accessed 1 December 2013].

Économistes Atterrés (2012) *L'Europe Maltraitée: Refuser le Pacte budgétaire et ouvrir d'autre perspectives.* Paris : Les liens qui libèrent.

EuroMemo Group (2013) *EuroMemorandum 2014: The Deepening Divisions in Europe and the Need for a Radical Alternative to EU Policies.* [Online] Available from www.euromemo.eu/euromemorandum/euromemorandum_2014/index.html [Accessed 20 December 2013].

European Commission (2001) *Realising the European Union's Potential: Consolidating and Extending the Lisbon Strategy – Contribution of the European Commission to the Spring European Council.* Stockholm, COM (2001) 79 final. [Online] Available from http://eur-lex.europa.eu/legal-content/EN/TXT/HTML/?uri=CELEX:52001DC0079&from=en [Accessed 20 December 2013].

European Commission (2009) *Quarterly Report on the Euro Area* 8(3), pp. October.

European Commission (2012) The Second Economic Adjustment Programme for Greece. *European Economy, Occasional Papers* 94. March.

European Commission (2014) *Economic and Social Developments in Europe 2013.* Luxembourg: European Commission.

European Union (1992) Treaty on European Union. *Official Journal.* 29 July.

Ewing, K. (2011) *The Draft Monti II Regulation: An Inadequate Response to Viking and Laval.* Liverpool: Institute of Employment Rights.

Ewing, K. and Hendy, J. (eds) (2009) *The New Spectre Haunting Europe – The ECJ, Trade Union Rights and the British Government.* Liverpool: Institute of Employment Rights.

Galbraith, J.K. (2007) *Maastricht 2042 and the Fate of Europe: Towards Convergence and Full Employment.* Levy Economic Institute, Public Policy Brief, 87A. [Online] Available from www.levyinstitute.org/pubs/hili_87a.pdf [Accessed 3 September 2014].

Grahl, J. and Teague, P. (2013) Reconstructing the Eurozone: The Role of EU Social Policy. *Cambridge Journal of Economics* 37(3), pp. 677–692.

Filoche, G. (2008) Tornade Patronale sur le Code du Travail. *Le Monde Diplomatique*, March, pp. 12–13.

Ireland (2013) *National Reform Programme 2014*. [Online] Available from http://ec.europa.eu/europe2020/pdf/csr2014/nrp2014_ireland_en.pdf [Accessed 9 January 2014].

Karamessini, M. (2012) Sovereign Debt Crisis: an Opportunity to Complete the Neoliberal Project and Dismantle the Greek Employment Model. In Lehndorf, S. (ed.) *The Triumph of Failed Ideas: European Models of Capitalism in the Crisis*. Brussels: ETUI, pp. 155–182.

Laskos, C. and Tsakalotos, E. (2013) *Crucible of Resistance: Greece, the Eurozone and the World Economic Crisis*. London: Pluto.

Milward, A. (2000) *The European Rescue of the Nation State*. 2nd edition. London: Routledge.

Nida-Rümelin, J. et al. (2013) We Need a Europe that is Truly Social and Democratic: The Case for a Fundamental Reform of the European Union. *Social Europe*. Occasional Paper. November.

Rodrik, D. (2011) *The Globalization Paradox: Why Global Markets, States and Democracy Can't Coexist*. Oxford: OUP.

Sapir, J. (2002) *Les économistes contre la démocratie*. Paris: Albin Michel.

Scharpf, F.W. (2011) Monetary Union, Fiscal Crisis and the Pre-emption of Democracy. *Zeitschrift für Staats- und Europawissenschaften* 2, pp. 163–198.

Shaw, J. and Wiener, A. (2000) The Paradox of the European Polity. In Green Cowles, M. and Smith, M. (eds) *The State of the European Union: Risks, Reform, Resistance, and Revival*. Oxford: OUP.

Standing, G. (1999) *Global Labour Flexibility: Seeking Distributive Justice*. Basingstoke: Macmillan.

Stockhammer, E. (2012) The Euro Crisis, European Neoliberalism and the Need for a European Welfare State. *Soundings* 50. Spring, pp. 121–130.

Streeck, W. (1993) *Gekaufte Zeit: die vertagte Krise des demokratischen Kapitalismus*. Berlin: Suhrkamp.

11 From new constitutionalism to authoritarian constitutionalism

New Economic Governance and the state of European democracy

Lukas Oberndorfer

> Finally, the crisis has shown the need to strengthen [the Economic and Monetary Union's] ability to take rapid executive decisions to improve crisis management in bad times and economic policymaking in good times.
>
> (Rompuy 2012: 17)

This avowal by the President of the European Council to 'solve' the crisis by means of executive decisions is reminiscent of the economic and judicial policies of the Weimar Republic. After the costs of the crisis (from 1929) had ripped a huge hole in the budget, German industrialist associations and intellectuals of the 'new liberalism' attempted to retell the crisis as one of state debt. The 'over-exploitation' of the state by welfare policies and the 'overburdening' of the economy with the tax burden had to be revised (Witt 1982: 388) by means of 'structural reforms' and a 'debt ceiling'. In the absence of parliamentary majorities for the introduction of these instruments, these policies, which involved drastic social consequences, were pushed through by 'presidential cabinets' assisted by Carl Schmitt as their legal adviser. Ultimately, all of the measures mentioned were adopted by the executive using emergency regulations, which were justified on the basis of an ongoing state of emergency (Oberndorfer 2012a).

Even if the current crisis in the European Union (EU) cannot be compared to the Weimar Republic in many aspects, some parallels are obvious: in Greece and Spain, the austerity policies ordered by the European executive have caused massive economic collapse. Unemployment in these two countries is above 25 per cent and more than 55 per cent of young people are without work, figures surpassed in the Weimar Republic in only one year (Eurostat 2013). With these developments, the 'rift between the represented and the representatives' (Gramsci 1996: 1577) is widening ever faster: the unfolding crisis of capitalism – the most severe since the 1930s – is taking the shine off neoliberal imaginaries and is eroding the aura of those neoliberal projects that were implemented in the context of the European Union (Bieling and Steinhilber 2000: 106). As a result, the present neoliberal mode of integration, which was based on consensus, is sliding into an ever deeper crisis of hegemony (Gramsci 1996: 1576, see also Bieling, Chapter 6 in this volume).

This becomes blatantly obvious when some of the 'organic intellectuals' (Gramsci 1996: 1557) of the dominant ideology, whose role it is to constantly universalize and rejuvenate it, are starting to defect from their previous beliefs. Discursive elements such as 'The left might actually be right' (Moore 2011)[1] and 'Among the bourgeoisie, doubts are growing whether they were right all their lives' (Schirrmacher 2011)[2] therefore represent much more than a storm in a newspaper teacup.

But the crisis is not just causing the production of a 'world view' (Gramsci 1992b: 719) and 'visions of Europe' to slow down; it is also affecting the second aspect of consensus-based rule: bank bailouts and the recession-induced reduction in tax revenues have made public debt explode, drastically reducing the scope for 'material concessions'. One after another, subaltern groups in various EU member states are being targeted by austerity programmes. In contrast, however, to the neoliberal austerity measures that accompanied the implementation of Economic and Monetary Union (EMU), current cuts are supported by neither the people's active nor their passive consent (cf. Gramsci 1992a: 481).

This can be seen in the increasingly vocal opposition and protest that has ignited strongly, parallel in spatial terms to the unequal but combined development of European capitalism. While things remained comparatively calm in the 'world champion export countries', which were able to externalize (Feigl and Zuckerstätter 2012: 1), the problem of insufficient demand by wage restraint and job market flexibility led to intense social battles in the economically peripheral countries (Horn and Wigger 2013: 202). Nevertheless, the political crisis, unfolding asymmetrically in the member states, is being felt at a European level. For, at the latest, the deep economic, monetary and political integration related to the euro has brought about the formation of a European ensemble of state apparatuses (Buckel et al. 2012) that closely entangles the national and European institutions and their (in-)stabilities, not least through European law. This crisis of hegemony, as the thesis goes, expresses itself in the replacement of consensus, which has become brittle, by executive legislation and force on various scale levels (Caceres and Oberndorfer 2013).

Because what has burst open with the slogan 'real democracy now!' is more than a small flurry of social protest (Candeias and Völpel 2014). For in this demand lies unease about a process of de-democratization and the reduction of social rights that has achieved a *new quality* with the greatest crisis in the world economy since the 1980s. While the neoliberalization of all fields of society and life since the beginning of the 1980s has been accompanied by a creeping erosion of the moment of substantive democracy fought for and won in the past – a process described by Colin Crouch as post-democracy (Crouch 2013)[3] – the attempts of the European ensemble of state apparatuses to manage the crisis are intensifying this process into an authoritarian turn that is also breaking with elements of *formal* democracy and is infringing fundamental rights (Fischer-Lescano 2014).

This is articulated not least in the fact that the central building blocks of neoliberal crisis policy – such as the so-called 'New Economic Governance' (and/or its constituent parts: the Six-pack passed in Autumn 2011 and the

Two-pack passed in May 2013) (Oberndorfer 2011), or the Fiscal Compact – have no adequate legal basis in the 'European Constitution' and could be established (Fischer-Lescano and Oberndorfer 2013) only through bypassing the ordinary revision procedure of the European Treaties (Article 48 TEU[4]). Not only the justifying statements made, such as that of Van Rompuy, but also the 'juristic' argumentation and techniques, such as the use of Article 136 Treaty on the Functioning of the European Union (TFEU) as a blanket clause for the creation of almost unlimited emergency law (Häde 2011a), seem to give Carl Schmitt 'alarming topicality' (Joerges 2012: 377). Characteristic of the previous instruments of crisis policy is also that they entail a massive upgrade of the executive apparatuses and have equipped them with comprehensive decision- and sanction-making competencies. At the same time, the parliamentary arena has been decisively weakened, at a national as well as a European level.

The suggestions made so far by leading figures of the European ensemble of state apparatuses within the framework of the debate started in June 2012 on deepening the Economic and Monetary Union (EMU)[5] are also marked by this direction of impact. After the rules for a strict austerity policy by means of an authoritarian constitutionalism all over Europe were given permanence, and thus made immune from a democratic challenge, we are now concerned with a Europeanization of structural reforms (Hermann 2012) tested in southern European laboratories. In 'contracts for competitiveness', according to German Chancellor Angela Merkel, member states should, with respect to the European Commission (COM), commit themselves to deregulating the labour market, to reforming their pension systems and to lowering their wages. The European Commission declares openly that the planned contracts aim at overcoming political resistance.

Legal structures are excellent indicators of shifts in the democratic system, as was emphasized from a neo-Gramscian perspective (Opratko and Prausmüller 2011) by Stephen Gill back in the 1990s, when he described the legal reframing of the neoliberal reorganization of economy and society at the transnational level with his concept of 'new constitutionalism'. According to him, new constitutionalism is leading to a European juridification, by which economic policies to a great extent evade popular-democratic controls (Gill 1998). This is occurring by the establishment of internal and external practical constraints, which include binding limits and rules for fiscal and economic policy and aim at making neoliberal capitalism the only model for the future. The new constitutionalism grants 'corporate capital' privileged rights, 'while constraining the democratic process that has involved struggles for representation for hundreds of years' (Gill 2003: 131). Thus an institutional and operational establishment of the independence of political and judicial decision-making processes is accompanied by a curtailment of democratic controlling rights (Bieling 2013: 216).

In light of the present social rupture, the concept of new constitutionalism must, however, be radicalized. The shifts taking place in the field of 'European law' have to be reconceptualized in parallel to developments across the whole society that are tending in the direction of 'authoritarian competitive statism' (Oberndorfer 2012b) and are increasingly difficult to describe with the topos of post-democracy, since it posits an incremental process up to the crisis that left the procedures and institutions of formal democracy untouched.[6] It is my view that the new constitutionalism, with which Gill described the legal codification of neoliberal dogmas in a manner that abides by European and international law and is supported by an at least passive consensus, is evolving into an *authoritarian* constitutionalism.

In order to be able to illustrate these developments and ruptures in the European judicial system, I shall depict the primary legal bases of European economic policy in Section 1. Here, on the one hand, those 'constitutionally legal' assurances of neoliberal policies will become tangible, which Stephen Gill terms 'new constitutionalism'. On the other hand, this is also an illustration of the legal foundations on which the legal acts of the New Economic Governance and the contracts for competitiveness lie. On this basis, the essential instruments of the crisis policy will be explained (Section 2) and legal issues will be addressed which show a pattern: in order to promote the neoliberal 'processing of the crisis', despite a collapsing consensus, the ordinary revision procedure is being circumvented and/or the appropriate instruments are being pressed into the 'European Constitution' illegally (Section 3). Theoretical deliberations on the character of the exposed authoritarian constitutionalism and the dangers and chances for democracy in Europe follow.

The new constitutionalism – or the European legal basis of economic policy

The primary legal structure of the economic policy of the European Union was set down by the Treaty of Maastricht (1992) and since then has essentially remained unchanged. The fact that the pertinent articles (120 to 126) of the Treaty on the Functioning of the European Union (TFEU) were conceived in the phase of 'euphoric neoliberalism' (Bieling and Steinhilber 2000: 112), becomes clear in the principles that prefix the chapter on economic policy. Thus the Union and the member states are obliged to create their economic policy in 'accordance with the principle of an open market economy with free competition' (Art. 120 TFEU) and to comply 'with the following guiding principles: stable prices, sound public finances and monetary conditions and a sustainable balance of payments' (Art. 119 para. 3 TFEU).

These elements of neoliberal theory petrified into a 'constitution' are complemented by the statement that through free competition 'an efficient allocation of resources' is favoured (Art. 120 TFEU). This is little more than a 'constitutional' reference to an economic theoretician who is known for supporting anti-democratic impulses in the name of the 'market' (Hayek 1969: 249). The conviction, clearly prominent in this principle, of constitutionally anchoring economic ideologies refers to the theory of 'economic constitution' (*Wirtschaftsverfassung*) (Joerges 1991: 225) that understands itself to be an overall decision about the economic life of a community and not to be subject to a democratic challenge. Ordoliberal intellectuals (Ptak 2004) developed this concept in the 1930s and brought it into position against the increasing demands for democratization of the economy (Oberndorfer 2012a). At the latest, by the 1970s a Europeanization of the theory of 'economic constitution' arose, in which a 'constitutionally legal' binding of economic policy on a European level was called for that should conform strictly to justiciable criteria in its execution (Mestmäcker 1973: 109). How much this conception could be realized in the EU's principles of economic policy is also reflected in the juridical commentary literature. In the face of the relevant provisions, Ulrich Häde comes to the conclusion that the European Treaties are close to the neoliberal concept of an 'economic constitution' (Behrens 1994: 73), understood as an anti-interventionist legal framework (Häde 2007a).

Apart from the economic principles, the chapter on economic policy has three essential objects of regulation. Article 121 TFEU contains the procedure for coordinating the economic policy of the member states and establishes the competences of the relevant institutions of the European Union. Article 126 regulates behaviour in case of excessive deficit. Art. 123 to 125 TFEU, finally, contain prohibitions of public refinancing away from the financial markets.

The comprehensive prohibition of public refinancing to release market power and for disciplining the welfare state

The last-mentioned prohibitions entail that those member states whose currency is the euro can no longer finance themselves 'cheaply' through their central banks. In addition, a direct injection of funds by the European Central Bank (ECB) and a common European debt and/or liability is forbidden. This monetary regime was described by legal science long before the economic crisis and its specific unfolding in the EU as the legal establishment of the disciplining of the public sector by the market: 'The state should … face the laws of the market when borrowing money. If the buyers of government bonds see the debt as problematic, then the state should be confronted with rising credit costs' (Gnan 1999: 3).

The fact that this constitutionalization of the 'monetarist revolution' (Brunner 1970) has not only been driven forward by the financial markets and the European Commission (especially by its Directorate General for Economic and Financial Affairs – DG ECFIN – see also Grahl, Chapter 10 in this volume), but also in a massive way by national state apparatuses, in particular the neoliberally oriented finance ministries, who thus try to weaken welfare state-oriented institutions, can be seen in the history of the origins of the provisions. It was the present Economic and Financial Committee, to which each member state sends two members, and who are to be selected 'from among senior officials from the administration and the national central bank',[7] who proposed the prohibition of financing away from the capital markets in the course of preparations for the Treaty of Maastricht (Gnan 1999: 12).

Beyond the prohibitions of public refinancing, the chapter on economic policy, as previously mentioned, regulates the process of economic coordination (Art. 121 TFEU) and the excessive deficit procedure (Art. 126 TFEU). Finally the chapter contains Art. 136 TFEU, which aims to enable the member states of the Eurozone to achieve a stronger coordination in the areas of Art. 121 and 126. The Commission has chosen those three provisions as a legal basis for the New Economic Governance (Six-pack and Two-pack) and is planning to propose a Regulation for establishing the 'contracts for competitiveness' on the basis of these articles as well.

Economic coordination – principles, proceedings and sanctions (Art. 121 TFEU)

The member states agreed in the Treaty of Maastricht that they would 'regard their economic policies as a matter of common concern and shall coordinate them within the Council' (Art. 121 para.1). The complete Communitization of monetary policy therefore finds in the field of economic policy no equivalent. The term 'their economic policies' rather expresses that this remains the responsibility of the member states (Koch 2010: 3). They still create and implement economic policy in their own jurisdiction but they are by law bound to fall in line with the procedures and content of a coordinated economic policy. This is evident from the fact that 'even the sharpest sanctions in the course of economic supervision consist of merely a warning' (Kempen 2012a: 1), which as a recommendation is not legally binding.

The pivotal point of the process is marked by the 'broad guidelines of the economic policies of the Member States and of the Union', which are adopted by the Council. If the Council reaches the conclusion, on the basis of reports by the Commission, that the economic policy of a member state does not correspond to the 'broad guidelines of the economic policies', or risks 'jeopardising the proper functioning of the economic and monetary union', then it can direct a recommendation to that member state. The Council is not obliged to give a recommendation ('may'). Rather, it is granted 'wide political discretionary power' (Hattenberger 2009: n. 15).

In order to create a certain 'pillory effect', the Council can also publish its recommendations. But the sanctions arsenal does not go beyond this 'naming and shaming': 'The Council can do no more; its possibilities end here' (Häde 2007b: 15). The Council makes decisions in the field of economic coordination by qualified majority.

Proceedings and sanctions regarding excessive deficits (Art. 126 TFEU)

The proceedings regulated by Art. 126 TFEU achieved fame through the co-called 'Maastricht Criteria'. According to this article, the member states are obliged to avoid excessive deficits. Significant for evaluation are two reference values: the government debt and government deficit as a percentage of GDP

(60 per cent and 3 per cent). The goal of this treaty determination is to make an 'expansive budgetary policy' impossible (Schulze-Steinen 1998: 234). Art. 126 contains a multi-staged procedure whose steps build on and depend on one another. To be able to justify 'hard sanctions' (for example, fines), which can be imposed by the Council in the excessive deficit procedure (in contrast to procedure for economic coordination, Art. 121 TFEU) and in order to give the member states the time and opportunity to reduce their excessive deficits, all procedural steps must be passed before the Council can finally decide about administering sanctions.

The Stability and Growth Pact

In order to further develop the procedure for economic coordination and the excessive deficit procedure, the Stability and Growth Pact was adopted in 1997. The Regulation 'on the strengthening of the surveillance of budgetary positions and the surveillance and coordination of economic policies',[8] also denoting the preventive component in the pact, was decreed on the basis of Art. 121 par. 6 TFEU, which authorizes the Council to determine the 'details' of proceedings. It makes the obligation to 'inform' on the part of the member states (Art. 121 para.3 TFEU) more concrete by prescribing the submission of so-called stability programmes containing medium-term budgetary objectives. In the case of substantial deviations from these objectives, the Council can direct a recommendation to the relevant member state 'at an early stage' to effect the implementation of necessary measures (Kempen 2012c: 20). The Regulation denoted as the corrective component[9] was decreed on the basis of Art. 126 para. 14 TFEU. The Regulation established, calculated from the announcement of the budget data, a ten-month time limit for the decision to level sanctions, as well as additional interim deadlines for the procedural steps of Art. 126 TFEU (Art. 7 Reg. 1467/97).

Surveillance and neoliberal normalisation

By means of this – now concluded – illustration of the primary law and secondary regulation of the economic policy until the crisis, we can confirm Stephen Gill's thesis: the new constitutionalism constructs a governmental surveillance system of national economic policy that corresponds to Michel Foucault's concept of control by 'surveillance and normalization' (Foucault 2007, 2008). Even when there is no direct control, economic policies are 'surveilled' by European and international financial institutions and thus are subject to a neoliberal 'self-rule' (Gill 1998: 13). This statement must, however, be differentiated: upon closer examination, we find in the chapter on economic policy two different logics that enable economic policy to divest itself of 'popular-democratic control'. In the procedure of economic coordination (Art. 121 TFEU), with regard to excessive deficits (Art. 126 TFEU) and intensified coordination and information in the Eurozone (Art. 136

TFEU), the member states retain certain discretionary powers, even if to differing degrees, within which they can shape their budgetary and economic policy. Popular-democratic powers still have the chance to problematize the respective policies of their national state apparatus, because they are, at least *formally*, responsible for them and have decision-making powers. Nevertheless, the fairly effective limitation and/or partitioning of these powers functions entirely in accordance with the governmental pattern of 'surveillance and normalisation' described by Gill: neoliberal path dependency is created by rule-based economic policy, competitive evaluation and self-evaluation and a discursive separation of member states into model students and sinners, although this cannot be imposed unconditionally.

However, the prohibition on public refinancing away from the financial markets (Art. 123 to 125 TFEU) extends beyond the logic of surveillance and normalization. In connection with the spatial shift of monetary policy to the European level laid down by the Maastricht Treaty (competence now lies with the explicitly independent ECB), access to public refinancing apart from the financial markets remains blocked for states even during crises and prohibited for the ECB – even if 'popular-democratic powers' could exercise effective pressure on their decision-makers. Regarding the blockade of public refinancing Stephen Gill's remarks therefore are to be put into concrete terms: the new constitutionalism in this area not only operates through surveillance and normalization but has in this field made national economic policy immediately subject to discipline by markets; a connection which became generally tangible during the crisis. In Foucault's terms, this area has rather become a system of 'surveillance and punishment' (Foucault 1977). This 'retardation' of governing technologies 'back' to direct domination, which detaches itself even more strongly from 'self-rule' and consensus, now comes to a head – as the following sections will show – in *authoritarian constitutionalism* and is transferred to other fields of economic policy.

New Economic Governance and contracts for competitiveness as authoritarian constitutionalism

> What is going on is a silent revolution – a silent revolution in terms of stronger governance by small steps. The member states have accepted – and I hope they understood it exactly – (…) very important powers of the European institutions regarding surveillance, and much stricter controls of the public finances'.
>
> (José Manuel Barroso, speech to the European University College, 18 June 2010)

This announcement by the President of the European Commission has become reality. In separate steps, and for the most part aside from public debate and academic discussion, a 'silent neoliberal revolution' (Klatzer and Schlager 2011: 61) is taking place, which will entail a profound restructuring of European economic policy. So far we can establish three stages in which the 'New Economic Governance' has been set up. In Autumn 2011, the so-called

Six-pack went into effect, a package of five regulations and a directive. In May 2013, the Two-pack, consisting of two regulations, followed, and in 2014 the next step is planned: the 'contracts for competitiveness'.

The tightening of the Stability and Growth Pact

Three of the six legal acts of the so-called Six-pack are aimed at tightening the Stability and Growth Pact.

With Regulation 1175/2011,[10] the *preventive* component of the SGP is tightened, especially by the following reforms: (i) If the debt level of a member state is higher than 60 per cent of GDP, the annual improvement of the cyclically adjusted budget balance must be at least 0.5 per cent of GDP; (ii) The Regulation introduces a rule to limit spending growth – the annual expenditure growth must not exceed the 'reference medium-term rate of the potential GDP growth'; (iii) In resolving whether the concerned member state has failed to take remedial measures, the Commission has received upgraded support from the 'introduction' of a Reverse Majority Voting. Thus the resolution 'shall be deemed to be adopted by Council unless it decides, by simple majority, to reject the recommendation within 10 days of its adoption by the Commission' (Art. 6 para. 2 as amended by Reg. 1466/97 Reg. 1175/2011). The *corrective* component of the SGP is tightened in particular by means of the Regulation 1177/2011,[11] so that in future the development of the government debt will have the same importance as that of the budget deficit. This was achieved by inserting a new section that more closely defines just what is to be understood by sufficient regressiveness of the level of government debt: it exists when the difference from the reference value (now 60 per cent) has decreased in the past three years 'on an annual average by one twentieth' (Art. 1a Reg. 1467/97 as amended by Reg. 1177/2011).

Ultimately, the SGP was 'effectuated' to effectively enforce budgetary surveillance by means of a new Regulation (1173/2011).[12] The Regulation determines a sanction system for the preventive and corrective components of the SGP, but it is valid 'only' for those member states whose currency is the euro (Art. 1 Reg. 1172/2011). In the preventive arm of the SGP, the concerned member state will be obliged to deposit an interest-bearing security of 0.2 per cent of GDP, when the decision has been made that it has failed to undertake appropriate measures against a considerable deviation from the adjustment path.

As an executive measure for the corrective component of the SGP, the Regulation further provides that, following the decision of the Council a fine of 0.2 per cent of GDP can be levied with a further decision (Art. 6 para. 1 Reg.). Here and in the preventive arm as well, the regulations impose a Reverse Majority Voting for the decision making concerning sanctions. In spite of the comprehensive enhancement of the role of the European executive branch (Directorate General for Economic and Financial Affairs of the European Commission – DG ECFIN), in the 'renewed' SGP and the tightening of its austerity rules, the abovementioned regulations provide for no co-decision rights for the European Parliament. Under the title of 'Economic Dialogue', the Parliament is granted only limited consultation rights in the preventive component.

At this point I would like to pause this presentation of the instruments of the New Economic Governance and subject the tightening of the Stability and Growth Pact (SGP) to a brief economic, democratic and judicial interim evaluation. If one observes the tightening of the SGP critically, it seems that the trend that Stephen Gill described as 'the new constitutionalism' is continuing. By tightening a rule-based economic and budgetary policy defined mainly by the European executive branch, this policy can avoid nearly all popular-democratic control. In addition, a turning from the path of neoliberal austerity policies – despite increasing criticism – is becoming ever more subject to preconditions. At the same time, the pro-cyclical effect of the illustrated provisions is further tightened with the 'reforms': the obligation to implement austerity measures even during an economic downturn leads to a further breakdown of (state) demand, and so to a continued decline in the economy and finally to a spiral of debt. This again emphasizes that the new constitutionalism, despite constant repetition of its 'saving' mantra, is not aimed primarily at debt reduction. Rather, it aims at preventing an expansive economic and social policy, which could shift the power relationship in favour of trade unions and social movements.

If one looks at the tightening of the Stability and Growth Pact from a legal and democratic perspective, it becomes clear that the central instruments of the new SGP were passed without the necessary legal competence. This 'radicalization' of the new to an authoritarian constitutionalism becomes particularly obvious in the Macroeconomic Imbalance Procedure (explained in detail below), but it appears even in the 'further development' of the SGP, because the most important components could only have been introduced in compliance with law, by an ordinary revision procedure of the European Treaties (Art. 48 TEU). The 'introduction' of a Reverse Majority Voting which strengthens the European executive (European Commission) is manifestly illegal. Art. 121 TFEU Sec. 6, used to substantiate these changes, allows only the possibility of adopting a Regulation with 'detailed rules for the multilateral surveillance procedure referred to in Art. 121'. But Art. 121 TFEU makes clear that here only the Council is granted the possibility to direct a recommendation to the member states. Art. 121 TFEU neither provides for the legal act of a decision, nor calls on the Commission to adopt such a decision, which consequently receives its validity through inactivity of the Council as provided by Reverse Majority Voting.

Macroeconomic Imbalance Procedure – neoliberal restructuring and interventionism in the area of wage policy

The official title of the 'Regulation on the prevention and correction of macroeconomic imbalances'[13] was purloined from heterodox economists who have stressed for decades that the introduction of EMU without common policies on wages, taxation, transfers and social welfare will accelerate capitalism's inherent tendency to create uneven development. They further argued that the imbalances in the distribution of income and foreign trade would have to be reduced to deal with this principal cause of crisis. To that end, the countries that are running a current account surplus due to wage moderation or labour market deregulation (for example, Hartz IV in Germany), and that are therefore partly responsible for the indebtedness of those countries with a current account deficit, should significantly increase their wages and thus labour costs (Stockhammer, Onaran and Ederer 2009; see also Flassbeck and Lapavitsas, Chapter 8 in this volume).

The above-mentioned Regulation, however, tries to establish an entirely different meaning of uneven development. This becomes obvious where the legal act declares that 'the need for policy action is particularly pressing in Member States showing persistently large current-account deficits and competitiveness losses'.[14] 'Corrections' in the area of 'wage policies' and deregulation of 'labour markets, product and service markets' are to be undertaken[15] until 'competitiveness'[16] is restored. The juridical interpretation of Macroeconomic Imbalance Procedure the regulation leaves little doubt that, by mandating a race to the bottom, 'Economic Governance' aims to create a permanent competition state in and through the legal form.

By drafting the regulation as a largely undetermined framework, the 'European legislature' makes the European executive the sole judge of what constitutes a macroeconomic imbalance. The executive enjoys an almost unlimited latitude to directly push through dominant interests. The European Commission (DG ECFIN) decides whether an imbalance exists in a member state through the use of a 'scoreboard' consisting of 'macroeconomic and macrofinancial indicators'. The Commission decides in an annual update[17] on the composition of these indicators that guide European economic policies. The Council and the European Parliament have the right only to comment.[18] According to the Regulation, the indicators will be used to detect imbalances 'in price and cost developments' as well as 'non-price competitiveness' at an early stage.[19] The wording is unambiguously neoliberal, too, with regard to the crucial question of the current account: the fairly neutral term 'current account positions', which would arguably include surpluses, is still used. In interpreting the Regulation, however, recitals have to be taken into account that require action primarily in the case of 'current-account deficits and competitiveness losses'.[20]

If the Commission reaches the conclusion that a macroeconomic imbalance exists in a member state, it initiates a thorough examination, combined with 'monitoring missions in the concerned Member State'.[21] If the Commission, during this examination, reaches the conclusion that an excessive imbalance exists, the Council can, at the suggestion of the Commission, adopt a recommendation with the statement that an excessive imbalance exists and that corrective action should be taken.[22] This leads to the consequence that the concerned state must present a 'corrective action plan' in which exact structural reforms and a timetable for their implementation must be included.[23]

If the Council reaches the conclusion that the plan for 'corrective action' is sufficient, it shall 'endorse the plan by way of a recommendation'[24] (sic!). Inasmuch as the intended action and the timetable for its implementation are considered insufficient, the Council directs a recommendation to the member state to present a new corrective action plan.[25] Formally, the decision on whether the member state is implementing the corrective action plan properly belongs to the Council; de facto, however, the Commission decides by Reverse Majority Voting: 'The Commission's recommendation on establishing non-compliance shall be deemed to have been adopted by the Council, unless it decides, by qualified majority, to reject the recommendation within 10 days of its adoption by the Commission'.[26]

In order to effect the orderly implementation of competitive restructuring in a timely manner within the Eurozone, the sixth legal provision of the so-called Six-pack was decreed.[27] By adoption of the Macroeconomic Imbalance Procedure, for the first time in European economic policy (aside from the excessive deficit procedure), sanctions have been provided that go beyond mere 'naming and shaming' by publicizing decisions.[28] For Eurozone countries, annual fines of 0.1 per cent of GDP, a substantial sum, can be levied if the corrective action is not implemented properly.[29] The preceding recitals entail that the fine should be imposed until the Council determines that the member state 'has taken corrective measures in compliance with its recommendations'.[30] And the sensitive decision about levying sanctions should take place according to the Regulation by way of Reverse Majority Voting and thus again mainly by the Commission alone.

Although the package of laws also contains some clauses that protect basic and fundamental human rights, closer examination reveals that 'Economic Governance' will interfere substantially with fundamental rights – such as the right to collective bargaining (Art. 28 of the EU Charter of Fundamental Rights). Through reciprocal references, the various levels of the European ensemble of state apparatuses mutually take the burden off each other. Article 1 of the Regulation on competitive restructuring declares that any recommendation must respect trade unions' right to collective bargaining. The Commission, however, does not need to interfere directly with fundamental rights: in keeping with the Regulation's wording,[31] it needs only to demand that 'competitiveness' be enhanced in the area of 'wage policies'. The national level within the European ensemble of state apparatuses (for example, a member state government), which, under this provision, is required to submit concrete corrective measures, can in turn invoke the 'implementation of EU requirements' when interfering with fundamental rights.

The fact that the DG ECFIN is willing to use the competences granted it by the Regulation for further neoliberal restructuring of Europe became apparent on close examination of the Communication[32] of May 2013, which will be dealt with in part here. The Communication recommends that Spain implements further employment market reforms because 'rigidities in product and labour markets contribute to high unemployment'.[33] In Slovenia and

France the minimum wage should be lowered; otherwise – according to DG ECFIN – further losses loom and the profits of corporations would be put under pressure.[34] Alluding to collective bargaining negotiations taking place mainly at sectoral level, the Commission demands that Italy creates a general framework that is friendlier to big business.[35] The DG ECFIN is here obviously attempting to convert its theory into practice outside the countries under the Troika regime: already in 2012, DG ECFIN recorded in a study that the new economic-political control instruments must be used to reduce the 'wage-setting power of trade unions'.[36] Thorsten Schulten and Torsten Müller therefore come to the conclusion that '(t)he new system of European economic governance with its newly introduced mechanisms for monitoring sanctions and intensified coordination has led to a new European interventionism in the area of wage policy' (Schulten and Müller 2013: 181).

Before submitting the Macroeconomic Imbalance Procedure to a legal and democratic analysis, I would first like to illustrate the latest plans for consolidating the Economic and Monetary Union by establishing 'contracts for competitiveness'. Because these are to be decided on the same deficient judicial foundation as the Macroeconomic Imbalance Procedure (Art 121 in conjunction with Art 136 TFEU), it is possible to show how both instruments feature the pattern that I conceptualize as authoritarian constitutionalism.

Contracts for competitiveness

The substance of crisis policy to date, especially of the planned 'contracts for competitiveness', is illustrated particularly well by a keynote speech on the future of the EU[37] given in Davos at the end of January 2013 by a central figure of the European ensemble of state apparatuses.

The European Union, according to Angela Merkel, has been coming along well on a stability path whose guardrails are strict fiscal discipline (tightening of the Stability and Growth Pact; Fiscal Compact) on the one hand, and structural reforms for more competitiveness (Macroeconomic Imbalance Procedure) on the other. The establishment of the necessary instruments would have been 'unimaginable' only a few years ago. But – according to the German Chancellor – what is missing now is an instrument for competitiveness throughout Europe that must create a global competitiveness. The time factor is central, because, on the one hand, it must be ensured that the structural reforms become effective before the political situation escalates further and, on the other hand, experience shows that pressure is needed for such reforms. The massive increase in unemployment in Europe is therefore according to Angela Merkel an opportunity, because in Germany, too, only the existence of five million unemployed made a competitiveness drive possible. Following the implementation of strict fiscal discipline, the next big European issue is the question of competitiveness. In this regard, areas such as 'unit wage costs (and) supplementary wage costs' must be focused upon (see Wigger, Chapter 7 in this volume).

What, exactly, is meant by 'pact for competitiveness' is made clear in, among other sources, a detailed Communication on the deepening of EMU, which the Commission completed by the end of 2012.[38] If the European executive branch has its way, the new instrument should be fitted into the Macroeconomic Imbalance Procedure.[39] Despite the largely unrestricted position on competitive restructuring of European economies accorded the Commission since the adoption of the New Economic Governance, the 'contracts for competitiveness' would once more strengthen the influence of the European executive and national governments in relation to the European Parliament. The 'contracts for competitiveness', according to the concept, are to be concluded directly between the member states and the Commission. In order to further the passing and implementation of reforms 'by overcoming … political and economic deterrents to reform,[40] financial support should be given if the timetable set in the treaty is met. In this way, the short-term impact of reforms raising the flexibility in the labour market could be compensated'.[41] With the 'contracts for competitiveness', a gap in previous crisis policy is to be filled: If a given country does not come under the sway of the Troika and has no 'excessive imbalances', the way to a corrective action plan and thus an eased crackdown on social rights and public services remains closed. This gap is now to be filled.

Even a brief look at these plans makes clear what is supposed to be achieved. The practice of 'Memoranda of Understanding', developed in the southern European laboratory of neoliberalism, which grants financial support in return for detailed 'structural reforms' (ranging from decentralizing collective bargaining to the privatization of the water supply) (Hermann 2012) should be Europeanized. While the 'contracts for competitiveness' seem largely undisputed amongst the leading figures of the European ensemble of state apparatuses, the judicial configuration will still be subject to struggle: in contrast to the German Chancellor, who would like to conclude 'a pact for competitiveness' in accordance with international law, analogous to the Fiscal Compact, the Commission prefers a solution through European secondary law (regulation).

Article 136 TFEU: an unrestricted general clause?

In its concept for the deepening of the EMU, the Commission explains that Art. 136 TFEU, upon which it had already based the Macroeconomic Imbalance Procedure, forms a suitable basis for the 'contracts for competitiveness'.[42] This argumentation is more than doubtful. Article 136 empowers the Council to enact measures for the euro area to (i) 'strengthen the coordination and surveillance of … budgetary discipline' and (ii) to 'set out economic policy guidelines for [the Eurozone states], while ensuring that they are compatible with those adopted for the whole of the Union'.[43] In addition, this must happen only within the framework of the relevant provisions (Art. 121 and 126 TFEU) and according to the procedure laid down therein. This means that the specific rules for the euro area must be within the framework of the boundaries established by the European Treaties, which 'reduces the meaning of the Regulation to a minimum' (Kempen 2012b: 2). Thus it follows that Art. 136 TFEU allows nothing more and nothing less than existing primary law (Louis 2011: 333). It is a matter of fact that it does not contain 'any authorisation for further intervention in the economic competences of the member states' (Häde 2011b: 4). On this basis, at the very most, more intensive coordination and information obligations for the euro area can be established (Kempen 2012b: 2).

Therefore it does not take a legally trained eye to recognize that Article 136 TFEU *does not establish a foundation* for either the essential components of the Macroeconomic Imbalance Procedure, already concluded, *or* for the intended 'contracts for competitiveness'. The relevant Art. 121, to which Art. 136 refers in matters of economic policy, does not provide either for sanctions in the form of fines in the Macroeconomic Imbalance Procedure, or for a Reverse Majority Voting. Just as little authorization can be found in Articles 121 and 126 for the Commission to conclude 'contracts for competitiveness' or any competences for surveillance of implementation of the 'reforms' agreed to. Furthermore, no financial support for the implementation of agreements can be drawn from the European Treaties. With regard to Art. 121 TFEU, the incompatibility with European law of these 'contracts for competitiveness' is thus obvious.

Out of the Pandora's box opened by the Fiscal Compact: the 'contracts for competitiveness'

Perhaps it is this obvious incompatibility with EU law that moved the Commission to leave a back door open in its concept: 'Intergovernmental solutions should therefore only be considered on an exceptional and transitional basis where an EU solution would necessitate a Treaty change'.[44] Here the Commission is alluding to the flight from European law according to the 'Fiscal Compact model'. In any case, a preference for this repeated use of a treaty of international law to circumvent those consensus requirements that are demanded to change the European Treaties can be inferred from the German Chancellor's Davos speech. But it is precisely because this approach would be congruent with the Fiscal Compact that the legal arguments (Fischer-Lescano and Oberndorfer 2013) brought against it can also be transferred to a great extent to a 'pact for competitiveness'. The verdict dominating amongst European law scholars that the Fiscal Compact is contrary to European Union law therefore applies to the 'contracts for competitiveness', too.

Two-pack: an attempt at legalising the Troika and the need for authorisation of national budget plans

In contrast to the 'contracts for competitiveness', the so-called Two-pack has been in effect since May 2013. The first of the two Regulations[45] represents, in essence, an attempt to put the previous role of the Commission within the framework of the Troika on a legal basis. The second Regulation[46] aims at surveillance and coordination of the budgetary policies of the Eurozone member states. The member states have to submit their draft budget to the Commission. If the Commission notes in their opinion a grave violation of the Stability and Growth Pact, it demands that the member state concerned *presents a revision* as soon as possible. In this way the Commission is granted substantial power in an area that was previously termed the 'royal right of parliaments' (Riedel 2012). This rests not on decision-making in a narrow sense, because the opinion is a non-binding 'legal act' of the Union, but the Commission can in future exercise considerable discursive pressure if it 'rejects' the draft budget of a member state as insufficient.

While most of the Regulations of the 'New Economic Governance', as far as their content is concerned, are at least *loosely* related to the legal basis they are built on, this is not discernible with regard to the regulation on draft budgetary plans. The basis for competence chosen by the Commission (Art. 121 TFEU in conjunction with 136 TFEU) deals with the coordination of economic policy, which includes 'employment policies, structural policies, innovation policies, as well as wage and income policies' (Kempen 2012d: 12), but not budgetary and fiscal policies (Schulze-Steinen 1998: 90). The only field in which EU competence exists in the area of budgetary policy – and this is very limited – is the procedure in case of an excessive deficit. Art. 126, relevant to this topic, has been however neither used as a legal basis for the Regulation and nor does it provide for the competence of the Commission to comment and reject draft budgets.

The obvious lack of effort made by the legal staffs of the Commission and the Council to even pretend to embed the two Regulations of the Two-pack in European law shows that the authoritarian constitutionalism within the European ensemble of state apparatuses is, for the most part, indisputable and has become the central strategy to deal with the eroding consensus for neoliberal integration. This is also shown by the fact that the legal means of the action for annulment, to which the member states and the institutions of the EU have privileged access, in contrast to natural persons (Art. 263), has until now not been brought into play against a single regulation of the New Economic Governance.

Conclusions: Constitutionalism as a contested, strategic project

The New Economic Governance, the Fiscal Compact and the intended 'contracts for competitiveness' without doubt display characteristic features of the new constitutionalism. Like the establishment of the EMU, these instruments are aimed at securing the neoliberal mode of integration 'by means of political and legal mechanisms that can be altered only with difficulty' (Gill 2000: 44). Yet neoliberal constitutionalism has become radicalized in several ways and is increasingly taking on an *authoritarian* form. In my concluding theses, I would like to discuss these shifts and the fact that such developments represent a challenge to and, at the same time, an opportunity for the establishment of European democracy.

With his conceptual approach, Gill has drawn attention to the introduction of neoliberal economic (constitutional) law in a manner that is legally permissible and has been supported by the at least passive consensus of the subaltern. However, since the consensus in favour of the neoliberal mode of integration and the deepening of the EMU is growing ever weaker, we are witnessing moves away from those sediments of law that are themselves the products of the new constitutionalism. In order to bypass a revision of the European Treaties and the requirements of consensus it would entail, instruments of neoliberal economic policy are being unlawfully inserted into the 'European constitution' or even – following the model of the Fiscal Compact – established in complete avoidance of European law. While up until the European crisis of hegemony, national compromise balances were circumvented and challenged by the shifting of policy fields into European law, now even the power relations condensed in the European legal form are becoming too tight for the radicalization of the neoliberal project. Since – as became apparent after the elections in Greece in June 2012 – the hegemonic crisis of the European ensemble of state apparatuses has resulted in whole states threatening to break out of the neoliberal consensus, it is to be expected that the deepening of EMU will be pursued for the time being using the methods of authoritarian constitutionalism. After all, each Member State has the power to veto any 'revision of the constitution' under the ordinary revision procedure.

New constitutionalism already aimed at making economic policy more independent of the necessity of subaltern agreement. However, the open resistance to the radicalization of the neoliberal mode of integration is now to be broken by an almost complete decoupling of the European ensemble of state apparatuses from the requirements of consensus. A return to new constitutionalism will only be made once the deepening of EMU has been widely completed by authoritarian constitutionalism. Authoritarian constitutionalism is associated with increasing encroachments on the procedures of formal democracy and the rule of law. Contrary to national-populist contentions, this is not directed at individual states. Rather, such encroachments are intended to place the European ensemble of state apparatuses, with its neoliberal configuration, of which the national executives are part, in a position to chip away at the social rights that are still anchored in the national legal systems.

This is another common denominator of the Fiscal Compact, the 'New Economic Governance' and the 'contracts for competitiveness': they weaken those terrains on which the subaltern are still able to assert their interests comparatively easily (in particular, national parliaments). At the same time, there has as yet been no enhancement of the European Parliament's status and power. The central axis of conflict in authoritarian constitutionalism is therefore not the European Union versus the nation-state, but the European ensemble of state apparatuses versus (representative) democracy. Moreover, the aforementioned upgrading of the executive must be further differentiated, because no general strengthening of the executive is occurring. Instead, it is especially those state apparatuses whose configuration is particularly neoliberal and masculinist that are gaining in status and power: the national finance ministries represented on the ECOFIN Council, and the Commission's Directorate General for Economic and Financial Affairs (DG ECFIN) (Klatzer and Schlager 2012).

Stephen Gill argues that the new constitutionalism sets up a governmental surveillance system of state economic policy that corresponds to Foucault's concept of control by 'surveillance and normalization' (Foucault 2007, 2008). Even though no direct intervention takes place, economic policies are being monitored and thus subject to neoliberal 'self-government' (Gill 1998: 13). The crisis of hegemony is leading to a shift in this area, too. With Economic Governance, repressive measures have been introduced into EU economic policy, and both the Fiscal Compact and the New Economic Governance *force* those member states which are affected by unequal development and deficits to present and gain approval for structural reforms. Because the neoliberal hegemony has become fragile, governmentality in the field of economy is no longer sufficient for the necessary control. In Foucault's terms, authoritarian constitutionalism involves a retardation, which leads to a system of 'surveillance and punishment' (Foucault 1977) in the area of European economic policy.

While the new constitutionalism left fundamental human rights for the most part untouched, at least in their formal dimension, its authoritarian intensification is aimed especially at breaking through at that point where defence of social rights is guaranteed. By establishing austerity and competitiveness as the new basic norms, authoritarian constitutionalism reclassifies basic and fundamental human rights, such as the right to collective bargaining (Art. 28 of the EU Charter of Fundamental Rights), and legitimizes their elimination. European interventionism, brought forth by authoritarian constitutionalism in the area of wage policy, therefore aims not coincidentally at those institutions and apparatuses (collective agreement systems, labour rights and unions) that are at least capable of protecting the interests of the subaltern and/or effectively representing them.

However, it is certainly open as to whether the authoritarian turn will succeed, or whether the new constitutionalism could actually be disrupted by the struggles for 'real democracy' in Europe. The demand raised by the movements for an assembly that would found Europe anew could be a project that paves the way to a form of progressive constitutionalism (Marterbauer and Oberndorfer 2013). One that would give the people of Europe the opportunity to argue about alternatives and shape their common future. In any event, the expansion of repressive techniques of rule and their constitutionalization must not be understood as purely strengthening the neoliberal societal formation. Even though it has probably never been more dominant than it is today, the loss of its leading, hegemonical moments is making it become brittle and ossified. Stephen Gill's thesis (Gill 2002: 47) that the new constitutionalism is much more a strategic project than a concluded historical process, which implies its existence is contingent and disputed, therefore remains valid as far as its authoritarian development is concerned.

Notes

1 Charles Moore is Thatcher biographer and former editor of the conservative Daily Telegraph.
2 Frank Schirrmacher is the editor of the leading conservative newspaper FAZ.
3 In this article Crouch, however, presents the argument, in contrast to those represented here, that the institutions of formal democracy remain intact during and after the crisis (2008–) and therefore can still be described in terms of 'post-democracy'.
4 Treaty on European Union.
5 http://ec.europa.eu/economy_finance/crisis/documents/131201_en.pdf (accessed 1 February 2013).
6 See fn. 4.
7 Cf. Art. 3 of Council Decision from 21 December 1998 on the detailed provisions concerning the composition of the Economic and Financial Committee, OJ 1998 L 358/109
8 Reg. (EC) 1466/97 of 7 July 1997.
9 Reg. 1466/97 (EC) 1467/97 of 7 July1997
10 Regulation (EU) 1175/2011, 16 November 2011 amending Council Regulation (EC) 1466/97 on the strengthening of the surveillance of budgetary positions and the surveillance and coordination of economic policies.
11 Regulation (EU) 1177/2011 of 8 November 2011 amending Regulation (EC) 1467/97 on speeding up and clarifying the implementation of the excessive deficit procedure.
12 Regulation (EU) 1173/2011 of 16 November 2011 on the effective enforcement of budgetary surveillance in the euro area.
13 Regulation (EU) 1176/2011 of 16 November 2011 on the prevention and correction of macroeconomic imbalances.
14 Recital 17.
15 Recital 20.
16 Recital 20.
17 Art. 4 para. 8.
18 Recital 12.
19 Art. 4 para. 3 lit b.
20 Recital 17.
21 Art. 5 para. 1.
22 Art. 7.
23 Art. 8 para. 1.
24 Art. 8 para. 2.
25 Art. 8 para. 2.
26 Art. 10 para. 4.
27 Regulation (EU) 1174/2011 of 16 November 2011 on the enforcement measures to correct of excessive macroeconomic imbalances in the euro area.
28 Regulation (EU) 1174/2011.
29 Art 3 para. 2 lit b in conj. With para. 5 Reg.(EU) 1174/2011.
30 Recital 12.

31 Recital 20.
32 Communication from the Commission of 10.4.2013 on the results of the in-depth review under Regulation 1176/2011 on the prevention and correction of macroeconomic imbalances, COM (2013) 199.
33 Ibid. 6.
34 Ibid. 8 and 11.
35 Ibid. 9.
36 European Commission, Labour Market Developments in Europe 2012 (2012), 104.
37 See www.bundesregierung.de/ContentArchiv/DE/Archiv17/Reden/2013/01/2013-01-24-merkel-davos.html (accessed 1 April 2014).
38 Communication from the Commission of 30.11.2012, A blueprint for a deep and genuine economic and monetary union, COM (2012) 777.
39 Reg. (EU) 1176/2011.
40 COM (2012) 777, 22.
41 Ibid. 22.
42 COM (2012) 777, 26.
43 Art. 136 para. 1 TFEU.
44 COM (2012) 777, 13.
45 Regulation (EU) 472/2013 of 21.05.2013 on the strengthening of economic and budgetary surveillance of Member States in the euro area experiencing or threatened with serious difficulties with respect to their financial stability.
46 Regulation (EU) 473/2013 of 21.05. 2013 on common provisions for monitoring and assessing draft budgetary plans and ensuring the correction of excessive deficit of the Member States in the euro area.

References

Behrens, P. (1994) Die Wirtschaftsverfassung der EG. In Bruggemeier, G. (ed.) *Verfassung für ein ziviles Europa*. Baden-Baden: Nomos, pp. 73–105.

Bieling, H.J. (2013) Europäische Verfassung als neuer Konstitutionalismus. *Europarecht*. Beiheft 1/2013, pp. 205–226.

Bieling, H.J. and Steinhilber, J. (2000) Hegemoniale Projekte im Prozess der europäischen Integration. In Bieling, H.J. and Steinhilber, J. (eds) *Die Konfiguration Europas. Dimensionen einer kritischen Integrationstheorie. Münster*: Westfälisches Dampfboot, pp. 102–130.

Brunner, K. (1970) 'The Monetarist Revolution' in Monetary Theory. *Weltwirtschaftliches Archiv* 105, pp. 1–30.

Buckel, S. et al. (2012) '…wenn das Alte stirbt und das Neue nicht zur Welt kommen kann.' – Kräfteverhältnisse in der europäischen Krise. In Forschungsgruppe Staatsprojekt Europa (ed.) *Die EU in der Krise. Zwischen autoritärem Etatismus und europäischem Frühling*. Münster: Westfälisches Dampfboot, pp. 11–48.

Caceres, I. and Oberndorfer, L. (2013) Verlangt das Gesetz der bürgerlichen Sicherheit die Einschränkung der politischen Freiheiten? – Spanien und die Neuzusammensetzung von Zwang und Konsens im autoritären Wettbewerbsetatismus. *Juridikum*, pp. 453–463.

Candeias, M. and Völpel, E. (2014) *Plätze sichern! – Über Occupy, Indignados, Syntagma und die Lernfähigkeit des Mosaiks*. Hamburg: VSA.

Crouch, C. (2013) Post-democracy and the Crisis. *Juridikum*, pp. 41–50.

Feigl, G. and Zuckerstätter, S. (2012) Wettbewerbsorientierung als europäischer Irrweg. *Infobrief EU & international* 4/2012, pp. 1–3.

Fischer-Lescano, A. (2014) Troika in der Austerität – Rechtsbindung der Unionsorgane beim Abschluss von Memoranda of Understanding. *Kritische Justiz*, pp. 2–25.

Fischer-Lescano, A. and Oberndorfer, L. (2013) Fiskalvertrag und Unionsrecht – Unionsrechtliche Grenzen völkerverträglicher Fiskalregulierung und Organleihe. *Neue Juristische Wochenschrift*, pp. 9–14.

Foucault, M. (1977) *Discipline and Punish – The Birth of the Prison*. New York: Vintage Books.

Foucault, M. (2007) *Security, Territory, Population*. London: Palgrave Macmillan.

Foucault, M. (2008) *The Birth of Biopolitics*. London: Palgrave Macmillan.

Gill, S. (1998) European Governance and New Constitutionalism. *New Political Economy* 10, pp. 5–26.

Gill, S. (2000) Theoretische Grundlagen einer neo-gramscianischen Analyse der europäischen Intergration. In Bieling, H.J. and Steinhilber, J. (eds) *Die Konfiguration Europas. Dimensionen einer kritischen Integrationstheorie*. Münster: Westfälisches Dampfboot, pp. 23–50.

Gill, S. (2002) Constitutionalizing Inequality and the Clash of Globalizations. *International Studies Review*, pp. 47–65.

Gill, S. (2003) *Power and Resistance in the New World Order*. Basingstoke: Palgrave Macmillan.

Gnan, E. (1999) Art. 104. In Groeben, H., Thiesing, J. and Ehlermann, C.D. (eds) *Kommentar zum EU-/EG-Vertrag*. Baden-Baden: Nomos.

Gramsci, A. (1992a) *Gefängnishefte, Band 3*. Berlin: Argument.

Gramsci, A. (1992b) *Gefängnishefte, Band 4*. Berlin: Argument.

Gramsci, A. (1996) *Gefängnishefte, Band 7*. Berlin: Argument.

Hattenberger, D. (2009) Art. 99 EGV. In Schwarze, J. (ed.) *EU-Kommentar*. München: CH Beck.

Häde, U. (2007a) Art. 4 EGV. In Calliess, C. and Ruffert, M. (eds) *EUV, AEUV – Kommentar*. München: CH Beck.

Häde, U. (2007b) Art. 99 EGV. In Calliess, C. and Ruffert, M. (eds) *EUV, AEUV – Kommentar*. München: CH Beck.

Häde, U. (2011a) Art. 136 AEUV – eine neue Generalklausel für die WWU? *JuristenZeitung*, pp. 333–340.

Häde, U. (2011b) Art. 136. In Calliess, C. and Ruffert, M. (eds) *EUV, AEUV – Kommentar*. München: CH Beck.

Hayek, F.A. (1969) Wettbewerb als Entdeckungsverfahren. In Hayek, F.A. (ed.) *Freiburger Studien*. Tübingen: Mohr, pp. 249–265.

Hermann, C. (2012) Die Finanzkrise und ihre Auswirkungen auf Sozialstaaten. *Infobrief EU & international* 5/2012, pp. 2–5.

Horn, L. and Wigger, A. (2013) Ungleiche Entwicklung und politischer Widerstand. *Das Argument* 301/302, pp. 200–209.

Joerges, C. (1991) Markt ohne Staat? Die Wirtschaftsverfassung der Gemeinschaft und die regulative Politik. In Wildenmann, R. (ed.) *Staatswerdung Europas?* Baden-Baden: Nomos, pp. 225–267.

Joerges, C. (2012) Europas Wirtschaftsverfassung in der Krise. *Der Staat*, pp. 357–385.

Kempen, B. (2012a) Art. 126. In Streinz, R. (ed.) *EUV/AEUV – Kommentar*. München: CH Beck.

Kempen, B. (2012b) Art. 121. In Streinz, R. (ed.) *EUV/AEUV – Kommentar*. München: CH Beck.

Kempen, B. (2012c) Art. 119. In Streinz, R. (ed.) *EUV/AEUV – Kommentar*. München: CH Beck.
Kempen, B. (2012d) Art. 125, N 1. In Streinz, R. (ed.) *EUV/AEUV – Kommentar*. München: CH Beck.
Klatzer, E. and Schlager, C. (2011) Europäische Wirtschaftsregierung – Eine stille neoliberale Revolution. *Kurswechsel* 1/2011, pp. 61–81.
Klatzer, E. and Schlager, C. (2012) Genderdimensionen der neuen EU Economic Governance. *Kurswechsel*. 1, pp. 23–35.
Koch, M. (2010) Art. 120–122. In Lenz, C.O. and Borchhardt, K.D. (eds) *EU-Verträge*. Köln: Linde.
Louis, J.V. (2011) The Economic and Monetary Union. *CMLRev* 2/2004, pp. 575–608.
Marterbauer, M. and Oberndorfer, L. (2013) Federating Competition States vs. Building Europe from Below – EU Treaty Revisions as an Opportunity for the Democratization of Economy and Politics. *Queries* 03(9), pp. 76–89.
Mestmäcker, E.J. (1973) Macht-Recht-Wirtschaftsverfassung. *Zeitschrift für das gesamte Handelsrecht und Wirtschaftsrecht* 2/1973, pp. 97–111.
Moore, C. (2011) I'm Starting to Think that the Left Might actually Be Right. *Daily Telegraph*. 22 July , p. 8.
Oberndorfer, L. (2011) Eine Krisenzählung ohne Kompetenz – Economic Governance rechtswidrig? *Infobrief EU & international* 3, pp. 7–12.
Oberndorfer, L. (2012a) Die Renaissance des autoritären Liberalismus? – Carl Schmitt und der deutsche Neoliberalismus. *PROKLA*, pp. 413–431.
Oberndorfer, L. (2012b) Hegemoniekrise in Europa – Auf dem Weg zu einem autoritären Wettbewerbetatismus? In Forschungsgruppe Staatsprojekt Europa (ed.) *Die EU in der Krise. Zwischen autoritärem Etatismus und europäischem Frühling*. Münster: Westfälisches Dampfboot, pp. 50–71.
Opratko, B. and Prausmüller, O. (2011) Neogramscianische Perspektiven in der IPÖ. In Opratko, B. and Prausmüller, O. (eds) *Gramsci Global*. Berlin: Argument, pp. 11–38.
Ptak, R. (2004) *Vom Ordoliberalismus zur Sozialen Marktwirtschaft – Stationen des Neoliberalismus in Deutschland*. Opladen: Leske and Budrich.
Riedel, D. (2012) Merkel verlangt Preis für Griechenlandrettung. *Handelsblatt*. 16 October 2012, p.16.
Rompuy, H. (2012) *Towards a Genuine Economic and Monetary Union*. 5 December 2012. [Online] Available from www.consilium.europa.eu/uedocs/cms_Data/docs/pressdata/en/ec/134069.pdf [Accessed 1 March 2014].
Schirrmacher, F. (2011) Ich beginne zu glauben, dass die Linke recht hat. *FAZ*. 15 August 2011, p. 15.
Schulten, T. and Müller, T. (2013) A New European Interventionism? The Impact of the New European Economic Governance on Wages and Collective Bargaining. In Natali, D. and Vanhercke, B. (eds) *Social Developments in the EU*. Brussels: ETUI.
Schulze-Steinen, M. (1998) *Rechtsfragen zur Wirtschaftsunion – Möglichkeiten der gemeinschaftlichen Gestaltung mitgliedsstaatlicher Wirtschaftspolitik nach dem EG-Vertrag*. Baden-Baden: Nomos.
Stockhammer, E., Onaran, Ö. and Ederer, S. (2009) Functional Income Distribution and Aggregate Demand in the Euro Area. *Cambridge Journal of Economics* 1/2009, pp. 139–159.
Witt, P.C. (1982) Finanzpolitik als Verfassungs- und Gesellschaftspolitik. Überlegungen zur Finanzpolitik des Deutschen Reiches in den Jahren 1930 bis 1932. *Geschichte und Gesellschaft* 8(1982), pp. 386–414.

12 Labour and the crisis in Europe[1]

Mònica Clua-Losada and Laura Horn

As of now, there is no concerted and sustained pan-European class-based struggle against the austerity governance and increasingly authoritarian neoliberalism manifesting at the European level. Some five years after the then-secretary general of the European Trade Union Confederation (ETUC), John Monks, (in)famously declared in 2009 that 'given the tough labour market, and desperate employers, this is not a time for huge militancy',[2] which new forms of labour resistance and alternative perspectives can we see emerging? How can we understand the uneven development of labour and the crisis in Europe with regard to the fundamental social relations that constitute the very fabric on which the European Union, and Europe, is built?

This chapter focuses on understanding the relationship between labour and the crisis at different levels and across variegated geographies of increasingly antagonistic class relationships in Europe. It seeks to contribute to the ongoing debate on the role and potential of labour in the social struggles that are characterizing the unfolding of the crisis worldwide (for example Burawoy 2010). In particular, the chapter addresses the fundamental theoretical-conceptual questions of the class character of crisis dynamics and responses, and, secondly, the need to reconceptualize the relationship between labour, the state and the economy. The chapter emphasizes that it is necessary to highlight the dialectic between material and ideational dimensions of social struggles when considering labour, in order to go beyond the voluntaristic nature of some analyses in this area. Related to this is the second key concern, that is a focus on whether we can conceptualize labour as an emancipatory agent, and, more fundamentally, a discussion of the difficulties in defining the meaning of 'labour' in the first place. As such, the chapter will offer a conceptualization of labour within the current crisis in Europe that goes beyond dichotomizing attempts which try to focus on either the co-option or the resistance of labour. Highlighting the asymmetrical nature of the crisis, the chapter also seeks to map the highly uneven development of labour positions and strategies in the EU.

Drawing on critical labour studies, geography and industrial relations, this chapter highlights the need for a deeper understanding of labour within critical political economy (CPE) approaches (for example Shields, Bruff and

Macartney 2011). We argue that most approaches to labour within CPE are linked to the concrete praxis of labour unions, which are then unable to move across different levels of abstraction. This leaves the capital and labour relation limping, on labour's side. Capital appears as systemic, abstract and transnational, whilst labour is only considered in terms of its agency and its concrete, specific location. In order to move beyond such conceptualizations of labour, and in keeping with the overall focus of this edited volume, this chapter aims to highlight the uneven development of labour within the crisis in Europe. In order to do so, it avoids the methodological nationalism that is inherent in much of the industrial relations literature, and which is often reproduced by others when analysing labour.

This has two key challenges, as pointed out by Kretsos (2011). On the one hand, much of the industrial relations literature focuses overwhelmingly on core European industrial relations system (such as the UK, Germany or France). On the other, and perhaps more importantly, 'most of those analyses treat militancy and activism as an attitudinal and behavioural issue ignoring its dynamic and contextual dependent character' (Kretsos 2011: 271). This leads to an understanding of labour based around organizational features, with trade unions becoming the channel for working class demands, and, as such, the unit of analysis within labour studies. We argue that this is problematic as, vis-à-vis capital interests, 'trade unions are … relatively powerless within the political sphere and have always been essentially defensive and reactive in terms of their political behaviour' (Taylor, Mathers and Upchurch 2011: 299). Therefore, if we focus on unions (rather than labour) we are forced to stay within national boundaries. This leads to two alternative, but complementary, options: either we upscale and focus on transnational union action (Bieler and Lindberg 2010), or we think of labour in a different, more abstract way (Silver 2003).

In relation to our understanding of labour we highlight another crucial aspect of discussions on the crisis. We propose an understanding of crisis as an intrinsic feature of capitalism. Capitalist social relations are in constant contention with moments of heightened conflict. This allows us to go beyond dichotomizing accounts of labour (pessimistic versus optimistic) and opens up possible avenues for class struggle.

Therefore, in this chapter, we discuss both traditional approaches to labour and the crisis in Europe, as well as alternative perspectives. As such, we consider *the challenges* labour faces and *the responses* it develops in concrete times and spaces before we then move towards a broader understanding which forces us to reconceptualize what we mean by labour. As challenges, we identify the role of corporatist structures and competitive wage pressures; we also consider the internal struggles that appear within labour organizations which are often due to either the concrete conditions of labour or the organizational traditions of labour unions. Moreover, we identify the structural shift towards atypical forms of employment as well as increasing sustained levels of unemployment: these highlight the contradictions and tensions between waged labour and non-waged labour. We highlight the divergent and often conflicting level of societal and union responses, in particular with reference to the class character mentioned above. Following from that, we point towards issues such as the importance of temporal/spatial dimensions and the possibilities for new coalitions, for example between trade unions and anti-austerity social movements. In this context, we emphasize the need to go beyond traditional organizational structures of labour, pointing towards the fact that co-option and resistance can be two sides of the same coin.

Dimensions of labour and the crisis

The challenges to labour from structural changes at the European and global level have been well documented (see for example Silver 2003; Dunn 2004; Peters 2011). Over the last decades, while there have been significant increases in labour productivity, labour's share of national incomes has been falling (ILO Global Wage Report 2013; *The Economist* 2013). Moreover, current developments in the financial and economic arena have had a direct and detrimental impact on workers, as many empirical studies show (for example, see the cross-country European study carried out by the ILO – Vaughan-Whitehead 2012; ETUI 2014, or country specific studies such as Clua-Losada and Navarro 2012). In such studies, the crisis is analysed in relation to which workers or sectors of society have been worse hit by the crisis. During the first few years of the crisis male, temporary, migrant, and/or young workers were the first to suffer layoffs and, as the crisis deepens, other groups are being affected (e.g. women and permanent workers). Additionally, and besides job losses, wage cuts are affecting those who are still in employment, whether as direct cuts or often as a reduction in performance-related bonuses or forced reductions in working hours.

However, as with previous periods of capital's offensive against labour, we need to be careful with pessimistic accounts that highlight how badly labour is faring vis-à-vis capital. During the long neoliberal period, debates around the globalization of capital were quick to emphasize capital's hypermobile capacities and a stark reduction in states' policy-making capacities which were rendering labour powerless. As Dunn (2004) argued, such approaches were often not sufficiently grounded in empirical evidence and were more often than not highly beneficial to capital's interests. 'If workers believe threats of plant closure, relocation, downsizing and global competition are the ineluctable products of economic change, they may become more willing to make concessions on pay, conditions and redundancies' (Dunn 2004: 5). This led to a 'common sense' based around capital's unlimited power to outflank labour (Anderson 1992), which had powerful implications for the ways in which the labour movement understood its position and possibilities.

In order to come to a more nuanced understanding of labour and the crisis, we draw on Cox (1981) to identify three dimensions of the challenges labour faces at the European level: material, institutional and ideational. As we will argue, these spheres are conceptually often seen as distinct – but we need to be aware of their simultaneous nature, and the dialectical relation between them. This also applies to the discussion of different sources of trade union power, such as associational, structural or organizational power (Wright 2000; Silver 2003; see also the literature on trade union revitalization, such as Phelan 2007).

Resources and material context

Key to trade union and wider working class challenges and responses are those that can be considered to fall within the arena of the material context, or at least where concerns over resources may acquire primacy. This often leads to an understanding of workers' interests in relation to their position within employment relationships and within economic or industrial sectors, and therefore subjected as to 'repeated challenges by employers as they try to redefine and realign worker interests with corporate goals' (Kelly 1998: 4). For example, workers in the car industry may favour subsidies to encourage car ownership, whilst workers in care services may see such subsidies as the removal of public funds. As such, industrial workers may be seen to have conflicting interests to those in the services industry or vice versa, or workers in some locations may be pitted against workers in another location in cases of companies moving across the border. However, there is an even more problematic distinction between different types of workers that is also becoming politically divisive, highlighting false dichotomies within the working class to benefit capital's interests, which is appearing with the rise of atypical forms of employment (for example, debates about insiders versus outsiders in the labour market).

Unsurprisingly, struggles over the level of wages and working hours have been key, historically and today, to understanding workers' organizational objectives. In the current period, wages have once again become the primary battlefield for the labour-capital relationship – even more so in specific geographical contexts in which there had been a steady increase in real wages prior to the crisis. In particular, in the European Mediterranean Member States', wage depression and outright cuts in both private and public sector wages have been central in the social struggles against austerity and crisis management. Even within advanced welfare states, there has been a dramatic rise in the number of the 'working poor' (Pradella 2013; ETUI 2014), combined with the dismantling of social protection across Europe, and a financialization of daily life which has affected workers' future hopes and organized labour in disproportionate ways (Peters 2011). These 'really existing conditions' matter as they highlight the need to consider struggles over 'bread and butter' issues as crucial to improving the concrete conditions of labour, but also as struggles that go to the heart of the conflict.

In organizational terms, related to labour's resources, it has become customary to accompany studies of labour agency with figures of the decline in trade union density. Therefore, as recent statistics indicate, overall we indeed see a steady fall in trade union density, at least on average in the OECD countries, with several European countries leading the trend (OECD 2014). However, we argue that to equate trade union density with 'the power of trade unions', or even labour as social category as such, means to foreclose a discussion of alternative forms of power. Moreover, and particularly in a conjuncture marked by increasingly antagonistic social relations as we see now emerging in Europe, where previous compromises and concessions are breaking down and can hence no longer veil the underlying power structures, it becomes all the more crucial not to subscribe to a determinist, almost fatalistic narrative of how organized labour has nowhere to turn because of its material weakness in declining resources and membership. Rather, we need to turn to the institutional and ideational/ideological dimensions of labour and class power, and hence bring attention to the changing relationship between labour and the institutional context it is embedded in (for example, the state), and more importantly still, the ideological and discursive conjuncture. In Silver's terms, this would necessitate a focus on associational rather than exclusively on structural power, for 'if the significance of associational bargaining power is growing, then the future trajectory of labour movements will be strongly conditioned by the broader political context of which they are a part' (Silver 2003: 173).

The institutional dimension

The ongoing crisis dynamics have thrown the changing relationship between organized labour and the institutional context, in form of state institutions or, in case of the EU, the supranational institutional ensemble, into sharp relief. Labour is increasingly marginalized from policy-making structures which it had previously been a member of. This means that labour has to fight on new terrains in order to achieve the improvement of working conditions (for example Gall 2014).

Corporatist structures are increasingly being rendered useless by structural changes in the labour market and concerted political action. Social dialogue in a labour market where more and more workers are not covered by it deepens the structural divisions that make labour solidarity difficult. 'Workers on the margins of the labour market, such as temporary workers, agency workers, domestic workers and the self-employed, are traditionally not covered by social dialogue, which has only aggravated the effects of the crisis on these more vulnerable categories' (Vaughan-Whitehead 2012: 20). The pressures on the social partnership model at national levels, as well as social dialogue at the supranational level, highlights the importance of considering institutional structures for an understanding of labour and the crisis, and at the same time shows the limits of current labour strategies. As Wahl (2014) argues, 'social partnership and social dialogue have largely been developed into an overall ideology in dominant parts of the labour movement … social dialogue has been given an exalted position as the way to promote workers' interests, completely decoupled from an analysis of specific power relations'. The institutional challenges and social terrain for responses are crucial indeed for an analysis of the constraints faced by labour's agency.

In particular, with regard to narratives about a 'window of opportunity' for alternatives for labour in the current crisis conjuncture, the limits of institutional structures have to be taken into account. That is, we need to interrogate the relationship between initiatives, strategies and alternatives, and the social terrain in which they are being formulated and initiated. The question of whether labour can indeed transcend institutional confines that are more conducive to neoliberal restructuring than social protection looms large here – and is one of the key battle grounds for strategies in the European crisis. The increasingly authoritarian character of EU economic governance, for instance, confines organized labour to an institutional straitjacket that significantly limits the political room for manoeuvre. A series of rulings by the European Court of Justice has highlighted the tension within the politico-legal framework of the European Union between the 'capitalist' freedoms of movement and establishment, and the fundamental right to industrial action that could potentially limit those freedoms. Organized labour is hence confined by the tendency to seek to work within institutional architectures which are increasingly neoliberal and therefore hostile (Bruff and Horn 2012: 165). We also see this play out in the role and strategies of global labour organizations such as the International Trade Union Confederation or the Global Union Federations (McBride and Smith 2013).

The social power relations at the heart of capitalist institutions need to be taken into account for understanding these struggles at various levels and with regard to idiosyncratic manifestations of crisis (Bruff and Horn 2012). This, however, is not the case in many perspectives that seem to take institutions as given, as channels that configure labour interests, identities and strategies. For example, with regard to developments in the European Union, Wahl points out that, 'in effect, labour has taken very specific historical experiences and behaved as if these were true for all time in terms of ideological guidance' (Wahl 2014). Labour responses to the crisis risk becoming like painting by numbers, pre-structured by the very institutions they are intended to change. To change this, a sustained engagement with the ideological undercurrents that engender and drive labour interests and agency is crucial. And it is at this level that the interlinkages between material conditions and institutional context have to be underwritten by a focus on the ideational and ideological dimensions. This also renders it possible to overcome the limitations of an overly determinist understanding of how worker interests are perceived exclusively through their material conditions – many approaches to labour studies, by focusing at the industry level, identify common material and institutional interests for groups of workers in similar industries, and antagonistic material and institutional aims for workers in different economic sectors or in different countries (for example Gumbrell-McCormick and Hyman 2013). In a sense, there is a deterministic expectation of shared or divergent ideas based on one's position within the labour market. We think this needs to, at least, be questioned.

Ideational and ideological vectors

As we have briefly explored when discussing the material and institutional dimensions of labour in relation to the crisis, material conditions and the type of formal institutions in existence in particular contexts matter. However, they are insufficient by themselves in explaining labour's key challenges and responses to the crisis. Material and institutional conditions structure labour's agency in particular ways, yet they do not determine it. As Simms points out (2012: 99), we should move beyond identifying workers' interests as being directly and uniquely 'related to the immediate conditions of work in a specific workplace'. Workers and labour unions are not always able, or willing, to articulate different types of interests at different organizational levels, which would highlight an initial difficulty with emphasizing material and institutional resources by themselves. Labour contestation, and co-option, is driven by a multitude of factors which include the two we have already explored as well as the ideological elements that relate to them.

Considering the role of ideational and ideological vectors when analysing labour becomes a crucial exercise, as there is an increasing differentiation and fragmentation in the categories of workers. The current crisis, and the neoliberal period that preceded it, are characterized by a combination of high levels of unemployment, and high levels of workers who live below the poverty line. The literature has often termed the increase in these workers as 'atypical workers', workers who may move interchangeably between being unemployed to being in precarious employment. This is a cause for concern as it erodes the sources of traditional trade union membership. Yet, it only does so if trade unions remain focused on the workplace. As Moody has argued, there is a need to move towards community-based unionism (or what has been termed social movement unionism). Experiences such as those of workers' centres in the USA, based around the community but yet dealing with workplace issues (Moody 2007: 216–223), can help overcome the moving ground in which unions are finding themselves.

Labour solidarity, following Hyman's concept of 'imagined solidarities' (1999) appears as something that is socially constructed, and therefore not inherent within labour. In a sense, it must be defined and worked at, otherwise divisions would be stronger than solidarity. Key divisions would appear between highly skilled and unskilled workers, or permanent and temporary workers, the latter much more characterized by marginalization but neither of the two being particularly keen on organizing jointly as they could feel threatened by the other. These internal divisions, these challenges to building imagined solidarities in Hyman's sense, appear as real problems in concrete struggles, as capital is able to exploit them for its advantage. Yet, neoliberalism's attempts to divide workers are at the same time uniting society. As Bieler and Lindberg argue, neoliberalism has extended 'into the sphere of social reproduction and has created the objective conditions for cooperation between trade unions and social movements, as it implies similar and related pressures at the workplace and within civil society' (2010: 10). Resistance to austerity in many European countries is increasingly being built around these similar pressures in the sphere of social reproduction.

Trade unions are often the awkward partners in these alliances, however, this is due to the fact that trade unions have developed within concrete contexts of institutionalization and struggle. This matters in terms of their future (and possible) choices for renewal, as 'inherited identities also shape the likely trajectory of union renewal' (Hyman 2011: 19). As such, it is not only the role of material and institutional resources, or the changes in such dimensions, that will help account for processes of resistance or co-option within unions, but also ideational aspects, which will be made up both from ideological choices but also unions' historical experiences.

In the European context, we can see this become manifest in the ambiguous position of the European Trade Union Confederation (ETUC). Having long been a firm part of the European project, the ETUC is showing signs of moving away from their role as 'professional labour diplomat[s]' (Hyman 2011: 27) and becoming unequivocal in their opposition to public sector cuts and wage competition within the EU. More importantly, in their recent response to the European Commission's communication on 'Strengthening the social dimension of the Economic and Monetary Union', the ETUC (2014) appears far more vocal than before in their criticism of the Commission. Yet, the criticism remains within the limits of acceptability. That is, the ETUC appears to still be accepting the way in which the crisis has been understood and managed (Horn 2012). What is more, with the 'authoritarian constitutionalism' that is now emerging at the EU level (see Oberndorfer, Chapter 11 in this volume), the institutional reconfiguration of Europe poses a formidable challenge for a fundamental reorientation of organized labour.

It is easy, however, to fall into dichotomizing trends when considering labour. Either trade unions become easily co-opted and therefore fail to present a real challenge to capital, or they are organizations that resist attempts to be integrated within capitalist social relations. Neither of the two options is sufficiently apt to explain trade union action in Europe. In fact, more often than not the material and institutional contexts in which trade unions operate lead to a combination of co-option and resistance strategies. Additionally, strategies are often nuanced. As Jakopovich (2011) points out there are clear differences, for example, between social dialogue and social partnership. Whilst the first 'is a necessary aspect of trade union activity' (ibid.: 68) the latter represents 'a status quo ideology that conceals the existence of class struggle' (ibid.).

Conceptualizing labour as an emancipatory agent

Bringing together the spheres of material resources, institutional contexts and ideational dimensions allows us to conceptualize labour as an emancipatory and solidaristic agent in historically specific conjunctures, as part of a contingent rather than an automatic process. We very much agree with Featherstone in that 'solidarities did not just produce abstracted political ideologies or identifications. Rather, they were interventions in the material relations between places' (Featherstone 2012: 18). Rather than a romanticized notion of labour solidarity and emancipation, our perspective should be on the simultaneous, fluid and dialectical relation between processes of solidarity, co-option and everyday organizing. That is, we appreciate the fundamental 'messiness' of labour as a social category and emancipatory actor at different levels and in different terrains. As Amoore argues (2002: 62), 'work (and by implication the restructuring of work) is conceived as everyday structured social practice through which the emerging social relations of globalisation may be enabled, contested or confounded'. It is possible to be reactive and emancipatory at the same time, for example participating in corporatist negotiations simultaneous with organizing general strikes. Hence 'the important issue is thus not how to transform partial and fragmented consciousness into a universal, critical consciousness, but to enquire into what is it about the nature of labour in capitalism that results in partial and contradictory forms of consciousness' (Taylor 2002: 93).

Moreover, it is only through a fundamental engagement with class, with regard to the social power relations in both production and reproduction, rather than with narrowly defined workplaces or social strata, that emancipation is engendered – even though material conditions might be divergent. For, as Martinez Lucio (2006: 206) points out:

> why should the changing nature of social boundaries, such as the emerging centrality of consumption, the changing nature of the workplace and the decline in traditional skill-based hierarchies at work be solely a challenge to labour? Do not the demands generated by rapid technological change, consumer identity, decentralized and global production and ongoing skill formation challenge the structures and identity of capital and management as well?

The ongoing debate about the 'new middle classes' in the global political economy has to be seen in this context (for example, see Radice 2014). It thus becomes crucial to point towards a relational understanding of class in line with E.P. Thompson's (1980: 213) reminder that 'the working class made itself as much as it was made, in order to begin to grasp concepts of labour solidarity and emancipation'. That is, it is through a focus on shared and common experiences, in the crisis but most importantly also beyond, that we can understand how these are articulated into identities and interests, becoming manifest in calls for resistance, cooption, indifference or acquiescence. It is here that the key for understanding the class character of the crisis lies, by focusing on the concrete responses of labour in concrete circumstances, engendered but never determined by the social relations of production. Therefore, we can only second Harvey when he insists that 'if it looks like class struggle and acts like class war then we have to name it unashamedly for what it is' (Harvey 2005: 202). In many perspectives and approaches, this fundamental class dimension is still lacking. As Dinnerstein and Neary (2002: 16) argue, 'the intellectual history of the 20th century is the history of avoidance of labour as a political category and its recreation as a sociological device which denies its critical capacity'. We would contend that this is still the case for many analyses of labour and the crisis – with this in mind, we now turn to a brief discussion of new avenues for labour in Europe in the current historical period.

We reject a view that would attribute labour, workers, organized labour, trade unions or any of these categories with innate, essential characteristics of solidarism and emancipation. Rather, these need to be formed, articulated, contested and reproduced, within the historical and social terrain in which labour as an agent is situated. At the same time, perspectives that would regard labour as at best a defensive actor, or mainly as the target of reforms in the context of the crisis, are clearly insufficient for understanding the ongoing developments in capitalist power relations in Europe – in particular with regard to investigating new avenues and alternatives for labour. This is not to suggest, though, that traditional terrains of struggle, for example attacks on collective bargaining and agreements, health and safety concerns, and worker representation at the shop floor should receive less attention. Quite to the contrary, it is here that trade unions are core actors for labour as a broader social group.

By pointing to a range of new avenues that have emerged as complementary to, synchronous with, or instead of some of these established struggles, we want to open a debate on the relationship between them. In particular, we would like to address 'new avenues' at interrelated levels, drawing on our relational understanding of class and highlighting their simultaneous and possibly contradictory nature. At the macro-level, it is crucial to give renewed attention to labour internationalism; at the meso-level, we need to address the social movement unionism some observers see as one of the most promising avenues for labour (for example Gindin 2013); lastly, we flag issues such as sabotage and everyday resistance at the micro-level. Europe here constitutes a particularly challenging terrain, due to its complex institutional configuration as well as the uneven development that characterizes it.

Exploring the contradictions and possibilities in labour internationalism offers the potential for a more nuanced discussion of solidarity. That is, one of the challenges here certainly lies in the reconciliation of established forms of trade union internationalism, and the more fluid and decentralized networks of labour activists that have emerged, often in concertation with social movements. De Angelis' comparison (2000: 11) between 'Old' and 'New' Internationalism here provides a useful angle for debate, where the distinction between the international/national/local becomes less pronounced, and the marginalization and subordination of other movements to labour movements gives way to the building of alliances and bridges. As he writes:

> an international process of recomposition of radical claims and social subjects has been under way, a process which is forcing every movement not only to seek alliances with others, but also to make the struggles of other movements their own, without first the need to submit the demands of other movements to an ideological test.
>
> (De Angelis 2000: 14)

This leads to an internationalism from below that is increasingly being researched (see for example Featherstone's (2012) historical review of internationalism) but, more importantly, that is also being practised. In this context, it becomes increasingly crucial for labour in Europe to go beyond the 'established' practices of organizing, both politically as well as socially, by taking in experiences from, for example, the Global South, in particular with regard to mobilizing (Pons-Vignon 2012).

The deepening and harmful consequences of austerity are bringing to the fore a plethora of resistance movements across Europe. The demands are far-ranging, from housing and other 'bread-and-butter' issues to the democratic capacity of existing institutions. These demands are not just being made to governments (whether at the national or at the European level) but also to the traditional organizations of working class representation, such as political parties and trade unions. For example, the outcry of Spanish people in May 2011, when they took to the major streets and squares in Spain's main cities, was primarily about the fact that people no longer felt represented by the organizations that were meant to carry out this task. This was a direct critique of existing Left parties and unions, creating in many cases locally based alliances of public sector workers and service users in order to resist austerity. For example, in Madrid, such alliances were successful in aborting the plans to privatize the management of health care services (*El País*, 27 January 2014). These types of alliances have placed additional pressures on trade union structures, as members are feeling that union bureaucratic structures have been incorporated within state structures for too long, and therefore are too slow and ineffective to react when required by circumstances. This has led to increased levels of discontent within trade union membership: people are more forcefully arguing for a different role for unions, one which is less concerned with bureaucratic state-union relationships and instead is more willing to resist when required. In a sense, this highlights a trend that the literature had already identified prior to the crisis. That is, the pressures on unions to change themselves are not just coming from neoliberal restructuring processes but also from within (see also Upchurch, Taylor and Mathers 2009)

Additionally, the crisis is highlighting the need for what Gumbrell-McCormick and Hyman (2013) have named 'collaborative power resources' to be created out of the cooperative relationships with other groups, movements and organizations. Whilst the appearance of these relationships is becoming more evident in certain contexts, it is by no means universal. For example, the General Strike of 14 November 2012 highlighted the uneven and variegated geographies of labour struggle and solidarity within the European context. Only Southern European countries (Portugal, Spain, Italy, Greece, Cyprus and Malta) seconded the General Strike, with its Northern European counterparts offering only limited (symbolic) support. In the Southern European countries where the strike took place it became a call for resistance, showing a high degree of dissatisfaction with traditional union structures. Overall, while there has been an increase in strikes in for example Greece and Portugal, overall austerity seems not to have 'triggered a pronounced upsurge' in the strike volume across Europe (ETUI 2014: 80). A distinction should be made here between industry-wide strikes, and political mass strikes. The recent example of the EU-level demonstrations organized in Brussels on 4 April 2014 in conjunction with several social movements is an interesting example of the potential and limits of these political mass strikes; violent struggles between participating dock workers and the Brussels police took place.

Social movement unionism is frequently put forward as a complementary or even alternative strategy for trade unions, and workers more broadly. This focus has increased in the current conjuncture, not least due to the emergence of 'new' social movements such as Occupy or the Indignados/15-M. While the characteristics of these movements are being widely discussed, their relationship with labour has been less studied. Most accounts highlight the ambivalent or even initially hostile attitude of many trade union organizations towards these horizontal social movements. The focus here is on the associational, and more specifically collaborative power resources of unions in the context of possible cooperative relationships with other groups, movements and organizations in Europe (Gumbrell-McCormick and Hyman 2013). The linkages and opportunities for campaigning and organizing are numerous, of course. The occupation of public space, for instance, echoes the debate about the occupation of production spaces. There is rather little attention, however, to the class character of these social movements, or rather, to the lack thereof. Moreover, as the current developments in Europe show, the actual organization of cross-linkages between organized labour and social movements is often rather limited due to questions of capacity, resources and ideological motivations (Wigger and Horn 2014).

One of our core concerns in this chapter is also to highlight the need to go beyond trade unions when analysing the agency of labour. In this context, one important avenue we would like to call attention to is the everyday forms of resistance, alternatives and muddling-through that we find across the broad spectrum of labour. Amoore contends (2002: 57):

> Global social change does not simply 'happen to' people, it is experienced, interpreted and lived. The thoughts and actions of those living in the production structure, for example, become at least as central to the reproduction or undermining of that structure as the abstract entities of states, firms and technologies are currently assumed to be.

Labour is increasingly acting in ways that go beyond traditional structures and into everyday practices of resistance. Grassroots organization of food distribution in Greece, disgruntled immigrant workers calling in sick, German workers blocking a supermarket by flashmob; these are everyday forms of agency that might even bear resemblance to notions of 'weapons of the weak' (cf. Scott 1985). In any case, they resist any totalizing attempts into broader, traditional patterns of labour organizing, and can stand in stark contrast, if not contradiction to, the other avenues mentioned above. Unlike in previous historical periods, there also often seems to be a lack of a sense of impending change; some of the struggles at the moment are no longer calling for immediate big changes, but are rather moments of disruption that may seem unconnected to each other. Yet, as Featherstone's reading of Gramsci suggests, 'Gramsci's stress on the practices through which solidarities are constructed situates such practices as transformative' (2012: 27). This means that, rather than analysing labour's agency in terms of its achievements, we could move towards an understanding of labour based around the emancipatory potential of its practices.

In lieu of a conclusion

It is with this fluid and contradictory, yet emancipatory, potential that we would like to end this chapter. There are no clear future scenarios as the crisis, and more importantly, the emancipatory reactions to it, are constantly evolving. Instead, we have attempted to open the door towards new ways of understanding labour and the crisis in Europe, by exploring the relationship between our conceptualizations of labour organizing and the uneven development of crisis management in Europe. It has become evident that we need to move beyond equating labour with trade unions if we are to grasp the complexity of class struggle at the European level in the current context. Moreover, the avenues we have pointed to also show how the 'scenarios' that can/should be expected in the crisis in Europe are actually far from distinct trajectories. Rather than an outlook that would focus on a predictive, clear path, we appreciate the development of contestation, resistance, cooptation and indifference in the context of labour and the crisis as also taking place in an interstitial and open-ended fashion.

Notes

1 We would like to thank the editors of this volume for their patience and comments. Parts of this chapter draw on Mònica Clua-Losada and Laura Horn (2014) Analysing Labour and the Crisis: Challenges, Responses and New Avenues. *Global Labour Journal*. 5(2): 102–13.
2 Cited in *The Economist* (2009) *Unions: In from the Cold?* 12 March 2009.

References

Amoore, L. (2002) *Globalisation Contested. An International Political Economy of Work*. Manchester: Manchester University Press.

Anderson, P. (1992) *A Zone of Engagement*. London: Verso.

Bieler, A. and Lindberg, I. (2010) *Global Restructuring, Labour and the Challenges for Transnational Solidarity*. London: Routledge

Bieler, A. and Lindberg, I. (2010) Globalisation and the New Challenges for Transnational Solidarity: An Introduction. In Bieler, A. and Lindberg, I. (eds) *Global Restructuring, Labour and the Challenges for Transnational Solidarity*. London: Routledge, pp. 3–15.

Bruff, I. and Horn, L. (2012) Varieties of Capitalism in Crisis? *Competition & Change* 16(3), pp. 161–168.

Burawoy, M. (2010) From Polanyi to Pollyanna: The False Optimism of Global Labor Studies. *Global Labour Journal* 1(2), pp. 301–313.

Clua-Losada, M. and Navarro, V. (eds) (2012) *El impacto de la crisis en las familias y en la infancia*. Barcelona: Editorial Ariel.

Cox, R.W. (1981) Social Forces, States and World Order: Beyond International Relations Theory. *Millennium: Journal of International Studies* 10(2), pp. 126–155.

De Angelis, M. (2000) Globalization, New Internationalism and the Zapatistas. *Capital & Class* 70, pp. 9–35.

Dinerstein, A.C. and Neary, M. (2002) From Here to Utopia: Finding Inspiration for the Labour Debate. In Dinerstein, A.C. and Neary, M. (eds) *The Labour Debate. An Investigation into the Theory and Reality of Capitalist Work*. Aldershot: Ashgate, pp. 1–26.

Dunn, B. (2004) *Global Restructuring and the Power of Labour*. Basingstoke: Palgrave.

El País (2014) *Madrid da marcha atrás a la privatización sanitaria tras el último revés judicial*. 27 January 2014. [Online] Available from http://ccaa.elpais.com/ccaa/2014/01/27/madrid/1390839012_137715.html [Accessed 14 February 2014].

ETUC (2014) *ETUC Position on the European Commission Communication on Strengthening the Social Dimension of Economic and Monetary Union*. [Online] Available from www.etuc.org/documents/etuc-position-european-commission-communication-strengthening-social-dimension-economic#.U2Ymy16sZJM [Accessed 25 April 2014].

ETUI (2014) *Benchmarking Working Europe*. Brussels: European Trade Union Institute.

Gall, G. (2014) New Forms of Labour Conflict: A Transnational Overview. In Atzeni, M. (ed.) *Workers and Labour in a Globalised Capitalism*. Basingstoke: Palgrave Macmillan, pp. 210–229.

Featherstone, D. (2012) *Solidarity: Hidden Histories and Geographies of Internationalism*. London: Zed Books.

Gindin, S. (2013) Beyond the Economic Crisis: The Crisis in Trade Unionism. *The Bullet* 878. 16 September 2013. [Online] Available from www.socialistproject.ca/bullet/878.php [Accessed 13 May 2014].

Gumbrell-McCormick, R. and Hyman, R. (2013) *Trade Unions in Western Europe: Hard Times, Hard Choices.* Oxford: Oxford University Press.

Harvey, D. (2005) *A Brief History of Neoliberalism.* Oxford: Oxford University Press.

Horn, L. (2012) Anatomy of a Critical Friendship: Organised Labour and the European State Formation. *Globalizations* 9(4), pp. 577–592.

Hyman, R. (1999) Imagined Solidarities: Can Trade Unions Resist Globalisation? In Leisink, P. (ed.) *Globalization and Labour Relations.* Cheltenham: Edward Elgar.

Hyman, R. (2011) Trade Unions, Global Competition and Options for Solidarity. In Bieler, A. and Lindberg, I. (eds) *Global Restructuring, Labour and the Challenges for Transnational Solidarity.* London: Routledge.

ILO (2013) *Global Wage Report 2012–13: Wages and Equitable Growth.* Geneva: International Labour Office.

Jokopovich, D. (2011) The Construction of a Trans-European Labour Movement. *Capital & Class* 35(1), pp. 63–77.

Kelly, J. (1998) *Rethinking Industrial Relations. Mobilization, Collectivism and Long Waves.* London: Routledge.

Kretsos, L. (2011) Grassroots Unionism in the Context of Economic Crisis in Greece. *Labor History* 52(3), pp. 265–286.

McBride, S. and Smith, S. (2013) In the Shadow of Crisis: Economic Orthodoxy and the Response of Global Labour. *Global Labour Journal* 4(3), pp. 206–229.

Martinez Lucio, M. (2006) Trade Unionism and the Realities of Change: Reframing the Language of Change. In Alonso, L.E. and Martinez Lucio, M. (eds) *Employment Relations in a Changing Society. Assessing the Post-Fordist Paradigm.* Basingstoke: Palgrave Macmillan, pp. 200–214.

Moody, K. (2007) *US Labor in Trouble and Transition. The Failure of Reform from Above, the Promise of Revival from Below.* London: Verso.

OECD (2014) *OECD Stats – Trade Union Density 1999–2012.* [Online] Available from http://stats.oecd.org/Index.aspx?DataSetCode=UN_DEN [Accessed 12 April 2014].

Peters, J. (2011) The Rise of Finance and the Decline of Organised Labour in the Advanced Capitalist Countries. *New Political Economy* 16(1), pp. 73–99.

Phelan, C. (2007) *Trade Union Revitalisation. Trends and Prospects in 34 Countries.* Oxford: Peter Lang.

Pons-Vignon, N. (2012) What Europe Can Learn from the South. *Global Labour Column.* 100. June 2012. [Online] Available from http://column.global-labour-university.org/2012/06/what-europe-can-learn-from-south.html [Accessed 24 June 2014].

Pradella, L. (2013) The Working Poor in Western Europe: A Global Political Economic Perspective. Paper presented at '*Structural Adjustment Comes to Europe*' workshop. 15–17 November 2013. Roskilde University.

Radice, H. (2014) The Middle Classes: Workers, not Owners. *New Left Project.* 20 February 2014. [Online] Available from www.newleftproject.org/index.php/site/article_comments/the_middle_classes_workers_not_owners [Accessed 13 May 2014].

Scott, J. (1985) *Weapons of the Weak: Everyday Forms of Peasant Resistance.* New Haven: Yale University Press.

Shields, S., Bruff, I. and Macartney, H. (eds) (2011) *Critical International Political Economy: Dialogue, Debate and Dissensus.* Basingstoke: Palgrave Macmillan.

Silver, B. (2003) *Forces of Labour. Workers' Movements and Globalisation Since 1870*. Cambridge: Cambridge University Press.

Simms, M. (2012) Imagined Solidarities: Where is Class in Union Organising? *Capital & Class* 36(1), pp. 97–115.Taylor, G. (2002) Labour and Subjectivity: Rethinking the Limits of Working Class Consciousness. In Dinerstein, A.C. and Neary, M. (eds) *The Labour Debate. An Investigation into the Theory and Reality of Capitalist Work*. Aldershot: Ashgate.

Taylor, G., Mathers, A. and Upchurch, M. (2011) Beyond the Chains that Bind: The Political Crisis of Unions in Western Europe. *Labor History* 52(3), pp. 287–305.

The Economist (2013) *Labour Pains. All around the World, Labour is Losing out to Capital*. 2 November 2013. [Online] Available from http://www.economist.com/news/finance-and-economics/21588900-all-around-world-labour-losing-out-capital-labour-pains [Accessed 24 June 2014].

Thompson, E.P. (1980) *The Making of the English Working Class*. London: Penguin.

Upchurch, M., Taylor, G. and Mathers, A. (2009) *The Crisis of Social Democratic Trade Unionism in Western Europe: And the Search for Alternatives*. Aldershot: Ashgate.

Vaughan-Whitehead, D. (2012) Introduction: Has the Crisis Exacerbated Work Inequalities? In Vaughan-Whitehead, D. (ed.) *Work Inequalities in the Crisis. Evidence from Europe*. Cheltenham: Edward Elgar and Geneva: International Labour Office.

Wahl, A. (2014) European Labour: Political and Ideological Crisis in an Increasingly More Authoritarian European Union. *Monthly Review* 65(8). [Online] Available from http://monthlyreview.org/2014/01/01/european-labor [Accessed 13 May 2014].

Wigger, A. and Horn, L. (2014) Uneven Development and Political Resistance against EU Austerity Politics. In Pradella, L. and Marois, T. (eds) *Polarizing Development. Alternatives to Neoliberalism and the Crisis*. London: Pluto Press (forthcoming).

Wright, E.O. (2000) Working Class Power, Capitalist-Class Interests, and Class Compromise. *American Journal of Sociology* 105, pp. 957–1002.

13 Conclusions and possible futures

Johannes Jäger and Elisabeth Springler

It is impossible to discuss the merits of critical political economy (CPE) and post-Keynesian (PK) perspectives in detail. However, we highlight some aspects in this concluding chapter. Whilst in general PK work shows 'what is wrong' with Europe's economy and what should be done in order to return to stable economic growth (Springler 2013), CPE explains why this does not happen and under which conditions it could happen. However, within the PK perspective especially the strand with a strong focus on Kalecki (1943) is very useful for understanding why the crisis was managed after 2010 in an anti-Keynesian way. The policies led to further increasing unemployment and thereby favoured capital over labour. Complementary to this, CPE insists that an abstract class interest does not transform itself automatically into class agency but is always mediated. Moreover, CPE points to some additional economic aspects, such as the material dimension of economic growth or the role of industry and productivity growth in development. A European development model also has to deal with the question of how productivity can be increased in the periphery, as for large parts of the periphery neoliberal strategies have failed. Contrary to PK approaches, CPE argues that growth is not an ultimate goal but at the best a means for emancipatory strategies which aim at the reduction of power asymmetries. However, from a PK perspective income policies in favour of workers and lower income groups are considered to be beneficial for economic growth and for counteracting measures such as strong austerity programmes which might account for even deeper recessions (see e.g. Ederer and Reschenhofer 2013; Stockhammer and Köhler, Chapter 2 in this volume).

There is another important difference between the way how CPE and PK perspectives understand the crisis. Whilst PK approaches mainly focus on the economic dimension of the crisis, that is, economic recession or stagnation, CPE points to the multiple dimensions of the crisis including a political crisis and a crisis of integration. Historically, a crisis such as the 1970s crisis of Fordism was a turning point in European integration (Ziltener 1999). While neoliberalism as the guiding principle for European integration, and the existence of finance-dominated regimes of accumulation alongside neo-mercantilist export-orientation, were the outcome of the crisis of Fordism, neoliberal accumulation strategies are in crisis now. However, neoliberal regulation has deepened further, and a transfer of regulations from the national to the EU level has taken place. In this understanding, PK and CPE perspectives formulate similar points of view. CPE, however, pins the argumentation down and understands this process as a politics of scale (Gough 2004) and of changing class relations. It particularly affects the wage relation and has implications for national welfare regimes. Both CPE and PK scholars claim that macroeconomic coordination and a deeper understanding of wage policies are necessary, but the latter refrain from a class analysis and from an acknowledgement of the power relations within the wage bargaining process.

Given the complexity of crisis processes it is difficult to foresee what the outcome will be, even more so given the dynamics of uneven development in Europe. The different contributions in the book have shown clearly the contradictory and fragile nature of the preliminary stabilization of the European economy. Whilst a totally chaotic crisis has been avoided, stagnation and uneven development of the crisis multiplied contradictions and centrifugal processes within the European Union. So-called anti-crisis polices aimed at restoring the pre-crisis status quo, and traditional power blocs and ruling classes have not changed significantly. Moreover, increasing dominance by these groups was used to compensate for a drastically diminishing hegemony. The central contradictions of European integration, which led to a crisis of over-accumulation from a CPE perspective or which cause a lack of effective demand and huge imbalances within the Eurozone from a PK perspective, have not been tackled yet. On the contrary, the development of wages in the context of record levels of unemployment and the overall European strategy to 'increase competitiveness' point to the opposite direction. The uneven nature of European development and thus the crisis, and the fragmented and asymmetrically linked national/regional modes of production, do not make a coherent and forceful response by organized labour likely. The weakness of labour, despite numerous but uneven (nationally) fragmented protests, the surge of new social movements, and the absence of a set of coherent national and/or regional regimes of accumulation for large parts of Europe, still represent important obstacles to progressive/emancipatory solutions to the crisis. However, the unfolding contradictions, and a strengthening power of subaltern classes, gives hope that, despite the authoritarian constitutionalism in the European Union, emancipatory forces at the national and the European scale may become more influential in the medium and long-term.

Possible and likely futures

Based on the contributions in the book, a closer look at different possible futures and the likelihood of their materializing is presented in the following. We analyse the conditions in which they may materialize, and which structural changes and the strategies of which agents will be required for this. The possible scenarios which we present here are inspired by the systematization developed by Buckel et al. (2012), but also by Niechoj's scenario analysis in Chapter 9 of this volume. Given the perspective of the present volume, we focus more on the material/economic side and the related dynamics and contradictions. In order to deal with this systematically, we outline different possible scenarios and distinguish three possible and one very likely future outcome.

Scenario 1: Total meltdown into the unknown

Although the contributions in this volume point to the fragility of the current situation, none of the chapters in this volume suggests that there will be a final crisis of capitalism in Europe or a total 'meltdown into the unknown' (Duménil and Lévy 2004). A very deep crisis such as in Greece might happen in other countries, but is not very likely for the European Union as a whole. In 2008/2009 a general and extremely deep recession in the EU was avoided by rescuing the financial sector with public money and by adopting Keynesian policies to stabilize the economy. Although public debts due to those measures are higher now, there is still the possibility of encountering another drastic collapse of economic activity. An even stronger focus on competition (see Wigger, Chapter 7 in this volume), and the new European economic governance according to the post-Keynesian contributions in this volume, show a very strong anti-Keynesian bias (Stockhammer and Köhler in Chapter 2 of this volume). This promotes stagnation and recession.

However, in a critical political economy perspective, despite this new authoritarian and neoliberal governance which has been institutionalized (see Oberndorfer, Chapter 11 in this volume), one may expect those rules to be violated and pragmatic heterodox Keynesian measures in fiscal and monetary policy to be implemented when necessary in order to prevent a total collapse of the system. Obviously, the ruling classes are interested in avoiding chaotic episodes which might not just drastically reduce their legitimacy but also end up in unforeseeable social upheavals and their own defeat. And it is the safeguarding of class power which is the ultimate goal of capitalist ruling classes. At least in the financial crisis of 2008/2009 but also during the eruption of the Eurozone crisis in 2011/2012 they have proven to be capable of this. However, due to the uneven nature of development, and the resultant complexity and divergence of European capitalist fractions and interests (Heinrich and Jessop 2013: 30), it is not certain that the ruling classes will be successful again. Hence, a total economic meltdown is not a very likely but still a possible European future.

Scenario 2: Social democratic Europe

Those contributions in the present volume inspired by a post-Keynesian perspective, at least at a very high level of abstraction, share a common vision of a desired European solution to the crisis. Most clearly this is summarized by

Torsten Niechoj's contribution (Chapter 9 in this volume). The desired scenario he describes is based on the implementation of Keynesian institutions and policies at the EU level. At its core is a co-ordinated fiscal policy with a strong European fiscal statehood. Complementary to this, Heiner Flassbeck and Costas Lapavitsas argue in their contribution (Chapter 8 in this volume) that wage co-ordination based on productivity increases is necessary to stabilize demand and therefore wage-led growth. In addition, in order to combat imbalances within the Eurozone, nominal wages should temporarily increase much stronger in surplus countries such as Germany until imbalances disappear. Moreover, unsustainable public debts in the periphery should be reduced in order to open up possibilities for fiscal policy, and also an exit from the Eurozone might be a necessary step for peripheral countries (Lapavitsas 2011). As John Grahl argues in this volume (Chapter 10), the implementation of a progressive European social welfare system would be desirable and could be part of this scenario.

In addition, adequate regulation of the financial sector is a necessary element of the PK agenda to stabilize the economy, but it cannot be the only one. Jan Toporowski reflects on this (Chapter 3), especially on the deficits in the current European debate on banking regulation, and introduces a two-fold view on European imbalances which allows for fiscal and monetary imbalances as a prerequisite for overall economic growth under the umbrella of, and strong institutional settings for, demand-side policies. Besides such demand-oriented post-Keynesian perspectives, a strategy which allows for a reconstruction of productive sectors, in particular of industry, is also essential for economic development in the periphery (Becker and Weissenbacher 2014: 27). Already before the crisis, large parts of the European periphery had been characterized by dramatic de-industrialization (Becker and Jäger 2010). These aspects are barely touched in a PK scenario. Hence, from a CPE perspective a European framework which allows for development of the periphery would be another essential element of this scenario.

This vision of a social democratic Europe and a further step of progressive integration have the Fordist national welfare states and the corresponding incomes policies as a reference. However, CPE perspectives point to the fact that Fordist (or at least peripheral) welfare states and respective incomes policies were implemented in most parts of Western Europe within a very specific historical and geo-political context. The basis for this was a social democratic class compromise between capital and labour after the Second World War and within the context of US hegemony and the Soviet challenge. The situation has completely changed. The power of capital vis-à-vis labour has increased and the national class compromises have eroded. Against this background it seems very unlikely that something similar to a Fordist class compromise can be institutionalized at the level of the European Union within a near future.

Although in the 1980s and 1990s there was an attempt to implement a social democratic project at the level of the EU, this by and large failed and neoliberal and neo-mercantilist interests succeeded. This has been manifested in the Maastricht Criteria and the Lisbon Agenda, and also during the recent crisis (van Apeldoorn, Drahokoupil and Horn 2009). Today, labour is even weaker and more fragmented. Although it is argued that there is a transnational European capitalist class (Van Apeldoorn 2013), we should not underestimate the importance of national capitalist classes (see Cafruny, Chapter 4 in this volume) within Europe and the existence of nationally fragmented working classes. Hence, from a CPE perspective it seems very unlikely that such a pro-European social democratic project (including some 'green' elements), which has a small and very weak social basis (see Buckel *et al.* 2012: 38), can be implemented within the foreseeable future.

Scenario 3: Radical reformism to overcome capitalism

CPE scholars usually are in favour of overcoming capitalism or, as a first step, of much-undesired forms of capitalism such as neoliberalism. Conversely to this, PK approaches stick to the latter aspect. Although this present volume does not comprise any contribution which discusses the crisis in such a more fundamental way and promotes respective alternatives, this is an important potential scenario which has to be dealt with. The reason for not including such a chapter into the book was the focus on an up-to-date analysis of concrete possible futures instead of a visionary or utopian discussion. However, the crisis has opened up the space for more radical critique and visionary proposals which question the capitalist organization of the economy in general and its neoliberal type in particular. Hence, within the context of an erosion of neoliberal hegemony and a surge of public discontent a fundamental critique and the discussion of alternative ideas are back on the agenda. Among them there is the questioning of economic growth as such, and the re-emergence of a broad development discourse.

In the tradition of critical political economy, the discussion should not be limited to the question of overcoming the crisis in terms of returning to economic growth based on the emergence of an ensemble of stable growth regimes in Europe. Whilst post-Keynesianism gives hints of how capitalism can be re-organized to overcome stagnation and turn back to economic growth (Davidson 2009), critical political economy provides a variety of more far-reaching alternatives to reduce exploitation, to eliminate power relations and to socialize production. Besides the questioning of economic growth, this does not just include the control of the financial sector and speculation but also a radically more equal income distribution, a shortening of working hours, the creation of decent jobs, investment in 'meaningful' areas, and strict public control in order to implement a new society and make the world a better place for all (Herrmann and Frangakis 2014: 192) In addition, the necessity of environmental sustainability means that new modes of production and of consumption are considered to be indispensable for providing a good life for all (Lipietz 2013; Novy 2013). Green capitalism is not necessarily progressive but may be a concrete solution to the current multiple crisis (Brand 2012).

Radical debates and visionary proposals are important for discursively expanding the room for possible alternatives. Hence, they may play their role for progressive long-term transformations towards post-capitalist societies. However, the agents promoting such a radical reformist approach are still very weak and fragmented, not least because of the uneven development of the crisis (Becker 2014; Buckel et al. 2012). Today, the coming of a radical reformist future within the medium-term is even more unlikely than a social democratic European Union. At the best, the latter could be a step towards more radical reforms because of shifting power relations implied by a social democratic Europe.

Scenario 4: Authoritarian neoliberalism and muddling through

The preliminary outcome of the crisis at the level of the European Union has been the implementation of an authoritarian neoliberalism which shows a strong anti-Keynesian bias. Whilst with the exception of a Kaleckian tradition this is difficult to explain from a PK perspective, CPE points to the fact that neoliberalism is less a strategy for growth but rather a mode to combat labour, and hence an expression of class struggle from above (Duménil and Lévy 2011; Stockhammer and Köhler in Chapter 2 of this volume). During the crisis, powerful export-oriented German capitalists (Heinrich and Jessop 2013; Cafruny, Chapter 4 in this volume) and well-organized transnational fractions of capital at the European level (van Apeldoorn 2013) have pushed for a deepening of neoliberalism at the European level. This has not just caused problems for the European periphery but even for the German economic model itself, which has become more export-dependent (Bruff 2015). Hence, as Hans-Jürgen Bieling shows in his contribution in this volume, these European developments can be called a passive revolution which is not yet completed but in trouble. However, capitalist fractions in the periphery have also supported neoliberal policies and a subordinate position because this at least secured their class position (Navarro 2011). Therefore, we observe dynamics in Europe's periphery which remind us of Latin American experiences (Cardoso and Faletto 1979 [1971]).

CPE points out not only the complexity of agents and process in particular but also the structural contradictions inherent to capitalism in general. Whilst it was possible to stabilize dynamic capitalist accumulation during the post-Second World War Fordist era on a national scale and within a very specific framework (US hegemony, Bretton Woods system, an EU supportive of national Fordist regimes of accumulation), and on the basis of a class compromise relatively favourable to labour, this is different today. There is a strategic selectivity (Jessop 2002) in favour of capital at the level of the European Union, and the crisis has led to a further shift of economic governance to this macro-regional level. Neoliberal European economic governance tends to reproduce and consolidate a very heterogeneous European economic space. Transnational European firms (usually their headquarters are located in the centre) may take advantage of persistently different productivities and wage levels within Europe in organizing their production chains. In line with this, the Transatlantic Trade and Investment Partnership might be understood as another way forward for the promotion of exports from the Germany-centred productive system (see Cafruny in Chapter 4 of this volume) beyond Europe to the rest of the world. However, given Europe's economic size it is very unlikely if not impossible that such an outward-oriented strategy can provide the basis for European-wide growth. Hence, the deepening of neoliberalism does not contribute to overcome capitalist contradictions, and the problem of realizing profits will be a constant feature in the future European trajectory.

Contradictions are likely to continue to be most visible in the European periphery, because the given economic governance structure in Europe tends to support the powerful interests of the European core countries and to shift the problems onto the periphery. However, as Drahokoupil and Myant (2012) and Becker, Jäger and Weissenbacher in Chapter 5 in this volume insist, peripheral European countries are integrated into the core in different ways. A single classical indicator such as penetration by foreign capital is not sufficient to grasp the dynamics. Those who are part of the Germany-centred productive core are in a better position than those countries in which the dominant patterns of accumulation were based on financialization. Particularly for countries which have a very weak industrial basis and which are not integrated into the productive core, the outlook is rather gloomy. This may promote the search for national development strategies and even imply a (partial) dissolution of the EU, because in many cases national development seems to be impossible within the EU's neoliberal competitive framework. Though, as (Bohle 2013: 118) insists, despite common external structures it is necessary to assess the specific internal processes and struggles. Moreover, persistently high unemployment may also cause centrifugal tendencies in less peripheral countries. Overall, a long-run persistence of instability, no early end of the crisis and increasing rift between the core and the periphery seem to be a very likely future.

Outlook and progressive strategies

Despite the discourses which proclaim the end of the crisis, so-called anti-crisis policies continue to deepen polarization in Europe. One example is the recent measures implemented by the European Central Bank in 2014 and 2015: now the central bank provides more and cheaper liquidity which is mainly beneficial to the financial sector. Those measures do not at all combat, and indeed actually reinforce, the uneven effects of the Euro as characterized by substantially higher real interest rates in peripheral countries suffering deflationary pressures. We will continue to see such unconventional measures as long as the European integration and major European economies are in crisis. However, the crisis has also caused a broad variety of responses and political strategies from 'below'. This has been mainly defensive struggles against wage reductions and welfare cuts, against rescuing the banking sector with public money, etc. Meanwhile, after in many cases often relatively unsuccessful protests many people at least passively have accepted austerity measures and the argument that there has been no alternative. Within this context, in many cases the extreme political right has been strengthened. However, leftist groups and parties have also become more important and part of emerging hegemonic projects (Buckel et al. 2012).

As Mònica Clua-Losada and Laura Horn have shown in this volume (Chapter 12), beyond the focus on traditional trade unions there is the necessity for different conceptualizations of labour organizing within the context of the uneven development of the European crisis. With regards to the European future, there is a broad variety across the aspired aims and the applied strategies (Demirovic and Sablowski 2012: 101; EuroMemoGroup 2014) and there is no consensus on the adequate strategy by progressive forces. Some groups are in favour of a social democratic solution at the European level (Scenario 2) and others demand a more radical change (Scenario 3). Moreover, on the one hand, there are many groups who argue that it is possible to reform the EU and demand a refoundation of Europe (Husson 2011). This view that the EU is the preferred scale for implementing progressive economic governance structures is usually supported by post-Keynesians. On the other hand, others argue that progressive reforms at the level of the EU are not possible and therefore national strategies are more promising. In addition, it is argued that leftist reforms in Greece, including an exit from the Eurozone, may trigger substantial changes in the EU.

CPE views on the preferred scale for progressive change are diverse. The labour movement is still fragmented by national borders. Social struggles at the local, the national and the European level seem necessary and should not be seen as opposing each other but as complementary and dialectically related. In addition, potentially progressive developments are a question of the time period considered. While in the short-term some social democratic elements might be implemented, this could provide the basis for more radical change in the future. However, it does not necessarily have to happen in this way. Social democratic reforms also could stabilize and cushion capitalist class power by providing some concessions to the working class. While the final outcome tends to be unforeseeable, it is for sure that struggles for progressive solutions do make the still very unlikely Scenarios 2 and 3 more realistic. The present edited volume can be seen as a contribution to those debates and provides a broad picture of the different and uneven aspects of the crisis. It has proven very fruitful for critical political economists and post-Keynesians to join forces and to discuss and support together progressive European developments. We hope that this book will help initiate and deepen an integrative debate within a period of rising contradictions in Europe.

References

Becker, J. (2014) Ist eine andere EU möglich? *Kurswechsel* 1/2014, pp. 92–96.

Becker, J. and Jäger, J. (2010) Development Trajectories in the Crisis in Europe. *Debatte: Journal of Contemporary Central and Eastern Europe* 18(1), pp. 5–27.

Becker, J. and Weissenbacher, R. (2014) Berlin Consensus and Disintegration. Monetary Regime and Uneven Development in the EU. In Dymarski, W., Frangakis, M. and Leaman, J. (eds) *The Deepening Crisis of the European Union: The Case for Radical Change*. Poznán: Poznán University, pp. 15–32.

Bohle, D. (2013) Euoropas andere Peripherie: Osteuropa in der Krise. *Das Argument* 55(1/2), pp. 118–129.

Brand, U. (2012) Green Economy and Green Capitalism: Some Theoretical Considerations. *Journal für Entwicklungspolitik* 28(3), pp. 118–137.

Bruff, I. (2015) Germany and the Crisis: Steady as she Goes? In Westra, R., Badeen, D. and Albritton, R. (eds) *The Future of Capitalism After the Financial Crisis: The Varieties of Capitalism Debate in the Age of Austerity*. Abingdon: Routledge, pp. 114–131.

Buckel, S. *et al.* (2012) '… wenn das Alte nicht stirbt und das Neue nicht zur Welt kommen kann.' Kräfteverhältnisse in der Europäischen Krise. In Forschungsgruppe Staatsprojekt Europa (ed.) *Die EU in der Krise*. Münster: Westfälisches Dampfboot, pp. 12–49.

Cardoso, F.H. and Faletto, E. (1979 [1971]) *Dependency and Development in Latin America*. Berkeley: University of California Press.

Davidson, P. (2009) *The Keynes Solution. The Path to Global Economic Prosperity*. New York: Palgrave MacMillan.

Demirovic, A. and Sablowski, T. (2012) Finanzdominierte Akkumulation und die Krise in Europa. *Prokla – Zeitschrift für kritische Sozialwissenschaft* 42(1), pp. 77–106.

Drahokoupil, J. and Myant, M. (2012) The European Sub-prime? Financial Crisis and the East-European Periphery. In Nousios, P., Overbeek, H. and Tsolakis, A. (eds) *Globalisation and European Integration. Critical Approaches to Regional Order and International Relations*. Abingdon: Routledge, pp. 130–153.

Duménil, G. and Lévy, D. (2004) *Capital Resurgent. Roots of the Neoliberal Revolution*. Cambridge, MA: Harvard University Press.

Duménil, G. and Lévy, D. (2011) *The Crisis of Neoliberalism*. Cambridge, MA: Harvard University Press.

Ederer, S. and Reschenhofer, P. (2013) *Macroeconomic Imbalances in the EU*. Working Paper No 42. WWW for Europe. [Online] Available from www.foreurope.eu/fileadmin/documents/pdf/Workingpapers/WWWforEurope_WPS_no042_MS71.pdf [Accessed 1 June 2014].

EuroMemogroup (2014) *EuroMemorandum 2014. The Deepening Divisions in Europe and the Need for a Radical Alternative to EU Policies*. [Online] Available from www2.euromemorandum.eu/uploads/euromemorandum_2014.pdf [Accessed 1 June 2014].

Gough, J. (2004) Changing Scale as Changing Class Relations: Variety and Contradiction in the Politics of Scale. *Political Geography* 23, pp. 185–211.

Heinrich, M. and Jessop, B. (2013) Die EU-Krise aus Sicht der Kulturellen Politischen Ökonomie. *Das Argument* 55(1/2), pp. 19–33.

Herrmann, P. and Frangakis, M. (2014) The Need for a Radical 'Growth Policy' Agenda for Europe at a Time of Crisis. In Dymarski, W., Frangakis, M. and

Leaman, J. (eds) *The Deepening Crisis of the European Union: The Case for Radical Change*. Poznán: Poznán University of Economics Press, pp. 179–194.

Husson, M. (2011) Exit or Voice? A European Strategy of Rupture. In Panitch, L., Albo, G. and Chibber, V. (eds) *The Crisis and the Left. Socialist Register 2012. Vol. 298–306*. London: Merlin Press.

Jessop, B. (2002) *The Future of the Capitalist State*. Cambridge: Polity.

Kalecki, M. (1943) Political Aspects of Full Employment. *Political Quarterly* 14, pp. 322–331.

Lapavitsas, C. *et al.* (2011) *Breaking Up? A Route Out of the Eurozone*. Occasional Report. RMF. London.

Lipietz, A. (2013) Fears and Hopes: The Crisis of the Liberal-Productivist Model and its Green Alternative. *Capital & Class* 37(1), pp. 127–141.

Navarro, V. (2011) Crisis and Class Struggle in the Eurozone. The Cases of Spain, Greece, Ireland and Portugal. *Counter Punch* (Weekend Edition 19–21 August).

Novy, A. (2013) Ein gutes Leben für alle – ein europäisches Entwicklungsmodell. *Journal für Entwicklungspolitik* 29(3), pp. 77–104.

Springler, E. (2013) Postkeynesianische Alternativen in Wirtschaftstheorie und Wirtschaftspolitik: Lösungsvorschläge zur globalen Finanz- und Wirtschaftskrise. *Wirtschaft und Gesellschaft* 39(2), pp. 125–151.

Van Apeldoorn, B. (2013) The European Capitalist Class and the Crisis of its Hegemonic Project. In Panitch, L., Albo, G. and Chibber, V. (eds) *Registering Class. Socialist Register 2014*. London: Merlin Press.

Van Apeldoorn, B., Drahokoupil, J. and Horn, L. (eds) (2009) *Contradictions and Limits of Neoliberal European Governance. From Lisbon to Lisbon*. Houndmills: Palgrave Macmillan.

Ziltener, P. (1999) *Strukturwandel der europäischen Integration. Die Europäische Union und die Veränderung von Staatlichkeit*. Münster: Westfälisches Dampfboot.

Index

For Product Safety Concerns and Information please contact our EU representative GPSR@taylorandfrancis.com Taylor & Francis Verlag GmbH, Kaufingerstraße 24, 80331 München, Germany

Batch number: 10725973

Printed by Printforce, the Netherlands